Race and Ethnicity in the Juvenile Justice System

ce and Ethnicity in the
enile Justice System

eiburger

ordan

hor.
iburger

, 2016. |

er)
ates. |
tates.
tates.
973--dc23

6

es of America

Library of Congress Cataloging-in-Publication Data

Names: Freiburger, Tina L., author. | Jordan, Kareem L., 1978- auth
Title: Race and ethnicity in the juvenile justice system / Tina L. Fr
and Kareem L. Jordan.
Description: Durham, North Carolina : Carolina Academic Pres
Includes bibliographical references and index.
Identifiers: LCCN 2015037802 | ISBN 9781611635348 (alk. pa
Subjects: LCSH: Juvenile justice, Administration of--United S
Discrimination in juvenile justice administration--United S
Classification: LCC HV9104 .F74 2016 | DDC 364.36089/00
LC record available at http://lccn.loc.gov/2015037802

Carolina Academic Press, LLC
700 Kent Street
Durham, NC 27701
Telephone (919) 489-748
Fax (919) 493-5668
www.cap-press.com

Printed in the United Stat

I dedicate this book to my husband, Dan Klein, and my son, Jonathan.

—Tina L. Freiburger

I dedicate this book to my wife, Tiffany Jordan, and our children, Jhailen, Anthony, and Kendall. I also dedicate the book to the memory of my mother, Barbara Lee.

—Kareem L. Jordan

Contents

Race and Ethnicity in the Juvenile Justice System

Chapter 1

Introduction: Race and Juvenile Crime

The idea of having a juvenile justice system that was separate from the adult criminal justice system began in the early nineteenth century (Platt, 1969; Bernard & Kurlychek, 2010; Ward, 2012). The House of Refuge was the first juvenile house of reform in the United States, opening in 1824 in New York. Later, in 1899, the first juvenile court was established in Cook County, Illinois. The idea of a juvenile system that was focused on treatment rather than punishment garnered widespread support, and within 30 years, every state had a separate juvenile justice system.

The juvenile system is based on a rehabilitative "parens patriae" (Latin for parent of the nation) philosophy, which stipulates that the state acts as a guardian or parent to youth whose parents are unable to care for them (Platt, 1969; Bernard & Kurlychek, 2010). Under this model, the juvenile court would intervene when juveniles engaged in delinquency and provide the necessary treatment and supervision. Treatment of juveniles' delinquency would be based on the needs of the youth and not on the offense. Therefore, juvenile justice actors were afforded a great deal of discretion in determining what was best for the juvenile. Unfortunately, with this discretion and little oversight, problems began to arise with the overrepresentation of minorities at every stage in the system.

The overrepresentation of minorities in the juvenile justice system has been a topic of concern for decades. In 1974, the Juvenile Justice and Delinquency Prevention Act established federal funds to states for their juvenile justice systems if they complied with four "core protections." The four core protections were: 1) the deinstitutionalization of status offenders, 2) the removal of juveniles from adult jails and detention centers, 3) keeping juvenile offenders out of sight and sound of adult offenders, and 4) disproportionate minority contact. The last core protection, disproportionate minority contact, demanded all states address the issue of minority overrepresentation in the juvenile justice system. Despite these efforts, however, minorities continue to be overrepresented in all parts of the juvenile justice system.

This text focuses on issues with minority overrepresentation in the system. It provides a largely comprehensive review of the research examining the treatment of juveniles of different races and ethnicities. In addition to providing a discussion of the research findings, the methodologies employed and data sources utilized in these studies are also discussed.

Measurement of Juvenile Crime

This text provides ample discussion on the research examining race and ethnic issues in the juvenile justice system. All research, however, is limited in its measurement of juvenile delinquency. Some research utilizes national official data sources, such as the Uniform Crime Reports (UCR). The UCR collects data from police departments across the United States on the incidences of arrests. This data is strong in that it provides a representation of arrests for the entire nation. It is weak, however, in that the UCR is a voluntary process in which police departments can elect out of reporting their arrests. An even larger limitation is that the UCR only contains information on crimes that are known to the police. It does not contain information on juvenile delinquency that occurs but does not result in arrest. This is especially problematic when examining racial and ethnic issues, as police bias can heavily affect these statistics. If police are more prone to arrest minorities than White juveniles, conclusions relying on UCR and other arrest data will present a biased picture of the rate at which minority juveniles offend compared to White juveniles.

Similar limitations exist with using official court records data, juvenile probation office data or detention center data. These data sources can provide accurate pictures of who is in the system and differences among those in the system. They are also important when determining whether differences exist in the treatment of juveniles of different races and ethnicities who are already in the system. They are not, however, able to identify biases that occurred when decisions were made regarding who entered the system. This can be most problematic when looking at decisions that are made further in the system. For example, when examining racial and ethnic differences in the petitioning of juveniles to the court, bias at the policing stage cannot be determined. When examining which juveniles receive placement as a final disposition, the juvenile has already been through multiple stages at which bias could have occurred, such as the decision to arrest, petition, detain, adjudicate, etc.

Arrests data also tend to underrepresent victimless crimes. Police are only made aware of crimes if the crime is reported or if the police officer witnessed the crime occur. It is less likely that police will receive a complaint regarding a victimless crime, such as drug use, unless it negatively impacts a third party (e.g., a parent might report a juvenile's drug use). Furthermore, most of these offenses are not within visible view of a police officer. These offenses, therefore, are largely underrepresented when examining arrests statistics.

Victimization surveys can provide a more accurate picture of crime because they are not limited to the requirement that an arrest was made for the offense to be counted. The Bureau of Justice Statistics (BJS) collects data for inclusion in the National Crime Victimization Survey (NCVS). The NCVS was developed to provide a more accurate picture of prevalence of crime in the United States. Each year the NCVS collects data from a sample of about 160,000 people from about 90,000 households that represent all households in the United States (Bureau of Justice Statistics, n.d.). Each household is interviewed every six months. The data includes information on victimizations for rape and sexual assault, robbery, aggravated and simple assault, theft, household burglary, and motor vehicle theft. In addition to estimates as to the rate at which juveniles experience victimizations, NCVS data can be used to measure juvenile offending by providing data on the frequency in which victims reported that their assailant was a juvenile. Victimizations surveys are limited, however, in that they do not collect information on all offenses. Because there is no victim, victimless crimes such as prostitution and drug use are not included. Status offenses are also not included. In addition, only individuals 12 and over are interviewed, so the data does not represent the victimization rates of juveniles under 12.

Other research attempts to get a clearer picture of youth offending by examining self-report surveys in which juveniles report their involvement in criminal activities. Several popular national self-report surveys exist that are commonly used in research on juvenile delinquency. They include the Pittsburgh Youth Survey, the Add Health data, Monitoring the Future, and the Gang Resistance Education and Training data. Other researchers collect original data from juveniles in schools, neighborhoods, or detention centers. Data collected from self-report surveys is not limited by police bias. In addition, self-report surveys provide an estimate of victimless crime. However, limitations do arise if juveniles do not accurately report involvement in delinquency, as self-report surveys are vulnerable to lying and memory issues. As discussed in Chapter 4, this can be especially problematic if juveniles of different racial and ethnic groups are less likely to accurately report offending.

Self-report surveys also commonly focus on more minor offending. When self-report surveys are administered in schools and other community settings, they typically asks juveniles about offenses such as drug, alcohol, and tobacco use, petty thefts, and simple assaults. More serious offending such as robberies, aggravated assaults, and major thefts are not examined because they are so rare among these populations.

Each source of juvenile data has strengths and limitations. It is important to keep the limitations of the data utilized in mind when examining research results. In this text, we attempt to identify limitations in our conclusions based on the data that is used. Conclusions that are derived from more than one type of data source are considered more tenable than those derived from only one type of data source.

Issues with Race and Ethnicity in the Juvenile Justice System

Race and Ethnicity in the Juvenile Justice System address the core areas of the research on this topic. In Chapter 2, the history of the juvenile justice system is reviewed. The chapter begins with a discussion of how the concept of childhood was developed, and how the meaning of childhood has changed throughout time. The development of the juvenile justice system through history is also reviewed. Intertwined within these topics is a discussion on the status of minority juveniles at that time and a description of how the reforms made within the juvenile court often did not apply to minority juveniles, especially Black juveniles in the South. Next, the chapter details how the juvenile system began to move beyond its original "parens patriae" philosophy to include due process safeguards in an attempt to rectify the seemingly unfair treatment of some juveniles in the court and the failure for treatment to effectively handle juveniles. Supreme Court cases that led this movement are also presented. The shift to incorporate more crime control measures which resulted in more juveniles being transferred to the adult court and to the harsher and more punishment-oriented treatment of youth in the juvenile court system is then reviewed. Lastly, disproportionate minority confinement/contact is discussed.

Chapter 3 is devoted to the theoretical explanations for the effect of race and ethnicity in decision-making in the juvenile justice system. The focal concerns perspective is the first theoretical explanation discussed. First developed to explain adult sentencing decisions, focal concerns is becoming an increasingly popular explanation for juvenile court processing. It is comprised of three main focal concerns which court actors consider when making case processing decisions. These concerns are the amount of danger the offender poses to society, how blameworthy the offender is, and the practical constraints and concerns that are associated with the processing of the offender. Each of these focal concerns is explained in the chapter. The empirical examinations of the focal concerns perspective in the juvenile court is discussed next. Attribution theory is then reviewed, as well as the empirical literature on attrition theory and its claim that internal factors are more often blamed for minority juveniles' acts of delinquency, while White juveniles' acts of delinquency are more often blamed on external factors. Racial and ethnic threat and conflict theories are also discussed, followed by reviews of their empirical validity. The formal legal perspective and its empirical support are discussed last in the chapter.

Chapter 4 is concerned with racial and ethnic issues in the policing of juveniles. The chapter begins with a general discussion of the roles that police officers perform. Next, police discretion is explained, with special attention being devoted to how police discretion affects minority youths. Special issues that arise when policing juveniles are presented, followed by juvenile arrests statistics delineated by race and ethnicity. The next section discusses the two contrasting hypotheses to explain minority overrepresentation in arrests. The first, differential involvement, points to differences in offending frequencies for White and minority youths. Differential selection, the second hypothesis, argues that police officer discretion explains minority overrepresentation. The research exploring the validity of each of these explanations is then presented. Explanations of the self-report surveys and the social systematic observations used in this research are also provided. The chapter then presents a discussion of juveniles' likelihood to waive their Fifth Amendment rights during the interrogation process. Lastly, recent research examining racial differences in the interrogation process is reviewed.

Racial and ethnic differences in juveniles' perceptions of the police and the juvenile justice system are the topics of Chapter 5. The chapter begins by discussing youths' perceptions of the police and how Black and Hispanic juveniles tend to view the police more negatively than White juveniles. Next, the chapter explores explanations for these racial and ethnic differences in juveniles' perceptions of the police. This section includes discussions of the group-position thesis, the importance of prior police contacts, the effect of being involved in deviant subcultures, the social bonding perspective as it can relate to police perceptions, and other relationships such as geographic location and membership in a gang that have been explored in empirical research. Four police programs that have been used to improve juveniles' perceptions of the police are presented next, as well as the empirical assessments of the effectiveness of each program. The last section then discusses the limited research that is available on juveniles' perceptions' of other parts of the juvenile justice system.

Chapter 6 focuses on juvenile court outcomes. More specifically, the chapter includes information on every major outcome after an arrest: intake, detention, petition, adjudication, and disposition. Each one of these decision points is discussed in depth, and race/ethnicity data are included within each of these discussions. Next, the empirical research is presented on the role of race and/or ethnicity within each of those decision points. The chapter concludes with an overview of the research, along with suggestions on how future research can address some of the weaknesses in the empirical literature.

Chapter 7 examines how community factors affect the processing of juvenile offenders and how juveniles of different race and ethnicities are differently impacted by community factors. The difference between community-level and individual-level factors is also explained. Theoretical perspectives stemming from conflict and symbolic threat theories explaining how structural factors influence individual juvenile processing decisions are then presented. Also in this section, attribution theory's ability to explain the effect of community factors is discussed. Next, the chapter covers Feld's (1994) introduction of the concept "justice by geography" and reviews the empirical research on the effect that level of urbanization has on juvenile processing decisions. Following this discussion, findings from research examining racial threat and juvenile processing decisions are assessed.

The waiver of juveniles into the adult court is the subject of Chapter 8. A history of the practice of transferring youth from the juvenile court into the adult court is discussed first. Next, a description of the characteristics of transferred youths is presented, and the issue of minority overrepresentation in the population of youth who are transferred into adult court is provided. Early research examining the effect of race on transfer decisions is then presented, followed by a review of the contemporary research that has considered the effect of race on juvenile transfer into adult court. Next, the chapter presents findings of research that compares the sentences that transferred Black and White juveniles receive in the adult court. Chapter 8 then examines the research that has compared the sentencing of transferred juveniles in the adult court with the sentencing of young adults in the adult court to determine whether age acts as a mitigating or aggregating factor. The last section in the chapter reviews the theoretical explanations for racial and ethnic differences in the transferring of juveniles and in the sentencing of transferred juveniles in the adult court.

In Chapter 9, issues surrounding girls in the juvenile justice system are discussed. The chapter begins by providing an overview of the arrests statistics for girls. This is followed by a discussion of the factors that affect girls' involvement in delinquency, including the factors that are similar to boys and those that are unique to girls. Next, the intersection of race and gender is discussed and an explanation of how both contribute to a juvenile's social placement in society. The importance of separately examining the experiences of girls of different races and ethnicities is also argued. This is followed by a discussion of girls' involvement in gangs and of the special needs that gang girls bring to the juvenile justice system. Next, an overview is provided of the changing rates of girls' delinquency rates as well as the explanations for these changes. The decision to arrests girls is then examined. The chapter follows with an examination of the research that has examined the treatment of girls of different races and ethnicities in the juvenile court system. A discussion of girls' programming and treatment needs is also provided, concluding with an assessment of the effectiveness of programs designed specifically for girls.

Chapter 10 discusses the special issues surrounding status offenders. Status offenses are behaviors that are prohibited for juveniles but not for adults, such as running away or being truant from school. In this chapter, there is discussion of the characteristics of status offenders and the racial and ethnic profiles of these offenders. Issues surrounding status offending and the escalation into more serious crimes are also discussed, as well as the effectiveness of using curfew laws to reduce juvenile offending and victimizations. Next, the chapter includes issues regarding the detention of status offenders. Although the Juvenile Justice and Delinquency Prevention Act of 1974 was supposed to end the practice of detaining status offenders, in many states status offenders are still being detained. The racial and ethnic make-up of these offenders in detention is also presented. The chapter further details the racial and ethnic disparities in the processing of status offenders in the juvenile system. It concludes with a review of new programming that provides alternatives to the formal processing and detention of chronic status offenders.

In Chapter 11, an overview of the issues surrounding race and ethnicity in the juvenile justice system is presented, paying special attention to concerns with the overrepresentation of juveniles at most stages. There is also discussion of specific techniques that are able to minimize Disproportionate Minority Contact in the juvenile system. Strengths and limitations in the current empirical examinations of these issues are further assessed. Lastly, directions for future research are presented.

References

Bernard, T.J. & Kurlychek, M.C. (2010). *The cycle of juvenile justice* (2nd ed.). New York: Oxford University Press.

Bureau of Justice Statistics (n.d.) National Crime Victimization Surveys Retrieved on June 26, 2005 from: http://www.bjs.gov/index.cfm?ty=dcdetail&iid=245.

Field, B.C. (1991). Justice by geography. Urban, Suburban, and rural variation in juvenile justice administration. *Journal of Law and Criminology*, 82(9), 156–210.

Platt, A. (1969). *The child savers.* Chicago, IL: University of Chicago Press.

Ward, G.K. (2012). *The Black child-savers: Racial democracy & juvenile justice.* Chicago: The University of Chicago Press.

Chapter 2

Race and Ethnicity and the History of the Juvenile Justice System

Goals of the Chapter

The purpose of this chapter is to examine the history of the juvenile justice system. More specifically, we trace the conditions that led to the creation of the juvenile court, along with the contextual race issues that were present in the United States at the time. We also discuss how the due process era provided youth more constitutional safeguards, but formalized the juvenile court into a system that was not originally intended. Finally, the chapter ends with a discussion of disproportionate minority confinement/contact and the steps that the federal government and individual states are taking to address minority overrepresentation in the juvenile justice system.

After reading the chapter, you will be able to do the following:

1. Understand why youth, at one point in history, were not viewed as needing protections;
2. Discuss the factors that led to juveniles being protected;
3. Discuss the differences in treatment between Black youth and White youth when delinquency was committed;
4. Explain how the U.S. Supreme Court formalized the juvenile court; and
5. Discuss disproportionate minority confinement/contact and explain why it is relevant to the juvenile court process.

Many people believe that the juvenile justice system began in 1899, when the first juvenile court was created. However, many events took place prior to that point which gave rise to a system that was created exclusively for juveniles who commit illegal acts. While it seems fairly normal in contemporary society to view youth as needing guidance, protection, and discipline, those actions were not always in place for juveniles. In fact, youth were often viewed as "little adults" or almost completely ignored at a very young age. While the views toward children were gradually changing toward how we view them today, *all* youth were not afforded such evolving perceptions. More specifically, immigrants and minority youth were still viewed with tough standards and often with degradation and abuse.

Prior to the inception of the juvenile court, there was only one formal justice system for offenders: the criminal justice system. Due to there being no Constitutional right to a juvenile court, there was no separate system for youth to be processed. They were prosecuted and housed with adult offenders. Conditions inside the adult facilities contributed to a strong movement (mainly in the northern states) to create a separate system to deal with issues that are specific to juveniles.

Ideas of Childhood

Prior to the 15th century, there was no true idea or appreciation of childhood (Bernard & Kurlychek, 2010). The infant mortality rate was very high during that time. In fact, most children aged six or under were dying (Empey, Stafford & Hay, 1999). During that period, approximately two-thirds of youth passed away by the age of four (Bernard & Kurlychek, 2010). Given this, many parents avoided getting attached to their children. Because youth were dying in great percentages, parents were afraid to become emotionally connected to their children out of fear they would eventually lose them. Once youth reached age seven, parents started to become close to their children and felt more confident their children would survive. Nevertheless, even when parents did begin to "enjoy" their young children, it was only to a small extent because the likelihood of death was still fairly high.

A more advanced idea of childhood developed in approximately 1600. While the first idea of childhood developed from parents, this idea developed from teachers and moralists (Empey et al., 1999; Bernard & Kurlychek, 2010). During this time, infant mortality was greatly decreasing. The teachers and moralists, however, were highly bothered that parents could practically ignore children from birth through age six. In addition, "Puritanism was on the rise, and they believe that humans had fallen from grace because of their sin in the Garden of Eden" (Bernard & Kurlychek, 2010, p. 42). Therefore, people were born "evil." Although adults were likely set in their ways, they believed that juveniles could be saved with proper intervention.

Origins of Juvenile Justice

Slowly, youth became viewed as innocent and fragile, but also as potentially corrupt and arrogant (Empey et al., 1999). In order for them to become productive adults, children had to be physically and morally protected, along with receiving a structured education. School teachers, moralists, the Catholic Church, and Protestant reformers were at the foundation of these changes. Generally, youth under seven were not considered capable of being guilty of crimes. Children between age seven and fourteen were presumed innocent of crimes, but could be punished if juries thought they recognized the nature of their sins. Youth over the age of fourteen were typically considered and treated as adults.

During the turn of the eighteenth century, children became a bit more central to the private family and to public policy (Ward, 2012). The way in which youth were raised (e.g., parenting skills, discipline, etc.) started to take more focus and prominence in society and in individual families. At this time, there was more concern over the literacy of children, of children behaving appropriately, and of parental responsibility. There were also discussions of the state playing a role to ensure that all of these goals were being accomplished, at least as much as possible.

During the eighteenth and nineteenth centuries, the industrial revolution had a growing impact on how youth were viewed in society (Taylor, Fritsch & Caeti, 2007). During this time, several events occurred almost at the same time: factories were being developed for work; people were moving in large masses to urban areas for jobs; there was massive European immigration; and the market economy was on the rise (Taylor et al., 2002; Ward, 2012). In addition, there was a growing societal perception that cities were unable to control inhabitants (especially youth). "Social disorganization" was also occuring, although the term was not coined until over a century later. The cities were rapidly growing due to immigration (rural people who wanted work at the factories and those from predominantly European countries) and racial heterogeneity. Because new work in the factories kept parents away from their children for longer periods of time, supervision of youth decreased. With all of these conditions in place, offenses committed by children progressively increased.

In the 1800s, Houses of Refuge were created to manage the unruly youth. Houses of Refuge were first developed in New York, Philadelphia, and Boston (Howell, 1997; Jordan, 2006). The purpose of these institutions was to take in and care for dependent, neglected, and delinquent youth. Those who supported these Houses generally believed that youth could be saved through hard work, education, and religion. Only youth who were "salvageable" were sent to the Houses of Refuge. Other youth were sent to the traditional (adult) criminal justice system for processing.

Houses of Refuge were built on the doctrine of *parens patriae* or "state as parent" (Taylor et al., 2007). Succinctly stated, under this doctrine, if parents were unable or unwilling to care for children, the state had the legal means to formally intervene in juveniles' lives. This doctrine was tested before the United States Supreme Court in 1839 in *Ex Parte Crouse* (Bernard & Kurlychek, 2010). In this case, Crouse was a poor child who was petitioned by her mother to be committed to the Philadelphia House of Refuge. Her mother asked for her to be committed out of fear that her daughter would grow up to be a pauper (poor person). Crouse's father, however, petitioned to have his daughter released because there was no crime committed and no trial was held. The Pennsylvania Supreme Court upheld the doctrine of *parens patriae*, saying the House of Refuge was helping the child and had the right to intervene. Following this ruling, Houses of Refuge started emerging all across the country.

Several decades after the Houses of Refuge were erected, they became overcrowded. Violence was also becoming more rampant, and children were being sent home to their parents more quickly (Platt, 1969). There was also a growing belief that Houses of Refuge were becoming training schools for learning delinquent behavior. For these reasons, a group of "prominent" women lobbied politicians in Chicago to establish a completely separate system for juveniles. This group of women was known as the "child savers." An additional explanation for the child savers wanting to establish a separate juvenile system was to protect their own lifestyle (Platt, 1969). The child savers were largely anti-immigrant and anti-minority, not trusting of those who lived in poverty. They also wanted others to accept their way of life. They believed that these "other" groups must assimilate into their culture in order to be productive members of society. Therefore, the best way to control this group was to have them under the control of the juvenile justice system. Eventually they were successful; in 1899, Illinois established the Juvenile Court Act, establishing the nation's first juvenile court in Cook County, Illinois. By the mid-1900s, every state within the nation created its own juvenile court system. The foundation of the court would be *parens patriae*.

(In)Justice of Blacks

The preceding discussion is an accurate depiction of the juvenile court's creation, and is the version most often told in scholarship that traces the creation of the juvenile court. Often missing from the discussion, however, is context. Given the minority overrepresentation that exists in the current juvenile system, it is important to trace some of that history, which may shed light on contemporary concerns. Only through this examination can people truly understand the role that race has played in the development of the juvenile court.

When the Houses of Refuge were intervening in the lives of youth to "help" during the 1800s, there was another "world" for Blacks in the United States (Ward, 2012). Slavery was still legal, and Blacks (men, women, and children) were legally denied equal protection under the law. They were not formally taken into consideration when children were being viewed as needing assistance and resources were being put in place to increase the likelihood of children's success. In fact, while free Blacks (mostly in northern states), including children, were counted equally for determining representation in the U.S. House of Representatives, slaves were counted as three-fifths of a person for determining such representation (U.S. Constitution). For example, five slaves would count as a population of only three persons.

An additional set of context to examine is the infamous *Dred Scott v. Sanford* case (1857). Again, this case was taking place while discussions and actions were occurring to save *some* youth who needed interventions. Dred Scott was once a slave who eventually lived in multiple "free" states. After his master's death, he made a claim of "freedom." The case made its way to the U.S. Supreme Court. In a 7–2 decision, the Supreme Court ruled against Mr. Scott. In delivering the majority opinion, Chief Justice Roger Taney stated the Court's threshold was to determine who was considered U.S. Citizens of the states when the Constitution was adopted. He stated, "In the opinion of the court, the legislation and histories of the times, and the language used in the Declaration of Independence, show, that neither the class of persons who had been imported as slaves, nor their descendants, whether they had become free or not, were then acknowledged as a part of the people, nor intended to be included in the general words used in that memorable instrument." He further declared:

> They [Blacks] had for more than a century before been regarded as beings of an inferior order, and altogether unfit to associate with the white race, either in social or political relations; and so far inferior, that they had no rights which the white man was bound to respect; and that the negro might justly and lawfully be reduced to slavery for his benefit. He was bought and sold, and treated as an ordinary article of merchandise and traffic, whenever a profit could be made by it. This opinion was at that time fixed and universal in the civilized portion of the white race. It was regarded as an axiom in morals as well

as in politics, which no one thought of disputing, or supposed to be open to dispute; and men in every grade and position in society daily and habitually acted upon it in their private pursuits, as well as in matters of public concern; without doubting for a moment the correctness of this opinion.

Finally, the Chief Justice quoted the Constitution of *all* men being created equal and being endowed with inalienable rights, including life, liberty, and the pursuit of happiness. He then stated:

The general words above quoted would seem to embrace the whole human family, and if they were used in a similar instrument at this day would be so understood. But it is too clear for dispute, that the enslaved African race were not intended to be included, and formed no part of the people who framed and adopted this declaration; for if the language, as understood in that day, would embrace them, the conduct of the distinguished men who framed the Declaration of Independence would have been utterly and flagrantly inconsistent with the principles they asserted; and instead of the sympathy of mankind, to which they so confidently appealed, they would have deserved and received universal rebuke and reprobation.

Yet the men who framed this declaration were great men—high in literary acquirements—high in their sense of honor, and incapable of asserting principles inconsistent with those on which they were acting. They perfectly understood the meaning of the language they used, and how it would be understood by others; and they knew that it would not in any part of the civilized world be supposed to embrace the negro race, which by common consent, had been excluded from civilized Governments and the family of nations, and doomed to slavery. They spoke and acted according to the then established doctrines and principles, and in the ordinary language of the day, and no one misunderstood them. The unhappy black race were separated from the white by indelible marks, and laws long before established, and were never thought of or spoken of except as property, and when the claims of the owner or the profit of the trader were supposed to need protection.

Again, this was the view toward Blacks (including Black children) during this time period. Therefore, one could ask whether Black children were being considered when politicians, teachers, moralists, and child-savers were discussing a justice system that was needed to help intervene in the lives of youth in a meaningful and positive way. Actually, it seems that Black youth were intentionally not meant to be served by this impending system, especially given the language of the time, the laws, and the Supreme Court decisions. Black youth were considered the children of inferior parents, all existing in a White-dominated society (Ward, 2012). Issues such as this indicate that Black children were never meant to be served by or benefit from a separate juvenile system.

In moving on to specifics, Black youth were not treated equally to Whites regarding the Houses of Refuge. The early Houses were open only to White males (Frey, 1981; Ward, 2012). Eventually, they did allow White females, in order to take care of traditional domestic responsibilities (e.g., cooking, cleaning, ironing, sewing, etc.). However, there still was not an option for Black youth to be residents of the Houses. The staff of the institutions felt that admitting Black youth would serve as a detriment to the White youth (Ward, 2012).

Nevertheless, in the mid-1830s, Houses of Refuge began taking in Black youth (Frey, 1981). Although Black children were now admitted into some Houses, they were either in their own section separated from the White youth or they had their own House of Refuge (e.g., House of Refuge for Colored Children, which was in Philadelphia). This was a reflection of the current and upcoming times (e.g., Jim Crow) regarding the views toward Blacks, generally, and Black youth, specifically. Within the House of Refuge, formal education was disproportionately provided to White youth, while Black youth were taught skills to make them good manual laborers (Ward, 2012). There was even an early hint of sentencing disparities during these times. While the average stay of White youth in the traditional House of Refuge was approximately one and a half years, the average stay of Black youth in the Colored Refuge was almost twice that length of time.

The Houses of Refuge (traditional and Black facilities) were not popular in southern states. In fact, most southern states resisted the calls for formal institutions to address juvenile concerns, because it would negatively influence the control the White residents had over their juvenile slaves. Slave owners already had a method of control for juveniles who stepped "out of line." Examples of methods for juvenile social control were whippings, lashings, raping of young girls, shootings, and hangings. Houses of Refuge and other institutions focused on reforming juveniles would have possibly removed youth from the homes of their masters, resulting in severely lowering the economic position of those Whites. Therefore, while Black juveniles in northern states were subjected to segregated juvenile facilities, Black juveniles in the south were subjected to the informal social control of slave owners. Even after the Civil War and the passage of the 13th Amendment that formally ended slavery, through legal segregation, mechanisms were in place to keep Blacks working on plantations. These mechanisms included Black codes that were focused on criminalizing behavior of newly freed Blacks and the convict leasing system that leased out inmates to private residents for a period of time. Black adults were not the only ones affected by these mechanisms. Juveniles also often ended up working back on plantations (see Figure 2.1) (Du Bois, 1901/2002; Myers, 1998; Ward, 2012; Gabbidon & Green, 2013). It is difficult, then, to see how Black juveniles were meant to be served by formal juvenile institutions.

Figure 2.1. "Juvenile convicts at work in the fields"

Library of Congress, Prints & Photographs Division, Detroit Publishing Company Collection [reproduction number, e.g., LC-D4-10865].

Although the first juvenile court was created in 1899 and many states followed suit in the immediate years thereafter, most of the beginning juvenile courts were created in northern states (Myers, 2005). Approximately 90% of all Blacks lived in southern states during 1900, in post-slavery times (Ward, 2012). Therefore, although there were juvenile courts being created, most Black juveniles did not have access to the new court system initially, even if only because of geography. However, this soon changed as a result of the Great Migration of Blacks to the northern cities and the Midwest for work opportunities.

Due Process Era

By the 1950s, people began to question whether the juvenile court could successfully rehabilitate youth (Snyder & Sickmund, 1999). Although the juvenile court's purpose of treatment was not necessarily in question, many believed that too many youth were being confined in the name of treatment. Juveniles, in large droves, were put in confinement for indefinite periods of time for fairly minor offenses. Also, there was an increasingly growing belief that the juvenile court was over-stepping its bounds. Related to this, many believed that youth were being denied their basic legal rights. The court was accused of not giving youth enough procedural safeguards, a practice that had been justified on the basis of *parens patriae.* Due to juvenile courts being implemented to do what was in the "best interests" of the child, it was thought that courts needed to have wide latitude in addressing the "needs" of youth. In response to growing criticisms, a series of landmark United States Supreme Court cases originating in the late 1960s sought to change juvenile court practices and procedures. Most of these cases fell under the infamous *Earl Warren* Court, which declared the doctrine of "Separate but Equal" (Jim Crow) unconstitutional in 1954.

The first of these cases was *Kent v. United States* (1966). Morris Kent (16 years old) was charged with rape and robbery, while he was on probation from a previous case. He confessed to the crimes. His attorney, assuming that the District of Columbia's juvenile court would transfer the case to criminal court, requested a hearing on the issue of which court should have jurisdiction. The juvenile court judge did not rule on Kent's motion, but later waived the case to criminal court, stating that a "full investigation" had occurred. Kent later was found guilty in criminal court and sentenced to 30 to 90 years in prison. Kent appealed, and the U.S. Supreme Court eventually ruled the waiver invalid, stating that Kent should have received a hearing that equated to the essentials of due process and fair treatment. In addition, the Court held that Kent's attorney should have had full access to the records involved in the waiver hearing, and that the juvenile court judge needed to provide written reasons to justify transferring the case to criminal court.

The next landmark case, *In re Gault* (1967), was ruled on by the U.S. Supreme Court a year later. This case resulted in juveniles being granted more due process rights when the case outcome could result in incarceration. These rights include the right to notice of the charges, the right to counsel, the right to question witnesses, and protection against self-incrimination. In this case, Gerald Gault (15 years old), while on probation, made a prank phone call to an adult neighbor. During his court hearing, the victim did not attend, and the court actually did not resolve the issue of whether or not Gault made any "obscene" comments. Gault then was sentenced to a training school until age 21. For a similar offense by an adult, the maximum sentence would have been 2 months in jail or a $50 fine. After the hearing, Gault obtained an attorney, stating his constitutional rights were denied.

The Court agreed with Gault, stating that he was being punished (not helped) by the juvenile court, and the doctrine of *parens patriae* was rejected. The majority opinion held that "juvenile court history has again demonstrated that unbridled discretion, however benevolently motivated, is frequently a poor substitute for principle and procedure" (Snyder & Sickmund, 1999, p. 90). The *Gault* case, along with the *Kent* decision, greatly expanded the procedural rights for juveniles that originally were granted only to adults.

The Supreme Court ruled on the next major juvenile case, *In re Winship*, in 1970. At that time, many juvenile courts used "by a preponderance of evidence" as the standard for burden of proof. When appealed to the U.S. Supreme Court, the Court found that although juvenile courts were implemented to save (rather than punish) children, they could not use that rationale to require a lesser burden of proof. The Court stated that "reasonable doubt" should be the standard of proof in all adjudicatory hearings. Two years following this case, the Court made its ruling retroactive, meaning all youth who were convicted by a preponderance of the evidence either had to be released from custody or adjudicated again using "beyond a reasonable doubt" as the burden of proof (Bernard & Kurlychek, 2010). However, because juveniles had no right to a jury trial, the juvenile court judge alone would make the subjective determination of whether the stronger burden of proof had been met.

The last salient due process case was *Breed v. Jones* (1975). In this case, Jones was arrested for an armed robbery in California (Snyder & Sickmund, 1999). He later was adjudicated delinquent in juvenile court on that charge, along with two other robbery charges. At the disposition hearing, the judge decided to waive Jones to adult court. Jones' attorney appealed the case, stating that because Jones already was "tried" in juvenile court for the offense, subsequently trying him for the same crime in adult court would constitute double jeopardy. On appeal, the U.S. Supreme Court agreed with Jones, stating that an adjudication hearing is equivalent to a trial in criminal court, meaning jeopardy attaches at the hearing when evidence is first presented. Therefore, if a youth is to be transferred to adult court, it must be done prior to evidence being presented at the adjudicatory stage in the juvenile court.

Although these cases granted juveniles many of the due process rights given to adults, not all procedural rights were granted. In *McKiever v. Pennsylvania* (1971), the Court stated that juveniles were not constitutionally entitled to a jury trial. Also, in *Schall v. Martin* (1984), the Court maintained that juveniles were not entitled to bail, meaning preventive detention was permissible. However, aside from these two cases, the Supreme Court's decisions appeared to change the original purpose of the juvenile court, by focusing more on formal procedures.

Many people may view these cases as historic victories for youth, because they granted a significant number of rights to juveniles in a system that was already dealing with issues of minority overrepresentation and a lack of respect toward those who entered that system (Feld, 2005). However, as the juvenile court became more formalized and similar to the adult system, it allowed itself to increasingly have some of the same problems the adult system faces (e.g., even more overrepresentation of minorities, punitive ideals, less rehabilitative efforts, etc.). Even in early research during the due process period, "Negro" and "Latin" youth were more likely than "Anglo" youth to have their cases formally referred to the juvenile court (Arnold, 1971). The author stated, "The data presented here certainly do not refute the view that our correctional system works to the disadvantage of lower-rank and minority-group members (or to the advantage of the dominant rank and race). Even differences that are not large numerically at any one stage in the correctional process could add up to very important differences for the system as a whole" (Arnold 1971, p. 226). In other words, during the early years of the juvenile court, race and ethnicity were playing a role in court outcomes, with the acknowledgment that those effects at one stage may very well influence subsequent stages of the judicial process. Although Black Migration resulted in a large influx of Blacks to northern cities during the due process era and after segregation was declared unconstitutional, the South continued to have its own method of social control (see Figure 2.2).

The Murder of Emmett Till

Figure 2.2. Emmett Till

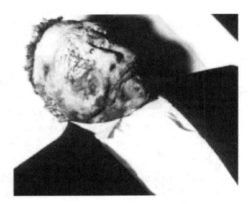

Picture on left is while alive, while picture on right is at his funeral.

Emmett Till was born in 1941 in Chicago. He was an only child, who grew up on Chicago's South Side, which at the time, was a middle-class neighborhood. According to Emmett's mother, "[He] had all the house responsibility. I mean everything was really on his shoulders, and Emmett took it upon himself. He told me if I would work, and make the money, he would take care of everything else. He cleaned, and he cooked quite a bit. And he even took over the laundry."

In August 1955, Till's uncle visited from Mississippi. After his stay, he took Emmett and his cousin back to Mississippi to visit other relatives. Prior to leaving from Chicago, Emmett's mother gave him his late father's ring, which was engraved with his father's initials. A few days after arriving in Mississippi, Emmett and a friend went to the store. While there, Emmett boasted about his integrated school in Chicago and an alleged White girlfriend. At this time, his friends dared Emmett to talk to Carolyn Bryant, who was the store owner's (Roy Bryant) wife.

At this point, the details are a bit conflicting, but Emmett did one of a few things toward Carolyn Bryant: whistled, used suggestive language, or touched her hand. Regardless of what happened, Rob Bryant found out what happened at the store. Four days later, Roy, his half-brother

John Milam, and another man kidnapped Emmett from the home where he was staying at 2:30 in the morning. They took Emmett and drove off with Emmett in the back of a pick-up truck.

Roy and John beat Emmett badly, dragged him to the bank of the Tallahatchie River, shot him in the head, tied him with barbed wire to a large metal fan, and shoved his body into the water. Emmett's body was found three days later, swollen with water, and badly damaged in the Tallahatchie River. His face and body was so disfigured, he was only able to be identified by the ring he wore, which his mom gave him before he left Chicago. Emmett Till was only 14 years old when he was killed.

Roy and John were eventually arrested and charged with Emmett's murder. At the time, Blacks and women were not allowed to serve on juries in Mississippi. Therefore, the trial had an all-White/all-male jury. After deliberating for 67 minutes, both men were acquitted, although they were openly identified as the kidnappers. A few months following the acquittal, both men admitted to the kidnapping and the murder to a magazine for $4,000.

Sources:
http://newsone.com/2032853/emmett-till-story/
http://www.biography.com/people/emmett-till-507515#impact-on-
    civil-rights

Crime Control Shift

The due process cases of the late 1960s and early 1970s coincided with a substantial increase in juvenile crime (Tanenhaus, 2000). This increase can be at least partially explained by the number of adolescents in the general population at this time. Following World War II, there was a large increase in the number of babies born (Myers, 2005). It also has been shown empirically that the most crime-prone years occur during mid to late adolescence, after which offending declines (Blumstein, 1995). Therefore, during the late 1960s and early 1970s, the "baby-boomers" were approaching and in their peak years of involvement in delinquent and criminal behavior, which undoubtedly contributed to the overall increase in juvenile crime.

In addition, by this time many people were losing faith in rehabilitation, and calls were being made for "just deserts" for juvenile offenders. The traditional belief in rehabilitation was challenged based on research suggesting that "nothing works" (Lipton, Martinson & Wilks, 1975; Martinson, 1974). Consequently, due to the increase in juvenile crime and the loss of faith in rehabilitation, it was believed by some that the juvenile court no longer was able to handle many youthful offenders. In order to remain consistent with the new focus of "just deserts," the juvenile court began to stiffen penalties for offenders, including mandatory minimums and determinant sentencing, as well as transferring more offenders to criminal court (Taylor et al., 2002). From the mid-1970s through the mid-1980s, juvenile crime rates remained relatively stable (Cook & Laub, 1998). However, beginning in 1985 and lasting until 1994, juvenile arrests for violent offenses increased (Snyder & Sickmund, 1999; Torbet & Szymanski, 1998). The overall rate of juveniles arrested for violent crimes rose by over 70% during the span of a decade. By 1994, juveniles constituted approximately one in six arrests for homicide, rape, and aggravated assault. Juveniles also made up about one-third of the robbery arrests in the country.

When examining these trends, it appears that there was a tremendous increase in overall violent juvenile offending. However, most noteworthy was the increase in criminal homicides committed by youth (Cook & Laub, 1998; Zimring, 1998). Until this time, juvenile arrests for all homicides committed was approximately 10%. However, beginning in the mid-1980s, this percentage started to increase, peaking in 1994 at 17%. Also, the increase in juvenile arrests for homicide far exceeded a slight rise in arrest rates for homicide committed by adults. In contrast to the increase in violent juvenile crime, juvenile property crime arrest rates remained steady or decreased during the same time period (Cook & Laub, 1998). Although more juveniles still were being arrested for property crime as compared to violent crime, property crime arrest rates did not follow the same upward trend. However, due to the increase in juvenile violent crime, and media sensationalism of violent events committed by young people (particular young Black males), many juveniles were thought to be extremely dangerous and generally were branded as "superpredators" (Cook & Laub, 1998).

Disproportionate Minority Confinement/Contact

The original acronym, DMC, stood for Disproportionate Minority Confinement. In 1988, the U.S. Congress amended the Juvenile Justice Delinquency and Prevention Act (JJDPA) to include DMC (Hsia, 2009). This amendment, required states to address DMC in their respective state plans. If minority (i.e., African American, Hispanic, American Indians, Asian, and Pacific Islander) youth were in confinement (including pre-adjudication detention) at a percentage that was higher than each's representation in the general population, the state was required to develop a plan to reduce those levels. For example, if Hispanic youth represented 16% of the population in the U.S., but made up any more than 16% of the confinement population, DMC was said to exist. In that case, the state would have to develop a plan to reduce Hispanic's representation among confined youth.

In 1992, the DMC Amendments were elevated to a core requirement in the JJDPA (Hsia, 2009). Through it being a core requirement, funding for states was tied to compliance. If states were not in compliance, they would not receive the JJDP Formula Grants, which many states needed to help fund their respective juvenile courts. In 1994, the Office of Juvenile Justice and Delinquency Prevention (OJJDP) published its first fact sheet on DMC. They found that in 1991, Blacks made up 43% of youth in juvenile detention centers, while Hispanics made up 19%. They also found that for those in public training schools, which were the most restrictive sanction a juvenile could receive, Black youth made up 47% of the population. In other words, Blacks and Hispanics were disproportionately over-represented among those confined through the juvenile justice system.

During 2002, Congress further amended the JJDPA through changing the meaning of DMC (Hsia, 2009). Instead of focusing on "confinement," the C was changed to mean "contact." OJJDP recognized that looking at confinement alone might not present the entire picture and may not fully capture the influence that race has in the juvenile justice system process. The section of the law now reads: "address juvenile delinquency prevention efforts and system improvement efforts designed to reduce, without establishing or requiring numerical standards or quotas, the disproportionate number of juvenile members of minority groups who come into *contact* with the juvenile justice system" (JJDPA of 1974, 2002).

The first OJJDP report following the change from "confinement" to "contact" stipulated that states must identify factors that contributed to DMC. These factors included such things as racial/ ethnic stereotyping/cultural insensitivity of criminal justice workers, lack of alternatives to detention and confinement, the existence of too much discretionary judicial power, education, social economic status, and lack of staff who speak a second language. Given how race (e.g., being Black) and ethnicity (e.g., being Hispanic) are tied to many of these issues, it is not surprising that these two groups, in particular, continue to be over-represented in the juvenile justice system.

While Blacks have a deep-rooted history in the United States and in the creation of the juvenile court, a similar history does not exist among Hispanics. However, Hispanics are currently the largest minority group, and are also over-represented in the juvenile justice system. Later chapters will detail the extent to which Hispanics are over-represented in the juvenile justice system. However, DMC documents were very specific on what could be done to reduce Hispanic DMC within the United States, including the following:

- assessment of language access needs of youth and their families, particularly the Hispanic population.
- access to services that meet linguistic needs of youth and their families.
- barriers to educational success for Hispanic youth including language proficiency issues, availability of educational advocacy assistance, and lack of academic supports.
- relationships of youth and their parents with the school and probation systems through providing bilingual probation staffing, services, and information to ensure that youth are enrolled in and attend school.

Conclusion

The juvenile court is often discussed as a system that was created to help all youth. Prior to the juvenile court's inception, youth were treated similarly to adults and/or put in juvenile facilities for indefinite periods of time. Due to a broader desire to protect youth and invest in making them productive adults, the juvenile court was created. While somewhat accurate, the history of the juvenile court's creation often ignored the racial dynamics going on at the time (e.g., slavery, Black codes, Jim Crow laws, etc.).

Some may argue that the juvenile court was not designed for non-White youth. At one time, there was not a large Hispanic/Latino representation in the United States, and Black youth (especially in the South) were generally handled by "Southern justice," instead of a formal social control system. It is also interesting that the current juvenile justice system is over-represented with Black and Hispanics. Given that these two groups were not initially served by the antecedents to the juvenile court (e.g., Houses of Refuge) and once served, had separate "colored" and inferior facilities, it then seems that non-Whites were not intended to fair well in this system. In addition, recall that Platt (1969) discussed how another reason for the juvenile court may have been to control the underprivileged, immigrants, and Black youth.

Regardless of the original intention, the federal government has taken steps to address the current disproportionate minority contact in the juvenile system. While confinement is important, expanding to overall contact with the system and making it a core requirement is a strong step in the right direction. It will be extremely difficult to fix a system that was flawed from the beginning. It is noteworthy to end this chapter with the words of Supreme Court Justice Thurgood Marshall. He gave a speech in 1987 about the Constitution, but it is also relevant to the juvenile court's creation, because he discusses a system designed from the very beginning and who the system was designed to serve (or not serve).

I do not believe that the meaning of the Constitution was forever "fixed" at the Philadelphia Convention. Nor do I find the wisdom, foresight, and sense of justice exhibited by the Framers particularly profound. To the contrary, the government they devised was defective from the start, requiring several amendments, a civil war, and momentous social transformation to attain the system of constitutional government, and its respect for the individual freedoms and human rights, we hold as fundamental today. When contemporary Americans cite "The Constitution," they invoke a concept that is vastly different from what the Framers barely began to construct two centuries ago.

For a sense of the evolving nature of the Constitution we need look no further than the first three words of the document's preamble: "We the People." When the Founding Fathers used this phrase in 1787, they did not have in mind the majority of America's citizens. "We the People" included, in the words of the Framers, "the whole Number of free Persons." On a matter so basic as the right to vote, for example, Negro slaves were excluded, although they were counted for representational purposes at three-fifths each. Women did not gain the right to vote for over a hundred and thirty years.

These omissions were intentional. The record of the Framers' debates on the slave question is especially clear: The Southern States acceded to the demands of the New England States for giving Congress broad power to regulate commerce, in exchange for the right to continue the slave trade. The economic interests of the regions coalesced: New Englanders engaged in the "carrying trade" would profit from transporting slaves from Africa as well as goods produced in America by slave labor. The perpetuation of slavery ensured the primary source of wealth in the Southern States.

Discussion Questions

1. Why were youth once thought not to need protection?
2. What were the different methods of addressing inappropriate/illegal behaviors by both Black and White youth prior to the juvenile court's inception?
3. Given the original goals of the juvenile court, did the rights given to juveniles by the Supreme Court help or hinder the goal of doing what is in the "best interest of the child"?
4. What efforts are the federal government utilizing to address disproportionate minority contact in the juvenile justice system?

References

Arnold, W.R. (1971). Race and ethnicity relative to other factors in juvenile court dispositions. *American Journal of Sociology, 77*(2), 211–227.

Bernard, T.J. & Kurlychek, M.C. (2010). *The cycle of juvenile justice* (2nd ed.). New York: Oxford University Press.

Blumstein, A. (1995). Youth violence, guns, and the illicit-drug industry. *The Journal of Criminal Law and Criminology, 86*(1), 10–36.

Breed v. Jones, 421 U.S. 519 (1975).

Chandler, D.L. (2012). Teen Emmett Till Victim of Kidnapping, Brutal Murder on this Day. Retrieved from http://newsone.com/2032853/emmett-till-story.

Cook, P.J. & Laub, J.H. (1998). The unprecedented epidemic in youth violence. In M. Tonry & M.H. Moore (Eds.), *Crime and justice: A review of research* (Vol. 24pp. 27–64). Chicago: University of Chicago Press.

Du Bois, W.E.B. (1901/2002). The spawn of slavery: The convict lease system in the South. In S.L. Gabbidon & H. Taylor Greene & V. Young (Eds.), *African American classics in criminology and criminal justice* (pp. 83–88). Thousand Oaks, CA: SAGE.

Dred Scott v. Stanford, 60 U.S. 393 (1857).

Emmett Till biography (n.d.) Retrieved from http://www.biography.com/people/emmett-till-507515#impact-on-civil-rights.

Empey, L.T., Stafford, M.C. & Hay, C.H. (1999). *American delinquency: Its meaning and construction* (4th ed.). Belmont, CA: Wadsworth Publishing Company.

Feld, B.C. (2005). Race and jurisprudence of juvenile justice: A tale in two parts, 1950–2000. In D.F. Hawkins & K. Kempf-Leonard (Eds.), *Our chil-*

dren, their children: Confronting racial and ethnic differences in American juvenile justice (pp. 122–163). Chicago: The University of Chicago Press.

Frey, C.P. (1981). The house of refuge for colored children. *The Journal of Negro History, 66*(1), 10–25.

Gabbidon, S.L. & Taylor Greene, H. (2013). *Race and crime* (3rd ed.). Thousand Oaks, CA: SAGE.

Howell, J.C. (1997). *Juvenile justice and youth violence.* Thousand Oaks, CA: SAGE.

Hsia, H. (2009). *Disproportionate minority cntact technical assistance manual* (4th ed.). Washington, DC: U.S. Department of Justice.

Jordan, K.J. (2006). *Violent youth in adult court: The decertification of transferred offenders.* New York: LFB Scholarly.

Juvenile Justice and Delinquency Prevention Act of 1974, 42 U.S.C §5633 (2002).

In re Gault, 387 U.S. (1967).

In re Winship, 397 U.S. 358 (1970).

Kent v. United States, 383 U.S. 541 (1966).

Lipton, D., Martinson, R. & Wilks, J. (1975). *The effectiveness of correctional treatment: A survey of treatment evaluation studies.* New York:Praeger.

Martinson, R. (1974). What works? Questions and answers about prison reform. *The Public Interest, 35,* 22–54.

McKiever v. Pennsylvania, 403 U.S. 528 (1971).

Myers, D.L. (2005). *Boys among men: Trying and sentencing juveniles as adults.* Westport, CT: Praeger.

Myers, M.A. (1998). *Race, labor & punishment in the New South.* Columbus, OH: Ohio State University Press.

Platt, A. (1969). *The child savers.* Chicago, IL: University of Chicago Press.

Schall v. Martin, 467 U.S. 253 (1984).

Snyder, H.N. & Sickmund, M. (1999). *Juvenile offenders and victims: 1999 national report.* (Report No. NCJ 178257). Washington, DC: Office of Juvenile Justice and Delinquency Prevention.

Tanenhaus, D.S. (2000). The evolution of transfer out of the juvenile court. In J. Fagan & F.E. Zimring (Eds.), *The changing borders of juvenile justice: Transfer of adolescents to the criminal court* (pp. 13–43). Chicago, IL: The University of Chicago Press.

Taylor, R.W., Fritsch, E.J., & Caeti, T.J. (2007). *Juvenile Justice: Policies, Programs, and Practices* (2nd ed.) Woodland Hills, CA:Glencoe Hills/McGraw-Hill.

The Bicenteennial Speech (n.d.) Retrieved from http://thurgoodmarshall.com/the-bicentennial-speech.

Torbet, P. & Szymanski, L. (1998). *State legislative responses to violent juvenile crime: 1996–97 update.* (Report No. NCJ 172835). Washington, DC: Office of Juvenile Justice and Delinquency Prevention.

Ward, G.K. (2012). *The Black child-savers: Racial democracy & juvenile justice.* Chicago: The University of Chicago Press.

Zimring, F.E. (1998). *American youth violence.* New York, NY: Oxford University Press, Inc.

Chapter 3

Race/Ethnicity and Theories of Juvenile Justice Decision-Making

Goals of the Chapter

The purpose of this chapter is to examine the leading theories that are used to explain the relationship between race and juvenile court decision-making. While criminological theories attempt to explain why crime and delinquency occurs, the theories we discuss explain the decisions that are made in the course of juvenile justice processing. In this chapter, we also discuss the empirical validity of these theories, along with their limitations. Finally, the chapter ends with a discussion of the value that theories have in understanding the role that race and ethnicity play in juvenile justice decision-making.

After reading the chapter, you will be able to do the following:

1. Recognize the leading theories that are used to explain racial and ethnic disparities in juvenile justice decision-making;
2. Discuss the empirical validity of these theories; and
3. Evaluate their usefulness to explain the effect that race and ethnicity have on decision-making.

Most theories that have been empirically tested, extensively, relate to theories of crime and/or delinquency. The focuses of these theories are on explaining why delinquency has taken place, and on the behavior of the offender. It is understandable why theories of delinquency receive the majority of attention. We live in a society in which we always want to know why offenders commit their crimes, especially when they commit violent crimes such as murder, rape, robbery, terrorist acts, etc. When one of the DC/Beltway Snipers, Lee Boyd Malvo, age 17 at the time of his crimes, committed a string of murders in 2002, we all wanted to understand why he engaged in those crimes. When

31

two 12-year-old girls in Wisconsin lured another girl into the woods and attempted to stab her to death (Slender Man case), we all wanted to understand why these girls would engage in such an act. Again, while having an understanding of why is very important, it should not end there.

Studying the decision-making of those who work in the juvenile justice system is equally important to studying the behavior of offenders. Kraska (2006), in discussing the criminal justice system, makes the point that we need "to start the process of re-orienting our discipline to approach the study of criminal justice/crime control as a legitimate and essential object of theorizing in and of itself; a second 'dependent variable' for our field alongside crime and crime rates. While still acknowledging their interconnections, crime and criminal justice would be treated as dual objects of study—as opposed to approaching criminal justice phenomena as the mere outcome or effect of crime" (p. 168). The same logic can be applied to the juvenile justice system. Instead of looking at the juvenile justice system as simply the place where delinquents go for processing, it can be studied as an entity worthy of theorizing about the reasoning behind the decisions its workers make.

There are a handful of theories that are used in the empirical research to help explain the effect of race/ethnicity on juvenile justice decision-making, from arrest through disposition of cases. While examining race/ethnicity effects on decision-making, theory is needed to provide guidance and context to help explain these findings. For instance, what is it about particular races that increase or decrease their likelihood of receiving certain outcomes in the juvenile justice system? Theory can place those results in proper context.

Walker, Spohn, and DeLone's
Discrimination-Disparity Continuum

Walker, Spohn, and DeLone (2012) developed a continuum to help explain the racial/ethnic disparity in the criminal justice system, that we can apply to the juvenile justice system. A disparity is a difference in observed outcomes (e.g., detention, adjudication, placements, etc.) that are based solely on the behavior of the people. Discrimination, however, is groups being treated differently without regard to the individual's behavior. Walker et al. (2012) make the argument that it is not as simple as there is either discrimination in the justice system or there is absolutely no discrimination. They indicate that there are additional categories that

fall between the two extremes. The Discrimination-Disparity continuum is below:

Systematic Discrimination	Institutionalized Discrimination	Contextual Discrimination	Individual Acts of Discrimination	Pure Justice

In focusing on juvenile justice, systematic discrimination is when there
is discrimination at all stages of the system. Institutionalized discrimination is disparities due to factors that appear to have no relevance to
race, such as prior record and offense severity. Contextual discrimination is "discrimination found in particular context or circumstance (for
example, certain regions, particular crimes, or special victim-offender relationships)" (p. 26). Individual acts of discrimination is when particular justice professionals (e.g., judges, prosecutors, intake officers, etc.)
act in a discriminatory manner, but it is not reflective of the agency or
system as a whole. Finally, pure justice means there is no race/ethnicity-
based discrimination at any point in the system.

Focal Concerns Theory

One of the most used theories to help explain the role of race/ethnicity in
the juvenile court decision-making is the focal concerns perspective. Originally, focal concerns theory was applied toward adult sentencing decisions, but
it is now often used to explain other decision points (e.g., arrests, prosecution,
detention, etc.). The rationale is that sentencing is one of multiple decisions
made in the system, so it can apply equally as well to other stages of the judicial process. Focal concerns posits that justice system workers (judges, prosecutors, etc.) make decisions based on three focal concerns: offender's
blameworthiness/degree of harm to victims, protection of the community, and
practical constraints and consequences (Steffensmeier, Ulmer & Kramer, 1998;
Steffensmeier & Demuth, 2000; 2006 Spohn & Holleran, 2000).

The first focal concern, blameworthiness, addresses an offender's culpability in the offense (e.g., Kramer & Steffensmeier, 1993; Steffensmeier et al.,

1998; Spohn & Holleran, 2000; Kramer & Ulmer, 2002). As the responsibility in the offense increases, along with injury caused to the victims, offenders will be perceived as more blameworthy and will be likely to receive a harsher outcome. This element of the perspective tends to focus on retribution, meaning the offenders get what is "deserved," based on their own actions. Research generally finds support for this element, as serious offenders are typically given harsher sentences than those who commit less serious offenses. Also, having a prior record implies more blameworthiness, because it is presumed to be an indicator of not learning from prior bad acts and continuing down the same path. Empirical studies tend to find that increased prior record tends to result in harsher court outcomes. In addition, research tends to find that those who played a primary role in the offense are sentenced more severely than those who played more of a secondary role. Finally, research also suggests that an increase in the number and/or injury of victims is associated with harsher sanctions.

The second element of focal concerns is protection of the community (e.g., Kramer & Steffensmeier, 1993; Steffensmeier et al., 1998; Spohn & Holleran, 2000; Kramer & Ulmer, 2002). Not only does this factor focus on incapacitation (locking up offenders so they do not have the opportunity to commit additional offenses), but it also means that judges and other practitioners consider deterring potential offenders. Justice system professionals are in a position where they are held accountable when crime/delinquency occurs in society. Therefore, when offenders enter the justice systems (both juvenile and adult) and decisions are being made, prosecutors and judges take into account what is needed to protect general society. In assessing this focal concern, justice system workers consider the risk of recidivism (i.e., reoffending). Because they cannot predict recidivism for the offenders, they usually focus on factors that may lead to recidivism (e.g., serious offense, more extensive prior record).

The final element of the perspective is practical constraints and consequences (e.g., Kramer & Steffensmeier, 1993; Steffensmeier et al., 1998; Spohn & Holleran, 2000; Kramer & Ulmer, 2002). With this focal concern, there are both organizational and individual concerns. At the organizational level, judges consider the correctional population (i.e., overcrowding), relationship with the courtroom workgroup, etc. At the individual level, judges consider offenders' ability to complete a punishment (e.g., incarceration, boot camp, etc.) and the impact of the sanction on the family (e.g., financially, being away from the home, etc.).

The combination of these elements represents focal concerns. The perspective also suggests that judges and other decision makers in the justice system do not have every piece of information about the offender or the offense that is needed to make a full assessment of these three focal concerns, especially at early decision points. Therefore, judges, prosecutors, and intake staff develop a "perceptual shorthand" in order to determine who may be dangerous and more likely to reoffend, who is more blameworthy and the practical constraints and consequences that would accompany each possible processing option. In other words, given the lack of certainty on the future behavior of offenders, practitioners usually make decisions on factors that they feel are associated with dangerousness and recidivism (e.g., offense seriousness and prior record). The problem is that stereotypes also tend to enter into that perceptual shorthand, namely with race and ethnicity.

Research has demonstrated that Blacks and Hispanics, specifically, are more likely to be viewed as threatening and violent (Dixon & Rosenbaum, 2004). One explanation is that Blacks and Hispanics are disproportionately over-represented in negative media images (Dixon & Linz, 2000a, 2000b). These negative images may influence people's perceptions, including those of criminal justice professionals, thereby resulting in a false link between race/ethnicity and criminality (Dixon & Maddox, 2005). Based on focal concerns, the association between being Black or Hispanic and criminality may influence perceived blameworthiness and protection of the community. Again, due to prosecutors and judges using a perceptual shorthand to make decisions at key points in the justice system, Black and Hispanics may be viewed more blameworthy. In addition, justice professionals may, even unintentionally, use race as a factor in determining offenders' threat to the community.

Empirical Research on Focal Concerns

Most of the empirical research on the focal concerns perspective focuses on adults (e.g., Kramer & Steffensmeier, 1993; Steffensmeier et al., 1998; Spohn & Holleran, 2000; Kramer & Ulmer, 2002), although some studies have also included juveniles. In addition, most of the empirical research has focused on judges regarding the sentencing of convicted offenders. Regardless of these two issues, it is still important to understand the empirical evidence on this perspective, especially since it directly relates to decision-making in the juvenile justice system. The bulk of the literature which tested this perspective does the following: 1) uses sentencing as an outcome, 2) statistically controls for legal factors (e.g., offense seriousness, prior record, etc.), and 3) includes race/ethnicity as a factor in the analyses and assesses whether it is significant in its effect on sentencing after legal variables are controlled. In theory, decision-making should be guided almost exclusively by legal factors. However, that is mainly true for the adult system. In the juvenile court, factors that are traditionally extralegal (e.g., school status, relationship with parents, and home environment) are actually relevant in the juvenile system (Bishop, Leiber, and Johnson, 2010). This somewhat "muddies" the waters because it makes it more difficult to assess which extralegal factors should be considered and which should not be considered in juvenile court decision-making. However, if race/ethnicity continues to significantly effect sentencing after legal factors are controlled, it is presumed to be support for focal concerns. Something else must be influencing decisions if race or ethnicity is still significant.

Because of this clarity issue, a critique of the empirical support for focal concerns is difficult. A plethora of research has been conducted that finds that Black and/or Hispanics experience more punitive outcomes in the juvenile justice system (Wordes, Byum & Corley, 1994; Bishop & Frazier, 1996; Secret & Johnson, 1997; Leiber & Mack, 2003; Guevara, Spohn & Herz, 2004; Leiber & Fox, 2005; Snyder, 2005; Leiber & Johnson, 2008; Jordan & Freiburger, 2015), and reviews of race research generally finds some support for this position (Pope & Feyerherm, 1990; Bishop, 2005). Given this, there does appear to be some support for the focal concerns perspective.

A limitation is that the perspective was generally not tested in its entirety. In addition, several indicators can represent more than one element of the perspective (e.g., offense severity being an indicator for blameworthiness and protection of the community). A more complete test of the theory was done by Hartley, Maddan, and Spohn (2007). Though their study focused on adults, it is relevant to the discussion of the perspective generally, and juveniles, specifically. They examined federal convictions from 2000, focusing on almost 60,000 offenders. The purpose of the study was to conduct a full test of focal concerns, and they used different indicators for each element of focal concerns. Race, gender, and age were indicators of a "perceptual shorthand." Based on the focal concerns perspective, due to prosecutors and judges having a limited amount of information on the offenders, a perceptual shorthand is used to make decisions and that is where stereotypes and other biases enter the decision-making in court outcomes. The findings suggest Hispanics and Blacks receive harsher sanctions, but did not find support for it being a perceptual shorthand. The authors indicated the following:

> The current research suggests that the focal concerns theory is not a theory at all. It has no set of testable propositions; most hypotheses that have been derived from this work have been extended over time. The primary concepts of this perspective are also underdeveloped. Different concepts can actually contain the same variables. Because

of this, and the fact that focal concerns theorists do not allude to how these concepts fit together, except in a "complex interaction," aspiring focal concerns empiricists are left to their own devices in testing extended analytic models. At this point, the "focal concerns theory" is no such thing; it is merely a perspective. (p. 73)

It then seems that focal concerns need additional clarity and development. It is not as though the theory/perspective is not useful. However, any significant race finding with juvenile court outcomes requires more explanation. In addition, there needs to be testable hypotheses before making the assumption that race effects are due to perceived dangerousness, perceptual shorthand, etc. For this reason, it is not known whether focal concerns is empirically supported. It very well may be, but until at least some of the very relevant concerns are addressed, it is difficult to make this claim.

Attribution Theory

Attribution theory is another perspective that is often discussed as a way to explain the effects of race and ethnicity in juvenile justice decision-making. This theory is actually from the social psychology literature (Kelley & Michela, 1980). Generally speaking, attribution theory focuses on the *perceived* causes of behavior. The term "attribution" relates to "perception or inference of cause" (p. 458). Related to juvenile justice, this theory can help explain prosecutors and judges perception of why youth engaged in delinquent behavior when exercising their decision making authorities. According to this theory, attributions of behavior are assumed to be due to either internal or external factors (Heider, 1944, 1958; Michotte, 1963). Internal factors are those within the individual and external factors are generally environmental, both of which have been shown to influence decision-making in the juvenile justice system (Albonetti, 1991; Bridges & Steen, 1998).

Examples of internal factors are bad character or attitude, lack of remorse, disrespect, etc. (Bridges & Steen, 1998). When internal factors are the cause of delinquent behavior, youth are viewed as more responsible for their actions. Conversely, external factors are those which are outside the direct control of individuals (Albonetti, 1991; Bridges & Steen, 1998; Rodriguez, 2013). Examples of external factors are neighborhood conditions, family circumstances, criminal friends/family, etc. External factors typically reduce offenders' culpability for delinquent acts because the illegality is presumed to be due mainly to forces outside of the juvenile's control. In other words, internal factors are viewed as within the control of individuals, while external factors are viewed as out of the control of individuals. Therefore, when assigning culpability (and ultimately punishment) to offenders, those who are presumed to have committed delinquency based on internal factors will be punished more harshly than those who are perceived to have committed illegal acts because of external factors. Even at the decision to arrest, youth who are perceived as more disrespectful (i.e., internal factor) have sometimes been found to have a greater likelihood of getting arrested (Allen, 2005). This link between internal factors and harsher outcomes then continue into the judicial system (Rodriguez, 2013).

Because the juvenile court was built on the doctrine of *parens patriae*, it is to operate in the best interests of the child. In order to determine what is in children's best interest, the court must examine all aspects of youth, including familial, environmental, school, and neighborhood. The court should use these factors, along with the other offense and offender categories, to best determine what is in juveniles' best interests. In other words, the juvenile court was largely built to assess the role of external factors in attributing responsibility and consequences for juvenile offenders. Therefore, it should be expected that external factors will be taken into account for all youth that come before the court. Bridges and Steen (1998) summed up the theory well: "To the extent that court officials perceive minority offenders differently than whites, they may be more likely to perceive minorities' crimes as caused by internal forces and crimes committed by whites as caused by external forces" (p. 556). As mentioned earlier, attributions due to internal factors are thought to result in harsher consequences because those illegal behaviors are due to factors in the control of youth. Conversely, attributions due to external factors will likely be accompanied by less harsh consequences because those behaviors are not thought to be within the control of the juvenile. In other words, Black youth are likely to be punished more harshly than White youth.

Empirical Research on Attribution Theory

Bridges and Steen (1998) examined over 230 predisposition reports (PDR) in a Western state. A predisposition report is a document constructed by probation officers to provide information on adjudicated (convicted) youth prior to formal disposition (sentencing). The PDR contains the probation officers' assessment of the youth, interviews with family, school record, along with information of the offense itself and its circumstance. Finally, the PDR contains the probations officers' recommendations to the judge on what the disposition should be regarding the juveniles. They found that probation officers were more likely to apply negative internal attributions to Black youth than White youth. They also found that probation officers were less likely to apply negative external attributions to Black juveniles than to their White counterparts. Based on the theory, negative internal attributions will result in more severe punishments, while negative external attributions will result in more lenient outcomes because it reduces offenders' culpability. They provided a narrative of the PDR for two different youth: one Black (name is Ed) and one White (name is Lou). With two friends, Ed held up a gas station, while Lou robbed multiple motels with two friends. The narrative is as follows:

> This robbery was very dangerous as Ed confronted the victim with a loaded shotgun. He pointed it at the victim and demanded that he place the money in a paper bag. This appears to be a premeditated and willful act by Ed.... There is an adult quality to this referral. In talking with Ed, what was evident was the relaxed and open way he discussed his life style. There didn't seem to be any desire to change. There was no expression of remorse from the young man. There was no moral content to his comment. (p. 564)
>
> Lou is the victim of a broken home. He is trying to be his own man, but ... is seemingly easily misled and follows other delinquents against his better judgment. Lou is a tall emaciated little boy who is terrified by his present predicament. It appears that he is in need of drug/alcohol evaluation and treatment. (p. 564)

The authors also examined the impact of internal and external attributions on the probation officers' recommendation to the judge and the perceived risk of reoffending for the youth (Bridges & Steen, 1998). They found that while both negative internal and external attributions influenced juveniles' risk of reoffending (as perceived by probation officers), internal attributions had a stronger effect. In light of the findings already pointing to Blacks being more likely to be labeled with negative internal attributions, it puts this group at a higher perception of risk for recidivism, in turn, leading to harsher court outcomes.

Rodriguez (2013) examined over 2,100 juvenile cases in Maricopa County, Arizona, from 2000–2002. Her focus was on correctional confinement. She examined a different type of external attribution: neighborhood concentrated disadvantage. While attribution theory and prior research suggests that external attributions lowers the culpability of youth, Rodriguez hypothesized that concentrated disadvantage may actually increase the likelihood of confinement for those youth living in a vulnerable situation. Juvenile court judges may then want to remove those youth from the community. First, she found that both Black and Hispanic youth had a greater likelihood of confinement than White youth. Regarding the external attribution, in areas of higher concentrated disadvantage, juveniles had a greater likelihood of confinement. This finding is consistent with the belief that these youth may be viewed as needing to be out of that environment, resulting in a greater probability of institutionalization. Finally, Rodriguez examined interactions between concentrated disadvantage (external attribution) and race/ethnicity. She predicted that individual Blacks and Hispanics with that specific external attribution would be punished more harshly than Whites. Her finding, though, was that in areas of higher concentrated disadvantage, Blacks, Hispanics, and Whites were treated similarly. Therefore the racial element of attribution theory was not supported, although individual Blacks and Hispanics still suffered harsher outcomes.

Racial/Ethnic Threat Hypothesis

Racial and ethnic threat, historically, are grounded in the early work of Blalock (1967). In this work, he presented a perspective on social control. He focused on how the mere presence of minority groups can impact social control in society. When minority groups increase in size, the dominant group (i.e., Whites) may view them as a threat to their status or social position. As the minority population size grows, there is increased competition for limited resources (e.g., employment, formal education, financial, etc.). Blalock also mentioned that political and economic competition is salient. As minority groups gain increased levels of political (e.g., voting) and economic (e.g., income, wealth, etc.) power, the dominant group will feel even more threatened. Therefore, discrimination against those minority groups can be used in order to limit their access to those scarce resources.

Research suggests that both criminal justice practitioners and general members of society stereotype Hispanics and Blacks as being more likely to be disrespectful, threatening, and commit violence (Bridges & Steen, 1998; Mann & Zatz, 1998; Spohn & Beichner, 2000). In other words, these specific minority groups carry negative stereotypes. The stereotypes associated with these groups have been used as one explanation to explain the sentencing patterns that places Blacks and Hispanics at a higher likelihood of receiving harsher sanctions than Whites (Kramer & Steffensmeier, 1993; Chiricos & Crawford, 1995; Steffensmeier, Ulmer & Kramer, 1998; Engen & Gainey, 2000; Spohn & Holleran, 2000; Steffensmeier & Demuth, 2000, 2001; Zatz, 2000; Ulmer & Johnson, 2004; Jordan & Freiburger, 2015), though not all research finds this, based on the sentence outcome examined (Freiburger & Hilinski, 2013; Wang, Mears, Spohn, and Dario, 2013).

Empirical Support for Racial/Ethnic Threat

Most of the research just cited focuses on the adult criminal justice system. Much less has been done on juvenile court outcomes. Armstrong and Rodriguez (2005) examined pre-adjudication detention in a northeastern state. They included a county measure for non-White population size. The results showed that as the non-White population increased, the likelihood of being detained also increased. While it was not typically desirable to have a generic non-White measure, apparently the effect was strong enough to withstand the grouping into one category.

Interesting findings were also found in West Virginia. Freiburger and Jordan (2011) examined over 3,300 cases in the state during 2005. They only included Black and White juveniles in their sample in order to assess the petition decision by prosecutors. While racial threat (percent Black population) did not significantly influence the petition decision, there was a significant interaction between poverty and race. Blacks who lived in areas of higher poverty had an increased likelihood of having a petition filed. This may be consistent with racial threat. Blacks who live in higher poverty are likely viewed as threatening to the dominant group. Therefore, one method of social control is a greater probability of being formally petitioned to the juvenile justice system.

Similar to Armstrong and Rodriguez (2005), other research also examined pre-adjudication detention (Thomas, Moak, and Walker, 2013). In this study, Thomas et al. (2013) included data on almost 64,000 youth in a Southeastern state from 2000–2008. They included multiple measures of racial and symbolic threat: county Black population, White-to-Black structural disadvantage, and the White-to-Black unemployment ratio. They found that none of the racial and symbolic threat factors had a significant direct effect on pre-adjudication detention. However, they did find that "Black youth in counties with more pronounced interracial socioeconomic equality are more likely to be detained than similarly situated White youth or Black juveniles in communities in which minorities are more affluent" (pp. 254–255). Therefore, with this research, it appears that symbolic threat was more salient than racial threat.

Conflict Theory

Conflict theory has been used to frame the relationship between race and crime, though it has mostly been applied to adults in the criminal justice system. However, it can inform and guide discussions on juvenile justice decision-making. Conflict theory can be traced to the works of Karl Marx and Max

Weber. According to the theory, laws are not designed based on general consensus amongst society's members or representatives. To the contrary, the laws are designed for the sole goal of reflecting the interest of those with power in society. In addition to the laws reflecting the interest of the powerful, laws are also designed to ensure other people (e.g., disadvantaged) are unable to attain power. The laws of the country, then, are meant to reflect the small group of people who have a significant amount of power.

A natural extension of this theory is behaviors that are defined as illegal may serve to benefit the most powerful, while there is little or no regulation on behaviors committed by the most powerful. Examples of this may be the federal drug law passed in the 1980s (Anti-Drug Abuse Act of 1986). During this period, crack cocaine was becoming widespread and *portrayed* as being associated with a new wave of violence in inner-city areas (e.g., gang wars). Crack was also portrayed as having higher addictive qualities than powdered cocaine. Crack cocaine was also significantly cheaper than powdered cocaine. Congress passed a law that is commonly referred to as the 100:1 rule. With a conviction for possession with the intent to distribute, a person would need either 500 grams of powdered cocaine or 5 grams of crack cocaine. In other words, it would take 100 times the amount of powdered cocaine to be eligible for the same sentence as someone in possession of crack. Given the cheapness of crack, it was mostly sold and used in poorer areas that were disproportionately minority. According to the U.S. Sentencing Commission, federal convictions for crack possession were 84.5% Black, 10.3% White, and 5.2% Hispanic. For federal convictions for trafficking, it was 88.3% Black, 7.1% Hispanic, and 4.1% White. Although many recognized, researched, and documented how the law disproportionately targets Black and Hispanics (especially in state prosecutions), the law was not changed until 24 years later in 2010. This change reduced the disparity, but did not eliminate it. The new disparity is 18:1.

Under a conflict perspective, it could be argued that these types of laws were designed specifically to oppress racially/ethnically underrepresented groups, while being lenient on the dominant group. While the drug law may be viewed as a logical and clear example, it may not always be that overt. In fact, Hawkins (1987) discusses a slightly different way to examine conflict theory in light of race and the justice system. He identifies four general problems regarding traditional conflict theory:

1. In testing the theory, researchers may find "anomalies" and identify them as such. Anomalies in the data (either in support or non-support of the theory) may be due to methodological concerns in the research.

2. The inconsistencies in examining the effect of discriminatory racial practices in the criminal justice system may be due to oversimplifying the theory.
3. The oversimplification is due to two factors. First, conflict theory does not fully explain the link between race and criminal sentencing. Second, researchers have routinely excluded the importance of "anomalies" found in the data when studying this issue.
4. The anomalies may point to problems with the actual theory, as there are other factors that can help explain the relationship between race and sentencing.

Generally speaking, Hawkins (1987) indicates that anomalies or inconsistencies are likely due to conflict theory traditionally not taking into account other factors that influence the offender race/sentencing outcome. One such factor is victim race. Some research does indicate that offender/victim race matters in sentencing. Hawkins (1987) also suggests that the "power-threat" dynamic must be taken into account, especially since racial groups have differing levels of power in various regions of the country. In addition, Hawkins advances the view that results must be examined in a historical and structural view. Stated differently, results are not simply a reflection of the moment at which data were collected. All of it can be explained in the context of what was going on both currently and historically.

Empirical Research on Conflict Theory

Most of the empirical research on conflict theory focuses on adults, while very little attention has focused on juveniles. However, one of the most heavily cited research studies was done by Tittle and Curran (1988). In this study, they examined juvenile outcomes across 31 counties in Florida. There sample included over 5,500 youth. Although it was not the most sophisticated measure, they did find support for conflict theory. As the threat of non-Whites increased (measured by percent of non-Whites in the county), it was accompanied by greater punishment severity for youth.

In a later study, Sampson and Laub (1993) examined a national sample of juveniles from 21 states during 1985. In total, they included almost 540,000 cases, covering over 300 counties across the United States. The outcomes they examined were formal petitioning to the juvenile court, pre-adjudication detention, and out-of-home placement for those convicted. The authors included multiple factors that, accordingly to conflict theory, influence juvenile court outcomes: underclass poverty, racial inequality, and wealth.

In terms of the formal petitioning to the juvenile justice system, they found that as racial inequality increased (for Blacks, specifically), there was a greater likelihood of juveniles being petitioned. There was also evidence that for pre-adjudication detention, those who are in underclass areas and those who live in greater areas of racial inequality were at a greater probability of being detained. Finally, for multiple types of offenses, those in underclass areas were at a greater probability of being placed out of the home if adjudicated delinquent (convicted). In separate analyses, Sampson and Laub also found that the conflict theory variables were more likely to play a role in these outcomes for Black youth as compared to White youth.

Formal Legal Perspective

Finally, there is one school of thought that denies racial discrimination in the juvenile justice system: formal legal perspective. With this perspective, the juvenile justice system and the decisions that stem from it are rationale (Dixon, 1995). Extralegal factors are irrelevant to the process, and decisions are made solely on the rule of law, policies, and precedence. Decisions on all levels, therefore, are predictable and not based on any factor other than legally relevant variables.

According to this view, Blacks and Hispanics are more likely to suffer harsher outcomes in the juvenile system because these two groups are the more serious offenders. In other words, Black and Hispanic youth are more likely to be charged and convicted of more serious offenses; they are also more likely to have an extensive prior record, all in comparison to White youth. In turn, those legal factors are the strongest determinants of juvenile justice decision making. Research does support that offense seriousness and prior record play the strongest role in juvenile court outcomes. In addition, research also supports that Black and Hispanic youth are more likely to be more serious offenders. Therefore, according to this perspective, there is no discrimination in the system. Instead, the disparity is due to differential offending (Walker, Spohn, and DeLone, 2012).

Empirical Support for Formal Legal Perspective

Several studies have tested the formal legal perspective, regarding whether race is relevant to juvenile court outcomes. If the perspective is accurate, the effect of race and/or ethnicity should not be significant after controlling for legal factors in statistical models. Secret and Johnson (1997) examined over

21,000 juvenile cases in Nebraska from 1988–1993. They examined the effect of race on multiple juvenile courts and found that race did play a significant effect on various court outcomes after legally relevant variables were controlled for in the model. However, race did not appear to impact the final disposition (sentencing) decision. While this may suggest some support for the theory, the authors performed additional analyses by year and found an inconsistent race effect.

Tracy (2002, 2005) examined juvenile court data within the state of Texas. While he did find that Blacks and Hispanics were more likely to experience some negative outcomes in the juvenile justice system, he did not find that there was a clear race/ethnicity effect with the disposition decision. According to Tracy, "The findings show an absence of strong and consistent race and ethnic differentials in juvenile processing in Texas. In fact, the findings indicate that even when such differentials occur, they do not affect the most important stage of juvenile justice decision making—the final disposition stage" (Tracy, 2002, p. 175).

Bishop (2005) reviewed the available research that examined race and juvenile court decision making at virtually all stages (arrest through disposition). She suggests that the race effects in court outcomes are due, in part, on differential levels of involvement in delinquency between the races. Based on conclusions drawn by Bishop, race effects may be more pronounced on the front end of the court process, as "minority youths are less often diverted, more often referred for formal processing, and more often held in secure detention than white youths who are legally similar" (p. 62).

Conclusion

The theoretical perspectives can be summarized fairly succinctly as seen in Table 3.1. Research generally shows that race and ethnicity play a role in explaining juvenile court outcomes. The issue, then, is which theory best explains the empirical relationship that is often observed. At this point, we think it is not clear which theoretical position has the most support. For instance, focal concerns theory is used in research a great deal to explain the race-outcome relationship, but it does not necessarily make it the best. As mentioned in research by Hartley et al. (2007), focal concerns theory is very difficult to test as a theory because the elements of the theory are ambiguous and the same indicators are often used for multiple elements of the theory. While this criticism may detract from the usefulness of the theory, researchers should spend time fully developing the theory into testable concepts to assess its true usefulness in explaining the link between race, ethnicity, and juvenile court outcomes.

Attribution theory is also a widely used theory that researchers use to examine the role of race in juvenile justice processing. The research is a bit more developed than focal concerns theory. There are clear internal and external attributions, with each having its own indicators without overlap. Researchers have also been clear in examining the role that race plays in the labeling of specific internal and external attributions, which in turn, influences court outcomes. Clearly there is more development of this theory needed, as the original interpretation of this theory regarding criminal justice outcomes projected external attributions insulating youth from culpability and resulting in more

Table 3.1. Theoretical Contexts to Race and Juvenile Justice Decision-Making

Theory	Context of Decision-Making
Focal Concerns	Based on perceptual shorthand, justice professionals make decisions on offenders' dangerousness. Decision-makers also balance protection of the community and practical constraints.
Attribution Theory	Judicial decision-makers attempt to attribute behavior to their perceived causes, which could be either internal or external.
Racial/Ethnic Threat	Larger percentages of minority populations are viewed as a threat, so court outcomes are used as a method of social control in light of that threat
Conflict Theory	Those who are in power create laws and punishment in order to maintain their power. In the process, they create laws to continually oppress those who are not in power.
Formal Legal Perspective	Decision-making is based purely on legally relevant factors, such as offense and prior record.

lenient sentencing. However, Rodriguez (2013) more recent research expands attribution theory, as she found that an external attribution may, in fact, serve as a way to result in a harsher sanction based on the vulnerability of the youth.

Racial/ethnic threat is also gaining some momentum in the juvenile justice research. While it has been used more with adults, it does indicate some support with outcomes in the juvenile justice system. While this perspective provides some guidance in understanding the contextual issue of whether the population of Blacks and Hispanics influences court outcomes for *all* youth, the adult court literature is a bit more developed. In that body of work, researchers not only examined the role of racial/ethnic threat, but they also tried to use it to explain individual racial differences in outcomes (Britt, 2000; Ulmer & Johnson, 2004; Wang & Mears, 2010; Feldmeyer & Ulmer, 2011; Feldmeyer, Warren, Sienneck & Neptune, 2015). They examined whether racial/ethnic threat interacted with individual race/ethnicity to produce a significant effect on outcomes. The juvenile justice research could benefit from some of these types of additional analyses when examining racial/ethnic threat.

Conflict theory is one of the most historical theories discussed, and it is used frequently to explain racial disparities in outcomes for both the criminal and juvenile justice systems. It is a popular theory, and its propositions are well set within the empirical literature. While popular, Hawkins (1987) brings up excellent points on how its application to the race and court outcome literature has been oversimplified. It does not take into account the dyad of offender race/victim race, regional difference, power-threat dynamics, or place findings in a true historical context. It may not necessarily be anything wrong with conflict theory, but rather how it has been reduced and tested in race and juvenile court outcomes' research.

Finally, the formal legal perspective also has empirical support, suggesting that race/ethnicity is not at all relevant in juvenile court decision-making. This may actually be considered, unofficially, the oldest of all perspectives. Originally, the juvenile court was thought to make decisions on purely legally relevant factors, independent of race and ethnicity. Therefore, this perspective was presumed to be at the foundation of the court system. Only when racial and ethnic differences in processing were observed did researchers and practitioners begin moving away from this perspective to embrace theories that incorporated potentially discriminatory elements as a method of explanation.

In summary, the body of theories to explain race/ethnicity in juvenile court outcomes is good, but still needs additional work. In addition to development in the areas discussed, theories should also include personal characteristics of the decision-makers: demographics, length of time employed in the system, role in the system, types of cases usually on their caseloads, etc. While there is research that includes these factors, it is not generally driven by or grounded in theory to help explain racial disparities in juvenile court processing. Criminology/delinquency theories incorporate characteristics of offenders to understand their behaviors; decision-making theories should include characteristics of the system's workers in order to understand their behaviors and decisions. Only then will theory truly shed light on explaining the role of race and ethnicity on juvenile court processing decisions.

Discussion Questions

1. Why are theories of decision-making important in juvenile justice research?
2. Focal concerns theory has been widely used as a foundation in research to understand the link between race/ethnicity and juvenile court outcomes. Is this theory more useful than conflict theory?
3. Compare and contrast focal concerns theory with attribution theory. Clearly discuss the similarities and differences.
4. The formal legal perspective is the one theory that indicates that race effect observed in court outcomes is a disparity, not discrimination. What factors could explain why some research finds support for this theory, while other research does not find support?
5. Examine a particular juvenile justice outcome (i.e., referral at intake, petition, detention, adjudication, or disposition) in terms of race and/or ethnicity effects. Read the articles discussed in the empirical research section. Justify where on the continuum the decision falls.

References

Albonetti, C.A. (1991). An integration of theories to explain judicial discretion. *Social Problems, 38,* 247–266.

Allen, T.T. (2005). Taking a juvenile into custody: Situational factors that influence police officers' decisions. *Journal of Sociology and Social Welfare, 32*(2), 121–129.

Armstrong, G.S. & Rodriguez, N. (2005). Effects of individual and contextual characteristics on preadjudication detention of juvenile delinquents. *Justice Quarterly, 22*(4), 521–539.

Bishop, D.M. (2005). The role of race and ethnicity in juvenile justice processing. In D.F. Hawkins & K. Kempf-Leonard (Eds.), *Our children, their chlidren: Confronting racial and ethnic differences in American juvenile justice* (pp. 23–82). Chicago: The University of Chicago Press.

Bishop, D.M. & Frazier, C.E. (1996). Race effects in juvenile justice decision-making: Findings of a statewide analysis. *Criminology, 86*(2), 392–414.

Bishop, D.M., Leiber, M. & Johnson, J. (2010). Contexts of decision making in the juvenile justice system: An organizational approach to understanding minority overrepresentation. *Youth Violence and Juvenile Justice, 8*(3), 213–233.

Blalock, H.M. (1967). *Toward a theory of minority-group relations.* New York: Capricorn Books.

Bridges, G.S. & Steen, S. (1998). Racial disparities in official assessments of juvenile offenders: Attributional stereotypes as mediating mechanisms. *American Sociological Review, 63,* 554–570.

Britt, C.L. (2000). Social context and racial disparities in punishment decisions. *Justice Quarterly, 17*(4), 707–732.

Chiricos, T.G. & Crawford, C. (1995). Race and imprisonment: A contextual assessment of the evidence. In D. Hawkins, *Ethnicity, race, and crime: Perspectives across time and place* (pp. 281–309). Albany, NY: State University of New York Press.

Dixon, J. (1995). The organizational context of criminal sentencing. *American Journal of Sociology, 100*(5), 1157–1198.

Dixon, J.C. & Rosenbaum, M.S. (2004). Nice to know you? Testing contact, cultural, and group threat theories of anti-Black and anti-Hispanic stereotypes. *Social Science Quarterly, 85*(2), 257–280.

Dixon, T.L. & Linz, D. (2000a). Overrepresentation and underrepresentation of African Americans and Latinos as lawbreakers on television news. *Journal of Communication, 50,* 131–154.

Dixon, T.L. & Linz, D. (2000b). Race and the misrepresentation of victimization on local television news. *Communicaiton Research, 27,* 547–573.

Dixon, T.L. & Maddox, K.B. (2005). Skin tone, crime news, and social reality judgments: Priming the sterotype of the dark and dangerous Black criminal. *Journal of Applied Social Psychology, 35*(8), 1555–1570.

Engen, R.L. & Gainey, R.R. (2000). Modeling the effects of legally relevant and extralegal factors under sentencing guidelines: The rules have changed. *Criminology, 38*(4), 1207–1230.

Feldmeyer, B. & Ulmer, J.T. (2011). Racial/ethnic threat and federal sentencing. *Journal of Research in Crime and Delinquency, 48*(2), 238–270.

Feldmeyer, B., Warren, P. Y., Sienneck, S. E. & Neptune, M. (2015). Racial, ethnic, and immigrant threat: Is there a new criminal threat on state sentencing? *Journal of Research in Crime and Delinquency, 52*(1), 62–92.

Freiburger, T.L. & Hilinski, C.M. (2013). An examination of the interactions of race and gender on sentencing decisions using a trichotomous dependent variable. *Crime and Delinquency, 59*, 59–86.

Freiburger, T.L. & Jordan, K.L. (2011). A multilevel analysis of race on the decision to petition a case in the juvenile court. *Race and Justice, 1*(2), 185–201.

Guevara, L., Spohn, C. & Herz, D. (2004). Race, legal representation, and juvenile justice: Issues and concerns. *Crime & Delinquency, 50*(3), 344–371.

Hartley, R.D., Maddan, S. & Spohn, C.C. (2007). Concerning conceptualization and operationalization: Sentencing data and the focal concerns perspective- A research note. *The Southwest Journal of Criminal Justice, 4*(1), 58–78.

Hawkins, D.F. (1987). Beyond anomalies: Rethinking the conflict perspective on race and criminal punishment. *Social Forces, 65*(3), 719–745.

Heider, F. (1944). Social perception and phenomenal causality. *Psychological Review, 51*, 358–374.

Heider, F. (1958). *The psychology of interpersonal relations.* New York: Wiley.

Jordan, K.L. & Freiburger, T.L. (2015). The effect of race/ethnicity on sentencing: Examining sentence type, jail length, and prison length. *Journal of Ethnicity in Criminal Justice, 13*(3), 179–196.

Kelley, H.H. & Michela, J.L. (1980). Attribution theory and research. *Annual Review of Psychology, 31*, 457–501.

Kramer, J.H & Steffensmeier, D. (1993). Race and imprisonment decisions. *The Sociological Quarterly, 34*(2), 357–376.

Kramer, J.H. & Ulmer, J.T. (2002). Downward departures for serious violence offenders: Local court "corrections" to Pennsylvania's sentencing guidelines. *Criminology, 40*(4), 897–932.

Kraska, P. B. (2006). Criminal justice theory: Toward legitimacy and an infrastructure. *Justice Quarterly, 23*(2), 167–185.

Leiber, M.J. & Fox, K.C. (2005). Race and the impact of detention on juvenile justice decision making. *Crime & Delinquency, 51*(4), 470–497.

Leiber, M.J. & Johnson, J.J. (2008). Being young and Black: What are their effects on juvenile justice decision making? *Crime & Delinquency, 54*(4), 560–581.

Leiber, M.J. & Mack, K.Y. (2003). The individual and joint effects of race, gender, and family status on juvenile justice decision-making. *Journal of Research in Crime & Delinquency, 40*(1), 34–70.

Mann, C.R. & Zatz, M.S. (1998). *Images of color, Images of crime.* Los Angeles: Roxbury.

Michotte, A. (1963). The Perception of Causality. New York: Basic Books.

Pope, C.E. & Feyerherm, W.H. (1990). Minority status and juvenile processing: An assessment of the research literature. *Criminal Justice Abstracts, 22*, 327–335.

Rodriguez, N. (2013). Concentrated disadvantage and the incarceration of youth: Examining how context affects juvenile justice. *Journal of Research in Crime and Delinquency, 50*, 189–215.

Sampson, R.J. & Laub, J.H. (1993). Structural variations in juvenile court processing: Inequality, the underclass, and social control. *Law & Society Review, 27*(2), 285–312.

Secret, P.E. & Johnson, J.B. (1997). The effect of race on juvenile justice decision making in Nebraska: Detention, adjudication, and disposition: 1988–1993. *Justice Quarterly, 14*(3), 445–478.

Snyder, H. (2005). *Juvenile arrests, 2003*. Washington, DC: U.S. Department of Justice, Office of Juvenile Justice and Delinquency Prevention.

Spohn, C. & Beichner, D. (2000). Is preferential treatment of the female offender a thing of the past? A multisite study of gender, race, and imprisonment. *Criminal Justice Policy Review, 11*(2), 149–184.

Spohn, C. & Holleran, D. (2000). The imprisonment penalty paid by young unemployed Black and Hispanic male offenders. *Criminology, 38*, 281–306.

Steffensmeier, D. & Demuth, S. (2000). Ethnicity and sentencing in U.S. federal courts: Who is punished more harshly? *American Sociological Review, 65*, 705–729.

Steffensmeier, D. & Demuth, S. (2001). Ethnicity and judges' sentencing decisions: Hispanic-White-Black comparisons. *Criminology, 39*, 145–178.

Steffensmeier, D. & Demuth, S. (2006). Does gender modify the effects of race-ethnicty on criminal sanctions? Sentences for male and female, White, Black, and Hispanic defendants. *Journal of Quantitative Criminology, 22*, 241–261.

Steffensmeier, D., Ulmer, J. & Kramer, J. (1998). The interaction of race, gender, and age in criminal sentencing: The punishment cost of being young, Black, and male. *Criminology, 36*, 763–798.

Thomas, S.A., Moak, S.C. & Walker, J. T. (2013). The contingent effect of race in juvenile court detention decisions: The role of racial and symbolic threat. *Race and Justice, 3*(3), 239–265.

Tittle, C.R. & Curran, D.A. (1988). Contingencies for dispositional disparities in juvenile justice. *Social Forces, 67*(1), 23–58.

Tracy, P.E. (2002). *Decision making and juvenile justice: An analysis of bias in case processing*. Westport, CT: Praeger.

Tracy, P.E. (2005). Race, ethnicity, and juvenile justice: Is there bias in postarrest decision making. In D.F. Hawkins & K. Kempf-Leonard (Eds.), *Our children, their children: Confronting racial and ethnic differences in American juvenile justice* (pp. 300–347). Chicago: The University of Chicago Press.

Ulmer, J.T. & Johnson, B. (2004). Sentencing in context: A multilevel analysis. *Criminology, 42,* 137–178.

Walker, S., Spohn, C. & DeLone, M. (2012). *The color of justice: Race, ethnicicty, and crime in America.* Belmont, CA: Wadsworth.

Wang, X. & Mears, D. P. (2010). Examining the direct and interactive effects of changes in racial and ethnic threat on sentencing decisions. *Journal of Research in Crime and Delinquency, 47*(4), 522–557.

Wang, X., Mears, D.P., Spohn, C. & Dario, L. (2013). Assessing the differential effects of race and ethnicity on sentence outcomes under different sentencing systems. *Crime and Delinquency, 59,* 87–114.

Wordes, M., Bynum, T.S. & Corley, C.J. (1994). Locking up youth: The impact of race on detention decisions. *Journal of Research in Crime and Delinquency, 31*(2), 149–165.

Zatz, M.S. (2000). The convergence of race, ethnicity, gender, and class on court decisionmaking: Looking toward the 21st century. In J. Horney (Ed.), *Criminal justice 2000, volume 3: Policies, processes, and decsions of the criminal justice system* (pp. 503–552). Washington, DC: U.S. Department of Justice.

Chapter 4

Minorities and Police

Goals of the Chapter

The purpose of this chapter is to examine issues with policing juveniles, and how race and ethnicity can influence police officers' arrests decisions. This chapter begins with a basic discussion of the roles that police officers perform and issues with policing juveniles. Next, arrests statistics and the explanations for the overrepresentation of minority juveniles in these statistics are reviewed. The research examining these explanations is then discussed. The chapter concludes with a discussion of the research examining racial differences in juveniles choosing to invoke their Fifth Amendment right to remain silent.

After reading this chapter, you will be able to do the following:

1. Be familiar with the roles performed by police;
2. Understand the differential involvement and differential selection hypotheses as explanations for racial disparities in arrests statistics; and
3. Critically assess the research on minority overrepresentation in arrest.

Police officers are the most visible part of the criminal justice system, and serve as the gatekeepers to the system. Although most people probably think of uniformed officers making arrests and pulling over traffic violators when they think of policing, policing actually involves a lot more than simply enforcing the law, issuing citations, and arresting those who violate the law. Police preform three roles in fulfilling their responsibilities in law enforcement. These three roles are to 1) enforce the law, 2) maintain order, and 3) serve the public (Green & Klockars, 1991).

When enforcing the law, law enforcement officers respond to victim and witness calls for police service. They also investigate crimes, gather evidence, interview witnesses and victims, interrogate suspects, prepare evidence for trial, and testify in court. Police further enforce the law by making arrests of those who violate the law. In one of their most visible law enforcement duties, they also enforce traffic laws and issue citations to violators.

To enforce the law, police also engage in activities to prevent crime. One such activity is patrols. Patrols make police visible to the community and deter potential offenders from engaging in crimes. In this role, police commonly have contact with juveniles, as juveniles are more likely than adults to hang out on the streets. Police also engage in other proactive activities to prevent crime, such as sting operations and problem-oriented policing activities. Sting operations are routinely used to address victimless crimes such as prostitution or drug activities. Problem-oriented policing activities, on the other hand, are used to combat a large array of crime and disorder issues. These activities involve the collecting of data on a specific crime problem, developing a solution to alleviate that problem, and evaluating the response to the problem (these steps are often conducted through the Scanning, Analysis, Response, and Assessment (SARA) model). Problem-oriented policing programs commonly involve other entities than the police, such as community organizations, schools, and local groups. Therefore, police must often work with members of the community when engaging in these types of policing activities.

In addition, police are expected to maintain the public order of society. Order maintenance duties can include directing traffic, controlling crowds at concerts and sporting events, or asking a loud group of teenagers to leave the street. Patrol officers actually spend the majority of their workday on these order maintenance activities (Brown, 1988), and there tends to be more ambiguity in this role than in the law enforcement role. Police must determine which behaviors are acceptable and which are "disorderly." Acts that are disorderly are disturbing public order to the point where police must intervene to restore order. Police officers are responsible for making decisions regarding how to handle all these situations they encounter.

In the service function, police are servants to the public. Duties under this function can include things like helping a lost child find his or her parents, distributing information on safety to the public, or providing directions to a lost tourist. It is apparent that some of these activities serve dual roles. For example, checking business doors after hours to make sure the owner remembered to lock them can be considered a service function. It can also be considered to be a law enforcement function by preventing a potential crime.

Police Discretion and Juveniles

The criminal justice system affords police a vast amount of discretion and autonomy when preforming their duties. Discretion is the decision-making authority that is given to officers to decide the best way to handle a situation. They can decide whether to give someone a warning, to issue a citation, or to make an arrest. They also use discretion to make numerous other decisions such as whether to conduct a search, to question a suspicious person on the street, to call for assistance, and to draw their weapon. Because police commonly work unsupervised when they are out in the streets, they often must make these decisions alone without the input of a supervisor.

When the police make contact with a juvenile they have several options available to them in the processing of that juvenile. One possibility is to use an informal option. Police officers have numerous informal options available to them. Some informal options are to 1) ignore the juveniles; 2) ask the juvenile to relocate or go home; 3) have an informal conversation with the juvenile and ask him or her to cease engagement in a behavior; 4) make an informal note of a juvenile's name and contact information in case another incident involving the juvenile occurs in the future; 5) take the juvenile to the station and talk to him or her there; 6) contact the juvenile's parents and ask for their assistance in addressing the juvenile's behaviors; 7) refer the juvenile to a community resource such as substance abuse treatment, anger management training, or a counseling program; or 8) work with another organization such as the juvenile's school or the juvenile probation office to find programming to meet the juvenile's needs.

Police also have many formal options available to them when processing juveniles. Most often this will involve arresting and booking the juvenile. Once the juvenile is arrested and booked, however, the police still have a number of options available to them. At that point, they could release the juvenile to his or her parents, release the juvenile with a warning, refer the juvenile to intake, or detain the juvenile in a secure facility. Police can also choose to use a combination of a formal and informal option. For example, an officer might arrest and book a juvenile only to release them without further action or release them with a warning. An officer could also arrest a juvenile and then simply contact another agency, such as juvenile probation, to handle the case informally.

Discretion is the greatest for lower-level offenses. Because juveniles often engage in low level offenses and status offenses, police typically have a greater degree of discretion in more situations involving juveniles than adults. For example, a police officer might accost a group of juveniles drinking underage. The officer can decide to simply give the juveniles a verbal warning, or the officer might decide to formally process the juveniles and refer them to the juvenile system. This decision has a great impact on the juveniles and can also heavily impact public safety. Imagine a scenario where an officer comes across a group of loitering teenagers outside a convenience store. The officer uses discretion and decides that the kids look harmless and does not engage with them. Later that evening, the teenagers rob the convenience store and injure the clerk. Now imagine the same scenario with an officer who instead decides to approach the teenagers. The officer does a quick pat-down of the teenagers and finds one has a weapon. The officer then takes the juvenile into custody and the robbery never occurs. From these scenarios, it is clear to see how a small decision made in the moment can have big consequences. Of course, this situation could easily go in the opposite direction too. The teenagers could have in fact been harmless. In this situation the first decision would have been the best one.

Police discretion is often viewed critically because there are concerns that police consider factors such as race and ethnicity, social class, age, and gender when making decisions. These considerations can lead to the unfair treatment of certain groups. This unfair treatment exacerbates disproportionate minority representation in the juvenile justice system. Indeed, examination of arrests statistics shows that minorities, especially Black juveniles, are overrepresented in arrests when compared to their rates in the general population.

Policing Juveniles

Complicating the relationship between juveniles and police is that police must serve a dual role with juveniles. Police are responsible for enforcing the law and maintaining order; therefore, they must address juvenile misconduct to protect the public from juvenile crime. They are also responsible, however, for protecting juveniles from being victimized and from becoming delinquent. Furthermore, juveniles engage in activities that place them in contact with police more often. Juveniles often "hang out" in public areas such as street corners and are more often out late at night. Police are also aware that juveniles engage in a disproportionate amount of crime, which can influence the way that police process juvenile offending and can even influence the way they approach juveniles on the street.

Most of the factors that impact officers' decisions to arrest adults also impact their decisions to arrest juveniles. Officers typically place the greatest emphasis on legal factors such as the severity of the offense, the amount of incriminating evidence, and the desires of the victim or complaining citizen (Black, 1971; Lundman, Sykes & Clark., 1978; Smith & Visher, 1981). Research has found some differences, however, in the way officers react to juveniles and adults. Brown, Novak, and Frank (2009) analyzed data from social systematic observations of patrol officers in Cincinnati, Ohio. Using this data, they found that juveniles were more likely to be arrested than adults. They further found that being disrespectful resulted in an increased likelihood of arrest for adults, but not for juveniles. The researchers speculated that officers might not react to disrespectful behavior from juveniles because they expect it from juveniles but not from adults. This finding contradicts Black and Reiss's (1970) early finding, however, that juveniles who were disrespectful to the police were more likely to be arrested.

Juvenile Arrest Statistics

Black juveniles make up 16.6% of people under the age of 18 in the United States. According to the Uniform Crime Reports (UCR), however, in 2012, Black juveniles accounted for 32.2% of juvenile arrests. They represented even more of the arrests for violent crime, accounting for 51.5%. For property crime, they account for 35.5%. As shown in Table 4.1, Black juveniles tend to be more represented in the most violent and serious offenses (i.e., Part I Crimes), such as homicide, robbery and aggravated assault.

These statistics raise concerns about the overrepresentation of minorities in arrests. Although a recent mandate of the Disproportionate Minority Contact initiative has called for a closer examination of racial disparities in the treatment of juveniles early in the system (i.e., at arrest), most research has focused on later decision points, namely those that occur in the juvenile court. This is an unfortunate oversight, as police officers' decisions often determine whether a juvenile enters the system or stays out of the system. For many juveniles entering the system, police are their first contact. In addition, the decision made by a patrol officer has a profound impact on the options available to decision makers further into the juvenile justice system (Wolcott, 2005).

A disparity in arrests statistics, however, does not necessarily indicate a disparity in offending. Myers (2004) found that in most police-juvenile encounters, police engage in unofficial contact with juveniles, in which they simply tell the juveniles to go home or to move to another location. Police only take juveniles into custody about 13% of the time during police and juvenile encounters. It is possible, therefore, that when White juveniles engage in delinquent acts, they are more likely to receive an informal response from police, while minority juveniles are more likely to receive a formal response (i.e., arrests).

Table 4.1. Arrests by Race

Offense	White		Black		American Indian		Asian Pacific Islander	
	Number	Percent	Number	Percent	Number	Percent	Number	Percent
Murder and non-negligent manslaughter	8,506	47.2	4,101	50.8	4,203	1.8	102	0.2
Part 1 Violent crimes[1]	402,470	46.6	236,394	51.5	155,088	0.8	5,198	1
Part 1 Property crime[2]	1,275,315	61.6	866,802	35.5	373,963	1.3	17,804	1.7
Forcible rape	13,886	64.1	9,027	33.9	4,512	1.1	183	0.9
Robbery	80,135	29.9	34,761	68.6	44,002	0.4	601	1.1
Aggravated assault	299,943	55.2	188,505	42.7	102,371	1.1	4,312	1.1
Burglary	219,232	59.1	147,156	38.8	67,554	0.9	1,966	1.2
Larceny-theft	994,304	62.2	677,895	34.6	288,025	1.4	15,052	1.8
Motor vehicle theft	52,952	57.9	35,251	39.3	16,301	1.4	645	1.3
Arson	8,827	73.5	6,500	24.8	2,083	0.6	141	1.1
Other assaults	924,839	59.1	606,048	38.9	294,678	1.2	13,898	.08

1. Part One violent offenses are classified by the FBI as murder, rape, robbery and aggravated assault.
2. Part One property offenses are classified by the FBI as burglary, larceny, motor vehicle theft, and arson.
Source: FBI Uniform Crime Reports. Available at: http://www.fbi.gov/about-us/cjis/ucr/crime-in-the-u.s/2012/crime-in-the-u.s.-2012/tables/43tabledatadecoverviewpdf.

Minority Overrepresentation

The overrepresentation of minority youth in the juvenile justice system has led to many inquiries into the reason for this overrepresentation. Two conflicting explanations are provided. The first argues that this overrepresentation is due to differences in offending. This is often referred to as the "differential involvement" hypothesis. It argues that police officers are more proactive than reactive, and that legally relevant factors such as severity of offense, and offender's prior record and frequency of offending drive police officers' decisions. Minorities are overrepresented in arrests, because minority youth engage in more delinquent acts, and in more serious and violent acts than White juveniles (Blumstein, 1982; 1993; Wilbanks, 1987). Hence their greater representation in arrest statistics is simply due to their differential involvement in criminal activities.

The other argument claims that minority, especially Black, overrepresentation in the system is actually due to systematic bias and not due to differences in offending propensities. This argument is referred to as the "differential selection" hypothesis. It suggests that extralegal factors such as race, age and gender influence police officers' decisions about whether to make an arrest (Chambliss, 1994; 1995; Tonry, 1995). Because police officers have discretion in how to handle juvenile offenders, officers are more likely to decide to arrest minority juveniles than White juveniles.

Sutphen, Kurtz, and Giddings (1993) used vignettes to study police officers' decisions to arrest White and Black juveniles. For this study, 126 male police officers in Georgia responded to eight scenarios that were developed from real police reports involving juveniles. Half of the vignettes portrayed a White juvenile and the other half portrayed a Black juvenile. Two sets of vignettes were created. In one set, vignettes one, three, four, and seven portrayed a White juvenile and two, five, six, and eight portrayed a Black juvenile. In the other set, the portrayal of race in the vignettes was reversed (i.e., vignettes one, three, four and seven portrayed a Black juvenile and two, five, six, and eight portrayed a White juvenile). Each police officer responded to only one of the sets; the set given to each officer was determined randomly. The results indicated that Black juveniles were treated more harshly than White juveniles when the vignette portrayed a juvenile stealing a bike, discharging a stolen weapon, or possessing marijuana. White juveniles, on the other hand, were treated more harshly for alcohol possession than Black youths. None of the other vignettes indicated a race effect. This study is informative because the use of vignettes allows the researcher to control other factors that might affect police officers' decisions. This comes with a limitation, however, as the researcher cannot be certain that an officer would act the same way in a real life situation as they indicated on the vignettes.

Pope and Snyder (2003) examined National Incident-Based Reporting System (NIBRS) data to determine whether minority juveniles did actually engage in more crimes than White juveniles. Their data represented police departments in 17 states and contained 102,905 juveniles. They found that race did not affect arrests decisions. They did, however, find several differences in the offending patterns of White and minority juveniles. Specifically, they found that minority juveniles were more likely to commit crimes with multiple victims, commit crimes against a victim of the opposite race, commit crimes when the victim was a stranger and an adult, commit more offenses outdoors, commit more crimes in groups, and were more likely to use a weapon in the commission of a crime, than White juveniles. All these factors increased the likelihood of arrests for both White and minority juveniles, except for victim race. When minority juveniles committed a crime of violence against a person of a different race it increased their likelihood of arrests. White juveniles who committed a violent offense in which the victim was a different race were not more likely to be arrested. These findings, therefore, suggest that the majority of variation found in Black and White juvenile arrests statistics is due to differences in offending and not in differences in police officer decision making.

While Pope and Snyder examined official arrest data to determine differences in Black and White juvenile offending characteristics, other methods are more commonly used. Ethnographic methodologies were used in several classic works to study police and juvenile relations. In these studies, researchers accompanied police officers on the streets and observed them as the police interacted with the community and performed their duties. These examinations were conducted in the 1960s and 1970s and laid the foundation for understanding how police interact with juveniles on the street. One important finding of these studies was that the majority of police-juvenile interactions were found to be for minor offenses and that the rate of arrest of juveniles was low, with most incidences being handled informally (Black & Reiss, 1970; Werthman & Piliavin, 1967). Therefore, most police-juvenile encounters were not included in formal arrest statistics, making conclusions based on official statistics misleading. To account for all police-juvenile encounters, therefore, the impact of race on arrest decisions are most typically examined using self-report studies or social systematic observations.

Self-Report Surveys of Offending

Self-report studies use survey or interview data collected from juveniles in which juveniles are asked about their involvement in delinquent activities. These surveys are sometimes collaborated with official records (i.e., police arrest records), but conclusions from these surveys are limited by the possibility that juveniles might not accurately report involvement in delinquency and arrests. Despite this limitation, self-report surveys are able to account for involvement in offenses for which there is not an official record. They are also able to determine whether differences in minority and White offending actually exist. If White and minority juveniles report similar rates of offending or if White youths report more offending than minority youth, it is likely that differences in arrests are due to disparities in the way these youths are treated by police. If minorities report greater involvement in criminal activities, then this supports the differential involvement hypothesis and the higher arrest of minority juveniles is simply an unavoidable byproduct.

Some self-report studies have found that White youth are more likely to use drugs or alcohol than minority youth. For example, Tapia (2010) found that White youth were more likely to use marijuana than minority youths. Watt and Rogers (2007) also examined Black and White juveniles' drug and alcohol use using the Adolescent Health Survey (Add Health) data. The Add Health Survey is a national, school-based, self-report survey administered to juveniles in grades seven to 12. They found that White juveniles were more likely to use alcohol than Black juveniles. For heavy drinking and other drug use, there were no significant differences in use for White and Black youth. It was further found that White youths' higher likelihood of drinking could be explained by the fact that they were more influenced by their peers than Black youth, and that White youths were less influenced by supportive families than Black youths.

When examining other crimes, however, research has found that Black juveniles engage in certain types of crime more often than White youths. Tapia (2010) found that White juveniles were less likely to engage in assaults than Black youths. Using the Add Health data, McNulty and Bellair (2003) also found that Black, Hispanic and Native American juveniles reported more involvement in serious offenses such as fighting, assault, and use of a weapon than White juveniles.

Additional self-report studies have examined the frequency at which juveniles have been arrested for their offenses. Tapia (2010) examined the effect of race on sentencing in combination with social economic status using data from the National Longitudinal Survey of Youth (NLSY). The NLSY collects data each year from a random sample of youths in the United States. The data includes self-report data as well as data from interviews with the youths' parents and through social observations conducted by the researcher in the youths' social environments. Using these data, Tapia found that race had the greatest effect on the decision to make an arrest for minor offenses. For serious offenses, police were more likely to make an arrest regardless of the race of the perpetrator. Overall, the race of the juvenile affected the likelihood of arrest even after controlling for relevant legal variables such as prior criminal records and severity of the offense and demographic factors such as gender and age. Both Black and Hispanic youth were more likely to be arrested than White youth, but the effect was stronger for Black youths. Social economic status also significantly affected the decision to arrest, with juveniles of low social economic status having a greater likelihood of arrest than those of middle and upper social class status. Overall, Black juveniles of low social economic status had the highest likelihood of arrest.

When examining the combination of race and social economic status, Tapia further found that race most heavily impacted Black juveniles of high social economic status, increasing their likelihood of arrests by 47%; for low economic status juveniles, being Black increased arrest by 19%. A similar pattern was found for Hispanic youths of high social class. Being Hispanic increased the likelihood of arrest by a significant 23% for these youths. For low economic class youths, however, being Hispanic did not significantly affect their likelihood of arrests.

There are two possible explanations for why being minority more negatively affects youths of high social economic status. The first possible explanation is that minority youth do not "fit the part" of high social economic status youth. In high economic areas, delinquency is less tolerated and their race signifies a dangerous juvenile offender. Therefore, they are not afforded the same leniency that is typically afforded White youths of higher economic status. The second explanation offered by Tapia (2010) is that these high economic status minority youths are hanging out in low social economic areas and committing their acts of delinquency there. Officers often know the juveniles who live in the areas they patrol. They know which juveniles are dangerous and which juveniles belong to gangs. They can use this information when making decisions. Juveniles who are not from the area, however, are unknown to police. In these situations, police might be more likely to make contact with these juveniles and to process them more formally in case the juvenile is dangerous.

The Pittsburgh Youth Survey (PYS) has also been used to examine racial differences in likelihood of arrest. The PYS is a longitudinal data source containing self-report data from a sample of boys in Pittsburgh public schools. Data were collected from the boys' caregivers and the boys' official records. The findings of this study indicated that Black youths were more likely to be arrested than White youth after controlling for relevant legal and demographic characteristics. Juveniles of low economic status were also more likely to be arrested (Hirschfield, Maschi, White, Traub & Loeber, 2006).

An earlier study conducted by Brownfield, Sorenson, and Thompson (2001) analyzed data from the Seattle Youth Study, which is also self-report data that was collected from students in the Seattle School District. They found that Black youths were 1.75 times more likely to be arrested than White youths after controlling for self-reported involvement in delinquency. Additionally, they found that juveniles of low economic states were also more likely to be arrested. Unlike Tapia (2010), however, they did not find that social class had a different effect on Black and White youths. Instead, being of lower social class increased both Black and White juveniles' likelihoods of arrests equally.

Not all studies, however, have found that race is a significant predictor of arrest. Pollock (2014) examined self-report data from the National Youth Survey Family Study to determine whether race persistently affects police contact across generations. She found that race was not a significant predictor of arrest or of a juvenile's likelihood of being questioned by the police for either the early or the late generation of juveniles examined. In other words, White and Black juveniles had the same likelihood of being arrested by the police and of being questioned by the police.

As mentioned earlier, a major concern with the use of self-report surveys is the validity of the information reported by the respondent. Although several studies have found a high level of agreement between juveniles' self-reports and official reports of criminal behavior (Hindelang Hirschi & Weis., 1981; Huizinga & Elliott, 1986), indicating that juveniles tend to honestly report their involvement in crime, it is possible that no differences are found in Black and White juveniles' self-reports of delinquent behavior because Black juveniles are less likely to report involvement in delinquent activities than White juveniles. In an early study, Hindelang, Hirishi and Weis (1981) found evidence of this. Their results indicated that Black youths in Seattle only reported 67% of the offenses that were listed on their official reports, while White juveniles reported 90%. They further found that Black juveniles were less likely to report their involvement in serious offenses than in minor offenses. Jolliffe et al. (2003) also found that White juveniles were more likely to report their delinquent activities than Black juveniles, and that Asian juveniles were the least likely to report delinquency (compared to White and Black juveniles). Maxfield, Weiler, and Widom (2000) produced similar findings, concluding that Black young adults were less likely to report arrests than Whites. They further found that as an individual's number of arrests increased, their likelihood of self-reporting arrests also increased. Therefore, prevalent offenders were more honest in reporting their arrests.

Not all research, however, has found that minority youths are less likely to self-report criminal involvement. Farrington, Loeber, Stouthamer-Loeber, Van Kammen, and Schmidt (1996) also analyzed the Pittsburgh Youth Survey data to examine differences in self-reported delinquency. They found that Black juveniles were actually more likely to admit past arrests than White juveniles. Piquero, Schuberty, and Brame (2014) also failed to find racial differences in self-reporting when they compared self-report surveys and official arrests data for a sample of serious delinquent offenders in Philadelphia, Pennsylvania, and Phoenix, Arizona. All of the juveniles in the study were sentenced for committing a serious offense; most had committed felonies. For these offenders, the researchers did not find significant differences in the self-reporting of criminal involvement and in the official arrest records of Black, White and Hispanic juveniles.

Overall, the research using self-report surveys indicates that Black juveniles are more likely to be arrested than White juveniles. These conclusions are limited, however, by the tendency for minority and White juveniles to differently report criminal involvement, with White juveniles often being found to more accurately report criminal involvement. When understanding the results of studies using self-reported data, it is also important to consider the source from which the data was collected. The Add Health data is collected from juveniles enrolled in school. Involvement in serious acts of delinquency is rare in these samples. It is unknown, therefore, whether the results can be generalized to juveniles who commit such acts.

Social Systematic Observations

Social systematic observations overcome the limitations of self-reported studies due to respondents being dishonest and under or over reporting involvement in criminal behavior. These observations rely on a predetermined data collection instrument that is used to collect and code data. Researchers are trained to use this instrument prior to conducting the observations. To conduct the observations, researchers accompany police officers and observe them performing their duties, while recording information with the instrument. Social systematic observations allow researchers to collect data on various types of police encounters that are not represented in official records, such as police-initiated encounters and informal conversations and encounters with citizens. They also allow for the collection of other data that is often not recorded in official reports such as the citizen's and officer's demeanor, length of an encounter, and presence of others at the scene. A disadvantage of social systematic observations, however, is that officers might change their behaviors because they know they are being observed.

Case Study: Police Officer Discretion and Public Disorder

On June 5, 2014, police officers arrived at the scene of a community swimming pool in McKinney, Texas, a suburb of Dallas. The officers were responding to calls of fighting and that uninvited teens were at the pool and refused to leave. During the encounter, an officer threw a 14-year-old teenage girl wearing a bikini to the ground and pushed her face into the ground. The officer then drew his gun and chased two teenage boys away who were approaching. He was heard yelling profanities at the other juveniles at the scene. The officer was White and many of the teenagers were Black. The girl was detained but later released to her parents. The day after the event, a video of the incident was posted on YouTube. Once the video surfaced, the officer was placed on administrative leave, and resigned a few days later. From the video, many in the media speculated that the officer's actions were in response to the girl's attitude and not a response to suspected criminal behavior (CNN Wire & Romero, 20115 June 7; Southall, 2005 June 9).

Black and Reis's (1970) study utilized systematic observations to examine police officers' decisions in Boston, Massachusetts, Chicago, Illinois, and Washington, D.C., in the summer of 1966. They found that Black juveniles had a higher rate of arrest than White juveniles. Lundman, Sykes and Clark (1978) replicated this study in a Midwest study in 1970. They also found that Black juveniles were more likely to be arrested than White juveniles. Both studies further found that juveniles who were disrespectful to the police were more likely to be arrested; this finding held for both Black and White juveniles. These studies also found that police are more likely to arrest a juvenile if a citizen requests that the juvenile be arrested. They further concluded that most police-juvenile encounters were citizen initiated and not police officer initiated. An example of a citizen initiated encounter could involve an officer responding to a citizen's complaint that juveniles on the street were making too much noise. Therefore, most police-juvenile contact was determined to be reactive and not proactive.

In addition to examining factors that influence arrests, Myers (2004) also examined police officers' use of authority and support. Use of authority included such things as officers issuing commands, threats, warnings, and using investigative tactics. Use of support included things like complying with a juvenile's request, providing information on how to deal with a problem, and providing sympathy or comfort. His study utilized data collected from social systematic observations of police-juvenile encounters and from interviews with police officers in Indianapolis, Indiana and St. Petersburg, Florida. Unlike earlier studies, he did not find that most police-juvenile encounters were reactive; instead he found that police initiated contact with juveniles as often as they responded to complaints. Also different from earlier studies, he did not find that minorities were subjected to more authoritative responses from police or that minority youths were more likely to be arrested than White youths. In fact, it appeared that minorities were treated more leniently than White juveniles. Race was also not a significant predictor of officers providing support. Officers were, however, more likely to provide support for juveniles in low social economic neighborhoods.

Liederbach's (2007) study also utilized data collected from social systematic observations to examine police encounters with juveniles. His study differs from previous studies in that he examined observations of police-juvenile encounters in 20 suburban and small towns, instead of an urban city. The observations took place in 1999 and 2000 in southwest Ohio. All of the 15 suburban cities surrounding Cincinnati. He found that minority juveniles were more likely to be arrested than White juveniles. Despite only committing 29% of the offenses observed, minorities accounted for 40% of the arrest observed.

Overall, it appears that the research from social systematic observations indicate that Black juveniles are more likely to be arrested than White juveniles. There is a limited amount of this research, however, and the existing research is limited to examining the treatment of Black and White juveniles. The treatment of other minority groups has not yet been examined.

Race, Gang Affiliation and Arrests

The reasons why police officers would be more likely to arrest Black juveniles is not clear. Research examining the factors that might impact the arrests decisions for White and Black youth are scarce. Research conducted by Tapia (2011a), however, suggests that gang membership might be a relevant factor, as youths who are members of gangs are expected to be viewed more dangerously and subsequently treated more harshly by police than juveniles who are not affiliated with gangs. Tapia utilized the National Longitudinal Survey of Youth (NLSY), the same dataset as in his earlier study, to empirically examine this possibility. He found that juveniles who were members of gangs were arrested more often, even after controlling for past involvement in delinquent activities. When considering the relationships between race/ethnicity and gang membership, he further found that being a gang member increased the number of arrests for Black juveniles by 62% and by 45% for Hispanic juveniles, but actually decreased the number of arrests for White juveniles by 38%. Tapia (2011b) expanded these findings with a later study in which he also considered the effect of social economic status with gang membership. This study indicated that gang membership still increased the number of arrests after social economic status was controlled. Gang membership had the greatest impact on juveniles of high social economic status, increasing their number of arrests more significantly than those of lower economic status.

These results are supported by an earlier study conducted by Curry (2000) in Chicago, Illinois. Survey data for this study was collected in the late 1980s in four middle schools located in low-income Chicago neighborhoods. All of the survey respondents were male and either Latino or African American. Additional official data was collected on the juveniles' arrests records five years after the surveys were administered. He found that those who were gang involved were more likely to be arrested in the five year follow-up. This relationship held for both African American and Latino juveniles. Brownfield et al. (2001), however, produced contradictory findings in his Seattle, Washington study. His analysis did not find an effect of gang membership on juveniles' likelihoods of being arrested. It is possible; however, that this finding could be specific to Seattle, as he pointed out that at the time of data collection, the Seattle police were not concerned about gangs in the city.

Overall, it appears that gang affiliation might partially explain the difference in arrests decisions for Black, White, and Hispanic youth. It further appears that gang membership has a larger negative impact on Black and Hispanic juveniles. This might be an indication that minority youth, and Black youths in particular, are viewed by the police as more dangerous and crime prone then their White counterparts. Because they fit the image of the dangerous juvenile, Black juveniles are more likely to be arrested, especially in cases where they have other indicators, like being gang-involved, of being dangerous, and of being a chronic offender.

Unfortunately, no recent social systematic observations have been conducted that examines how gang affiliation affects patrol officers' decision-making on the street. Therefore, our understanding is limited to self-report studies, which are not able to determine with certainty that a juvenile's gang affiliation was known to the police at the time that the arrest decision was made. In addition, conclusions on the effects of gang membership are often dependent on the assumption that the juveniles surveyed correctly identified themselves as gang members or non-gang members. According to Esbensen, Winfree, He, and Taylor (2001) this can be problematic as some juveniles, termed "wannabe" gang members, will self-identify as gang members even though they are not truly affiliated with a gang and do not engage in the same types of serious delinquency as fully affil-iated gang members. Although Curry's method did not rely on juveniles iden-tifying themselves as gang members, largely because only 20 juveniles identified themselves as such, he relied on the juveniles' reports of involvement in gang ac-tivities, some of which were as mundane as flashing gang symbols, wearing gang colors, and perceiving gang membership as advantageous. It is likely, there-fore, that some of the youths classified as gang-involved were not established gang members. Furthermore, Curry's analysis did not control for involvement in delinquency during the five year follow-up period. Therefore, it is impossible to determine how much of the difference in arrest rates between gang-involved and non-gang-involved youth can be explained by disparities in offending and not due to police officers' decision-making.

Racial Differences during Police Interrogation

The Fifth Amendment of the United States Constitution protects a person from having to be a "witness against himself." On television we commonly hear people reference this right when they say, "I plead the fifth," indicating that they are not talking to police or answering a question. This right applies to ju-veniles the same as it applies to adults. Juveniles have the right to remain silent and not provide police with statements that are self-incriminating. Juveniles also have the right to due process if they are in custody. If juveniles are arrested and held in custody, they must be aware of their Miranda rights. You have probably heard the Miranda warning recited in crime shows on television. The warning stipulates the following general principles:

- You have the right to remain silent.
- If you give up that right, anything you say can and will be used against you in a court of law.
- You have the right to an attorney.
- If you cannot afford an attorney, one will be provided to you at no cost.
- You have the right to exercise these rights at any time and can refuse to answer any questions.

Although these rights may not seem especially complicated, they can be dif-ficult for citizens to understand. One confusing aspect is that, unlike other rights, they stipulate things citizens do *not* have to do, instead of things that they *can* do. In addition, the nature of remaining silent when an authoritar-ian figure asks for assistance violates the values with which most citizens are socialized, as society teaches children to tell the truth and listen to authority.

Given these points, it is not surprising that research on interrogations often finds that juveniles, especially younger juveniles, do not fully understand the provisions of the Miranda warning (Woolard, Cleary, Harvell & Chen, 2008). Although the court has acknowledge the fact that juveniles might be disadvantaged in their capacities to understand the magnitude of waiving their right to remain silent, the Supreme Court has stopped short of stipulating special provisions for juveniles in the interrogation process.

After being notified of their Fifth Amendment rights, juveniles can decide to waive their rights and talk to the police or they can refuse to waive their rights and not talk to the police. If the juvenile decides to talk to the police, the information they provide to the police can be used as evidence against them in subsequent criminal justice system decisions. It is typically to the advantage of juveniles to remain silent and not respond to police questioning. Those who make statements to the police often make self-incriminating statements that work to their disadvantage as they are being processed through the system. Therefore if there are racial disparities in the likelihood of juveniles waiving their rights, it could contribute to the overrepresentation of minorities in the juvenile justice system.

Feld (2013) examined racial differences in the interrogations of juveniles in four Minnesota Counties (Anoka County, Dakota County, Hennepin County, and Ramsey County). Two of the counties were urban (Hennepin and Ramsey) and two were suburban (Anoka and Dakota). All the juveniles in the four counties had been charged with a felony. He found that although the majority of juveniles (92.8%) waived their rights during interrogations, there were several racial differences in the circumstances of the interrogations for juveniles of different races. Black juveniles and juveniles of other races were more likely than Whites to be interrogated in urban counties than suburban counties. There were also racial differences in the types of crimes for which juveniles were interrogated. Black juveniles were less likely to be questioned for a property or drug offense than White youth, but were more likely to be questioned for a violent crime and twice as likely to be questioned for a firearm offense. White juveniles were also less likely to have had a prior offense or be under the supervision of the court than Black juveniles or juveniles of other racial status. White juveniles were also less likely to be questioned at the police department or at a detention center. Fewer Black and juveniles of other races had their parents present during the interrogation than White juveniles.

Despite these differences, Feld did not find any significant differences in the likelihood of White, Black and other race juveniles waiving their Miranda rights. Instead, the majority of juveniles in each racial category (Black, White, and other) waived their rights. In all three groups, those who waived their rights less often were those with prior contact with the system and those located in urban counties. He further found that police did *not* use different techniques to interrogate juveniles of different races. Police interrogated all the juveniles for similar lengths of time.

Feld did, however, find differences in the way juveniles responded to the interrogations. White juveniles were more likely to be forthcoming with incriminating information and to be cooperative. They provided lengthier responses to questions and were less likely to deny involvement in criminal behavior than Black juveniles and juveniles of other races. In fact, 72% of White youths gave full confessions compared to 43.9% of Black juveniles and 40% of juveniles of other races.

Case Study: Police Guidelines for Interacting with Juveniles

The Office of Juvenile Justice and Delinquency Prevention released an informational report in partnership with the International Association of Chiefs of Police (IACP) in 2015 aimed at helping law enforcement officials better understand juveniles. The report contained information on why adolescents behave the way they do and linked adolescents' behaviors to brain development, and how brain development hinders juveniles' abilities to calculate long-term consequences in stressful situations. Protective factors that can prevent delinquency are also discussed, and law enforcement officers are encouraged to become a protective factor by developing relationships with juveniles. Issues with juveniles during interviews and interrogations are also discussed, and law enforcement officers are warned that juveniles are more susceptible to falsely confessing. The report further presents 10 strategies to improve police-juvenile interactions.

The 10 strategies are:

1. Approach youth with a calm demeanor, conveying that you are there to help them.
2. Establish rapport.
3. Be patient.
4. Model the respect you expect in return.
5. Use age-appropriate language.
6. Repeat or paraphrase their statements. Affirm their emotions.
7. Take caution with nonverbal communication.

8. Model and praise calm confidence.
9. Empower them through choices.
10. Serve as a positive adult role model.
(IACP, 2015, p., 4)

Although tension between juveniles and police is still a problem, steps are being taken to adopting policing styles to consider the special circumstances surrounding juveniles. As these initiatives grow, police-juveniles interactions will hopefully improve.

Conclusion

It is still not clear whether minority overrepresentation in arrest is due to differences in offending or differences in the treatment of juveniles. It is very possible that both play a role in arrest disparities. The majority of research that has attempted to determine which perspective has the greatest impact has relied on self-report surveys or systematic observations. Although not all the findings are consistent, overall it appears that race does have some impact on arrest decisions, at least in some situations and in some locations. Additional research, however, is needed to really understand the root cause of disparities in the processing of juveniles. It is possible that officers are reacting to other situational factors through which race indirectly affects outcomes. Empirical examinations in the interrogation process do not indicate that minority and White juveniles are treated differently. More research should be conducted, however, of possible racial disparities in the handling of juveniles in additional investigative stages (e.g., decision to search or interrogate a juvenile), as differences that might be present at these points could be contributing to the overrepresentation of minorities.

Discussion Questions

1. Summarize the "differential involvement" and the "differential selection" hypotheses. Which do you think is best at explaining the overrepresentation of minorities in arrest statistics? Use examples from recent news and media reports to support your argument.

2. Many of the studies that examined likelihood of arrest using self-report data used data that was collected from juveniles in public schools. How does this limit the generalizability of these findings? How might the results be different if juveniles who were not enrolled in schools were included?
3. From the standpoint of the police, what factors could make encounters with juveniles more difficult than other encounters? What strategies can police utilize to better handle juvenile encounters?
4. Given the research on juveniles' lack of understanding of their Miranda rights, should all states be required to consult with juveniles' parents before being allowed to waive their right to remain silent?
5. Do you think the report released by the Office of Juvenile Justice and Delinquency Prevention and the International Association of Chiefs of police will be helpful to law enforcement agencies? Why or why not? Is there any additional information they could have included to make it more helpful?

References

Black, D. (1971). The social organization of arrest. *Stanford Law Review, 23,* 1087–1111.

Black, D.J. & Reiss, A.J. (1970). Police control of juveniles. *American Sociological Review, 35*(1), 63–77.

Blumstein, A. (1982). On the racial disproportionality of U.S. prison populations. *Journal of Criminal Law and Criminology, 73*(3), 1259–1281.

Blumstein, A. (1993). Racial disproportionality of U.S. populations revisited. *University of Colorado Law Review, 64*(3), 743–760.

Brown, M.K. (1988). *Working the street: Police discretion and dilemmas of reform.* New York: Russel Sage Foundation.

Brown, R.A., Novak, K.J. & Frank, J. (2009). Identifying variation in police officer behavior between juveniles and adults. *Journal of Crime and Justice, 37,* 200–208.

Brownfield, D., Sorenson, A. M. & Thomson, K. (2001). Gang membership, race, and social class: A test of the group hazard and master status hypothesis. *Deviant Behavior: An Interdisciplinary Journal, 22,* 73–89.

Chambliss, W.J. (1994). Policing the ghetto underclass: The politics of law and law enforcement. *Social Problems, 41*(2), 177–194.

Chambliss, W.J. (1995). The institutionalization of racism through law. In Darnell Hawkins (Ed.). *Race, ethnicity, and crime* (pp. 235–258). Albany, NY: State University of New York Press.

CNN Wire & Romero, L. (2015 June 7). Texas officer suspended after video appears to shows him pulling gun on juveniles outside pool. KTLA 5, Available at: http://ktla.com/2015/06/07/texas-police-officer-placed-on-leave-after-video-appears-to-shows-him-pulling-gun-on-juveniles-outside-pool/.

Curry, G.D. (2000). Self-reported gang involvement and officially recorded delinquency. *Criminology, 38*(4), 1253–1274.

Esbensen, F., Winfree, T., He, N., Taylor, T. (2001). Youth gangs and definitional issues: When is a gang a gang and why does it matter? *Crime & Delinquency, 47,* 105–130.

Farrington DP, Loeber R, Stouthamer-Loeber M, Van Kammen WB & Schmidt L. (1996). Self-reported delinquency and a combined delinquency seriousness scale based on boys, mothers, and teachers: Concurrent and predictive validity for African-Americans and Caucasians. *Criminology, 34,* 493–514.

Feld, B.C. (2013). *Kids, cops, and confessions: Inside the interrogation room.* NY: New York University Press.

Greene, J.R. & Klockars, C.B. (1991). What police do. In *Thinking about police. 2nd ed.* Edited by C.B. Klockars and S.D. Mastrofski. New York: McGraw-Hill.

Hindelang, M.J., Hirschi, T. & Weis, J.G. (1981). *Measuring delinquency.* Beverly Hills, CA: Sage.

Hirschfield, P., Maschi, T., White, H. R., Traub, L. G. & Loeber, R. (2006). Mental health and juvenile arrests: Criminality, criminalization, or compassion? *Criminology, 44,* 593–627.

Huizinga, D. & Elliott, D.S. (1986). Reassessing the reliability and validity of self-report delinquency measures. *Journal of Quantitative Criminology, 2*(4), 293–327.

International Association of Chiefs of Police (IACP) (2015). *The effects of adolescent* development on policing. Washington D.C.: Office of Juvenile Justice and Delinquency Prevention (OJJDP). Available at: http://www.theiacp.org/Portals/0/documents/pdfs/IACPBriefEffectsofAdolescentDevelopmentonPolicing.pdf.

Jolliffe, D., Farrington, D.P., Hawkins, J.D., Catalano, R.F., Hill, K.G. & Kosterman, R. (2003). Predictive, concurrent, prospective and retrospective validity self-reported delinquency. *Criminal Behaviour and Mental Health, 13,* 179–197.

Liederbach, J. (2007). Controlling suburban and small-town hoods: An examination of police encounters with juveniles. *Youth Violence and Juvenile Justice, 5*(2), 107–124.

Lundman, R., Sykes, R. & Clark, J. (1978). Police control of juveniles: A replication. *Journal of Research in Crime & Delinquency, 15*(1), 74–91.

Maxfield, M.G., Weiler, B.L. & Widom, C.S. (2000). Comparing self-reports and official records of arrests. *Journal of Quantitative Criminology, 16,* 87–110.

McNulty, T.L. & Bellair, P.E. (2003). Explaining racial and ethnic differences in serious adolescent violent behavior. *Criminology, 41*(3), 709–748.

Myers, S.M. (2004). Police encounters with juvenile suspects: Explaining the use of authority and provision of support [Executive Summary Report submitted to the National Institute of Justice]. Available at: https://www.ncjrs.gov/pdffiles1/nij/grants/205125.pdf.

New York Times, Available at: http://www.nytimes.com/2015/06/10/us/police-officer-in-mckinney-tex-resigns-over-incident-caught-on-video.html?_r=1.

Piquero, A.R., Schubert, C.A. & Brame, R. (2014). Comparing official and self-report records of offending across gender and race/ethnicity in a longitudinal study of serious youthful offenders. *Journal of Research in Crime and Delinquency, 51*(4), 526–556.

Pollock, W. (2014). Things change: An intergenerational examination of the correlates of police contact. *Crime & Delinquency, 60*(8), 1183–1208.

Pope, C,E, & Snyder, H.N. (2003). *Race as a factor in juvenile arrests.* Office of Juvenile Justice Delinquency Prevention Juvenile Justice Bulletin. Washington, D.C.: U.S. Department of Justice.

Smith, D.A. & Visher, C.A. (1981). Street-level justice: Situational determinants of police arrest decisions. *Social Problems, 29*(2), 167–177.

Stephen, R., Kurtz, P.D. & Giddings, M. (1993). The influence of juveniles' race on police decision-making: An exploratory study. *Juvenile & Family Court Journal, 44*(2), 69–78.

Southall, A. (2015 June 9). McKinney, Tex., Police officer resigns over incident caught on video. The New York Times.

Tapia, M. (2010). Untangling race and class effects on juvenile arrests. *Journal of Criminal Justice, 38,* 255–265.

Tapia, M. (2011a). Gang membership and race as risk factors for juvenile arrest. *Journal of Research in Crime and Delinquency, 48*(3), 364–395.

Tapia, M. (2011b). U.S. juvenile arrests: Gang membership, social class, and labeling effects. *Youth & Society, 43*(4), 1407–1432.

Tonry, M.H. (1995). *Malign neglect: Race, crime, and punishment in America.* New York: Oxford University Press.

Watt, T. & Rogers, J. M. (2007). Factors contributing to differences in substance abuse among Black and White adolescents. *Youth and Society, 39,* 54–74.

Werthman C, Piliavin I. (1967). Gang members and the police. In: Bordua D, editor. *The police: Six sociological essays.* New York: Wiley.

Wilkbanks, W. (1987). *The myth of a racist criminal justice system.* Monterey, CA: Brooks/Cole.

Wolcott, D. B. (2005). *Cops and kids: Policing juvenile delinquency in urban America, 1890–1940.* Columbus, OH: Ohio State University Press.

Woolard, J.L., Cleary, H.M.D., Harvell, S.A.S. & Chen, R. (2008). Examining adolescents' and their parents' conceptual and practical knowledge of police interrogation: A family dyad approach. *Journal of Youth Adolescence, 37,* 685–698.

Chapter 5

Minority Youths' Perception of the Police and the Juvenile Justice System

Goals of the Chapter

The purpose of this chapter is to examine youths' perceptions of the police and the juvenile justice system, and how minority juveniles' views differ from White juveniles'. This chapter begins with a discussion of youths' perceptions of the police. Next, broad explanations for racial differences in White and minority youths' views of the police are explored. The research examining programs to improve youths' perceptions of the police are then discussed. The chapter concludes with a discussion of the research examining youths' views of other parts of the juvenile justice system.

After reading this chapter, you will be able to do the following:

1. Understand the differences in White and minority youths' perceptions of the police;
2. Demonstrate knowledge in the explanations for racial and ethnic differences in perceptions;
3. Critically assess programs aimed at improving youths' perceptions of the police; and
4. Understand the research on youths' perceptions of other parts of the juvenile justice system.

After a late school event, a young Black youth is standing on the corner waiting for his ride. He is wearing what kids typically wear in his neighborhood—dark jeans, a white t-shirt, and a black hoodie. As he waits, two police officers approach him. First, they demand to see his hands. Startled and nervous, he complies. Next, they ask him a series of questions regarding what he is doing on the corner. Their demeanor is sharp and accusatory. Satisfied that the youth is not causing any problems, the officers continue on down the street. The officers view this as a routine encounter with a citizen in a high-crime neighborhood. The youth, however, feels violated and picked on; he was simply waiting for his ride, not bothering anyone, in his own neighborhood. He cannot help but think that this does not happen in other neighborhoods; it does not happen to White kids.

This type of encounter happens every day in urban areas. In fact, oftentimes these encounters are much more dramatic, with youth being frisked, asked to sit on the curb, strongly interrogated, insulted, or disrespected. It is also not uncommon for youths to react in a more resistant manner, cursing at the police, calling the police a derogatory name, or simply being rude and disrespectful. These types of encounters, coupled with negative media reports of police behavior, feed an environment of distrust and disrespect between youths and the police, and can lead to larger issues with youths and the police.

Youths' Perceptions of the Police

Research on juveniles' perceptions of the juvenile justice system has largely focused on juveniles' perceptions of the police. This research has suggested that youths tend to hold more negative perceptions of the police than adults (Leiber, Nalla & Farnworth, 1998; Snyder & Sickmund, 1996). Considering the issues surrounding youth offending and victimizations, how youths view the police may seem like a less pressing issue. Several research studies, however, have shown the importance of views towards the system, as those with more positive views are more likely to obey the law and to cooperate with policing efforts (Fagan & Tyler, 2005; Piquero, Fagan, Mulvey, Steinberg, & Ogers 2005; Sunshine & Tyler, 2003; Tyler, 2006). Citizen cooperation with policing efforts is important as the police must often rely on the public for assistance in reporting crimes and providing information. Therefore, if more people view the police as fair, the police can be more effective.

In addition, research shows that juveniles are more likely than adults to have contact with the police, especially in field stops and frisks (Hurst, Frank & Browning, 2000; Leiber, Nalla & Farnworth, 1998). Because of this frequent police contact, youths begin to feel that police will bother them regardless of their behaviors. Therefore, there is nothing to lose from being disrespectful to the police and giving the police a hard time (Bittner, 1990). Unfortunately, being disrespectful can then increase juveniles' likelihoods of being arrested during a police encounter (Black & Reis, 1970; Lundman, Sykes & Clark, 1978).

Perceptions of the police are heavily tied to race and ethnicity. Youths' perceptions of the police are not the same across White and minority groups. Black youths, in particular, tend to hold more negative views of the police (Hurst, Frank & Browning, 2000) and to report negative experiences with police (Hagan, Spedd & Payne, 2005; Taylor, Turner, Esbensen, & Winfree 2001). Not only is there a culture of distrust between the Black community and the police, but Black juveniles are also more likely to be stopped by the police than White youths (Black & Riess, 1970; Leiber, Nalla & Farnworth, 1998). Hurst et al. (2000) surveyed 852 high school students in and around Cincinnati, Ohio to determine whether Black and White youths had different perceptions of the police. Their results indicated that Black youths' held more negative overall perceptions of police. When the researchers asked questions regarding police behavior in specific situations, the kids had actually experienced with the police, however, Black and White youths held similar attitudes.

Jones-Brown (2000) also examined the views of Black male youths toward the police. Her data was collected from youths enrolled in three high schools and two summer youth programs in three towns in New Jersey. A total of 125 Black males age 15 to 18 (with 90% being age 16 or 17) were included in the study. Data was collected through interviews that lasted between 45 minutes and one hour. The interviews asked about police contact and the juvenile's perception of that contact as either favorable or unfavorable. Whether the contact was favorable or unfavorable was assessed using two questions. The first question was more general and asked if the juvenile thought the officer acted the way she/he were supposed to act. The second question was more specific, asking if there was anything the juvenile did not like about the way the officer acted. Additional questions were also asked regarding the youths' attitudes towards the police.

The results indicated that all of the respondents had contact with the police in the last year, and the majority (92.1%) had been stopped by the police in the last year. Over 37% reported their police encounter to be unfavorable. Of those, a little less than half specified that they did not like the police officer's attitude. Another one-third were unsatisfied with the physical treatment they received from the police officer (e.g., being handcuffed, grabbed, pushed, or punched), and one-fourth believed they were unfairly targeted because they were Black. An additional 34 participants reported some indirect experience with the police through a friend and 61 reported indirect experience through a relative. Few of the indirect experiences reported were favorable (1 for friends and 3 for relatives). For the attitude measures, police were rated low for equity and fairness, with 80% of respondents reporting that police do not always have a good reason when stopping people and 60% believing that police do not give all young people an even break. Over one-half of the respondents, however, indicated that they respected the police in their town.

Carr, Napolitano, and Keating (2007) conducted interviews with juveniles and young adults in three Philadelphia neighborhoods. One neighborhood was predominantly White, another predominantly Black, and the third predominantly Latino. The researchers found that less than 10% of the youths interviewed would call the police in any situation. Similar to other studies, they also found that youths tended to hold more negative than positive dispositions of police. Most of these negative dispositions stemmed from personal negative encounters with police, and focused on the unfair practices by the police instead of the outcome of the encounter. When asked how crime should be better controlled, however, most youths argued that a greater police presence and stricter enforcement of laws was necessary to reduce crime. One juvenile interviewed said this about the necessity of police:

> If there was no police round every corner there would be a riot or a mob. That would be like there is no rules. And the police need to set rules and laws, because if there was none there would be chaos around this world. (Carr et al. 2007, p. 468)

The researchers did not find a statistically significant relationship between police dispositions and likelihood of supporting a punitive response to crime.

Another study by Brunson and Weitzer (2009) conducted qualitative interviews with young men in three disadvantaged neighborhoods in St. Louis. One neighborhood was predominately Black, another predominately White and the last was racially mixed. They found that the Black youths they spoke with reported higher rates of being stopped by the police and higher rates of being treated poorly by the police. One Black youth reported the following incident:

> A friend of mine and me were in the community, we were outside and it was a late night and I guess the officer that approached took us as gang bangers or whatever. He asked us what we were doing and we looked at each other and we said, "Nothing," and he [said] that we looked real suspicious.... He used the excuse that we had drugs in our mouth[s] and told us to take whatever we had in our mouths out. We had grills [decorative dental molds] in our mouth[s] and he made us take them out, we showed them to him in our hand[s] and [the officer] smacked 'em out and when they [hit] the ground, he stomped on them and laughed. But he was showing us that he had more power, authority over us at the time, so there was nothing we could do or say. (Brunson & Weitzer, 2009 p. 866)

The White youths reported a higher rate of police harassment and being stopped by the police when they were in predominately Black neighborhoods, with Black friends, or dressed in urban clothing. It appeared to these young White men that while in the company of Black youths they were guilty by association. One White youth reported this incident while with Black friends:

> [We] was on a corner during school hours and a cop talked to us about what we were doing, and then took us back to school. We got in trouble for it at school, it sucked.... The cop that stopped us was being a dick at first. He kept asking us if we were going on a booty call together. You know, like we were gay. Then kept making jokes about booty calls and then ask[ed] if we left school because of the "brothers." Then he asked if we were scared of the "brothers" and if that is why we left school or if the "brothers" booty call[ed] us and that is why we left. The cop finally quit giving us shit, took us back to school, and we got three days of in-school suspension. (Brunson & Weitzer, 2009 p. 867)

Another White youth discussed a similar incident of being harassed while in a Black neighborhood:

> [The police] asked me what I was doing in a Black neighborhood, 'cause I'm a White boy. They said, "You ain't sellin' drugs are you?" and he tried to plant drugs on me. I didn't have weed on me 'cause I never sold it or smoked it but the [officer] put it in my pocket, put his hand in my pocket and pulled it out. I felt his thumb was folded under his hand, there's a lump. And then when he touched me I felt a bag under his thumb, he pulled it out and then said, "Aha, what's this?" (Brunson & Weitzer, 2009 p. 867)

Brunson and Weitzer also found that youths from the three different communities reported different treatment. Youths in the neighborhood that was predominately Black reported being stopped the most, those in the racially mixed neighborhood reported being stopped the second most frequently, and those in the predominately White neighborhood reported experiencing the fewest police stops. Those in the predominately White neighborhood also believed that most police stops were justified.

When considering racial differences in juveniles' perceptions of the police, it is also important to examine differences across gender. Although boys are more likely to come into contact with the police than girls, the number of girls entering the criminal justice system is growing at a faster rate than any other group. Therefore, more girls are having contact with the police than ever before. In addition, research has found that the treatment of girls in the criminal justice system varies by race, making it important to recognize the fact that girls of different racial and ethnic backgrounds have different experiences in the criminal justice system and throughout their lives.

Hurst, DcDermott, and Thomas (2005) examined racial differences in girls' perceptions of the police. Their study found that Black girls had less positive perceptions of the police. They also found that Black girls were more likely than White girls to hear about police physically mistreating someone, of police covering up another officer's misconduct, and officers not performing their duties. They also found that girls who reported a police contact that they rated as "positive" had better perceptions of the police, while girls who reported a police contact that they rated as "negative" had more negative general perceptions of the police.

Explanations for Racial Differences in Juvenile Police Perceptions

Research examining youths' perceptions of the police and the racial and ethnic differences in youths' perceptions has been extended to explore the factors that contribute to these differences. Several possible explanations have been explored. They include the group-position thesis, differences in past experiences with the police, involvement in subcultures, neighborhood social context, and differences in the strength of social bonds. In addition, several other factors have been identified that could account for the racial and ethnic variation in youths' perceptions of the police, such as experiences with victimization, geographic location, and gang affiliation.

Group-Position Thesis

The group-position thesis stems from conflict theory and contends that different groups hold different positions in society. Race is an indicator of group membership (Blumer, 1958). Because Whites are the dominant group, their interest is best served by upholding the current status quo and preventing minorities from gaining equal access to resources. Minorities, however, are disadvantaged by the current division of resources. Therefore, it would be advantageous to them to challenge the existing racial order.

According to this thesis, Whites are supportive of the police as they see opposition to the police as a threat to their dominant position. Because Whites view police as a regulatory force against minorities, they identify with the police and are less troubled by acts of police misconduct. Minorities, on the other hand, view the police as a symbol of White domination. Police are often viewed as the authority who upholds the subordination of the Black population. Their interests are better served, therefore, if police authority is more controlled (Weitzer & Tuch, 2004). It would then be expected that minority juveniles would hold more critical views of the police, especially of incidences of police misconduct, than White juveniles.

Hagan, Shedd, and Payne (2005) analyzed survey data regarding juveniles perceptions of police injustice. The surveys contained information collected from 18,251 juveniles enrolled in 91 Chicago Public Schools that examined how the racial make-up of a juvenile's school affected his or her perceptions of police. Hagan et al. (2005) speculated that greater exposure to White students at school might cause minority students to better recognize their position of subordination, resulting in more negative views of the police. Their results indicated that Black and Latino juveniles' perceptions of unfairness did indeed increase if they were in schools with larger White populations. They argued that as Black and Latino youth became more segregated with White youth, White privilege became more visible to them and this allowed them to better recognize the racial differences in police treatment. This argument is also consistent with Schuck's (2013) finding that Black youths living in predominately White neighborhoods experienced a more rapid decline in their perceptions of the police than Black youths living in areas with lower White populations. In Hagan et al.'s (2005) study, however, this effect did not sustain once the population of White students reached about one-third of the school population. At that point, further increases in White enrollment had the opposite effect on Black and Latino youths' perceptions of injustice, and led to improved perceptions.

Lee, Steinberg, Piquero, and Knight (2011) examined the perceptions of Black youths who had been identified as serious offenders. Given the arguments presented in the group-position thesis, we would expect to find that minority youth who are more closely tied to their ethnic group would have the most negative perceptions of the police. Their findings did indicate that youths' perceptions of the police were influenced by how much they identified with their ethnic group but in the opposite direction. Those who were more closely tied to their ethnic group identity had more positive perceptions of the police and the law. It is possible, however, that this finding does not contradict the group-position thesis. As suggested by Hagan et al. (2005), juveniles who are more ingrained with their ethnic group may be less aware of the differential treatment that minorities receive compared to Whites than juveniles who are more exposed to the dominant (White) culture.

Case Study: Black Lives Matter

The Black Lives Matter campaign began in 2012 after George Zimmerman was acquitted of killing Trayvon Martin. The campaign gained more attention in 2014 when Michael Brown, an unarmed 18-year-old Black man, was shot by Darren Wilson, a White police officer in Ferguson, MO. When the prosecutor announced that the grand jury decided not to indict Wilson, riots erupted that lasted for weeks. Later incidences of unarmed Black men being killed by police in Baltimore, Maryland, New York, New York, and Milwaukee, Wisconsin, have further brought the Black Lives Matter campaign into public attention.

Sources:
http://blacklivesmatter.com/about/
http://www.nytimes.com/interactive/2014/08/13/us/ferguson-missouri-town-under-siege-after-police-shooting.html?_r=0

Past Police Contact

Past experiences with the police have also been found to influence juveniles' perceptions of the police. It is easy to understand how an incident in which a juvenile receives lenient treatment from a police officer can be viewed positively by the juvenile. Imagine a scenario when a teenager is speeding. An officer pulls him over and writes him a ticket. Do you think that juvenile will have a more negative view of the police after that encounter? According to research, it depends. Tyler (1990) found that it is not as much the outcome of the encounter (i.e., getting a ticket versus a warning) that influences citizens' perceptions of the police. What is more impactful is the manner in which the citizen is treated by the police officer. If the officer treated the juvenile fairly and with respect, the juvenile is more likely to hold a favorable opinion of the police and of the encounter. If the juvenile views his treatment as unfair and the officer as disrespectful, however, he is more likely to express negative views of the police.

Research further indicates that the impact of police encounters is greater for Black individuals than for White individuals. Black individuals are also more likely to feel that they were not treated with procedural justice during a police encounter than Whites (Tyler & Huo, 2002). Another study found that Hispanics held positive attitudes about the police until they had contact with the police. After having contact, their perceptions of the police decreased and continued to do so as they had more contact with the police (Carter, 1985).

Past experiences with the police can also impact peoples' perceptions indirectly. Hearing about another individual's either positive or negative encounter with the police can impact how an individual perceives the police. Additionally, witnessing police encounters in the community can affect perceptions. These encounters can be witnessed first-hand or through the media. Media portrayal of police can be through news reports of police misconduct or brutality or through reality television shows such as COPS. Escholz, Blackwell, Gertz, and Chiricos (2002) examined the effects of watching these shows (specifically COPS, America's Most Wanted, and Highway Patrol) and found that they can work to increase the racial divide in confidence in the police. For White males without a college education, watching these shows improved their confidence in the police. Viewing these shows, however, did not affect Black respondents confidence in the police.

In the Chicago school study discussed earlier, Hagan et al. (2005) examined youths' perceptions of the police and how police contacts shaped youths' perceptions. The results indicated that Black, Latino, and American Indian youths had lower perceptions of police fairness than White juveniles. The largest gap was found between White and Black juveniles followed by White and Latino juveniles. No significant difference was found between White and Asian juveniles. They further found that although Black juveniles experienced more contacts with the police, their perceptions of police fairness were less influenced by these encounters than White and Latino juveniles' perceptions. For White and Latino juveniles, increased police encounters decreased their perceptions of the police as fair, with the effect being greater for Latino juveniles.

Involvement in Subcultures

Involvement in subcultures (e.g., participation in a gang) has also been explored as a cause of negative attitudes toward the police. Leiber, Nalla and Farnworth (1998) argued that subcultural deviance theories could explain juveniles' perceptions of the police. Subcultural theories posit that negative views of authority figures and formal control agents, such as the police, are part of the shared norms in deviant subcultures. Subcultural theories also stipulate that lower class youths will be more susceptible to subcultures, and because minorities comprise a large portion of lower-class youths, they will be overrepresented in subcultures.

Leiber, Nalla, and Farnworth (1998) examined these relationships empirically using survey data from 337 male youths in four Iowa counties. Subcultural values were measured through attitudes and behavior. Attitudes were measured by asking youths how wrong they thought it was to engage in a number of criminal behaviors, and behavior was measured by asking youth about their involvement in delinquent behaviors. The results indicated that juveniles who had delinquent attitudes and who engaged in juvenile delinquency held more negative views of the police, with attitudes having a stronger impact on police perceptions than behaviors. They also found that delinquent attitudes decreased White and minority youths' respect for the police, but involvement in delinquent activities only reduced White juveniles' respect for the police.

Brick, Taylor, and Esbensen (2009) also examined the relationships between youths' involvement in a subculture and attitudes toward the police. They used data collected from 1,289 sixth- through ninth-grade students in 15 schools in four states in 2005. Subcultural involvement was examined through two measures. One measured juveniles' commitment to delinquent peers, and the other measured attitudes favorable to involvement in delinquent activities. Their examination also included measures of community structure. They included 1) community disorder, 2) ties to the community, 3) strain, 4) fear of criminal victimization and 5) risks of criminal victimization.

Their results indicated that Black and Hispanic juveniles had more negative perceptions of the police than White juveniles. Involvement in delinquent activities also had a strong effect on attitudes toward the police, with those juveniles involved in delinquency having more negative views of the police. Having been arrested had the strongest effect on attitudes, with juveniles who had an arrest history, holding significantly more negative views of the police. None of the other police contact variables were significant (having an officer as an instructor for a past prevention program, having contact with police and a victim, or being stopped and questioned). Subculture involvement did in fact influence police perceptions, with those juveniles more closely tied to deviant peers and those holding more pro-delinquency attitudes having more negative perceptions of the police. Juveniles who lived in areas with high levels of strain, weak community ties, and less fear of crime also had more negative views of the police. Community disorder and risks of criminal victimization, however, did not significantly affect police perceptions.

Social Bonds and Perceptions

Another explanation proposed by Wu, Lake, and Cao (2015) argues that social bonds are indicative of juveniles' perceptions of the police. Social bonding theory, proposed by Travis Hirshi (1969), was originally developed to explain why some juveniles do not engage in delinquency. It stipulates that the likelihood of juveniles being delinquent rests on the strength of four social bonds: attachment, commitment, involvement and belief. Attachment refers to the junction one has for prosocial others. For juveniles, this might involve concern over disappointing one's parents who stress to the juvenile the importance of staying out of trouble. Commitment refers to the investment a juvenile has in conventional activities. An example of this might be a juvenile being concerned that involvement in delinquent activities will hurt his or her chances of getting into college. Involvement is simply the time a youth spends engaged in non-criminal behaviors; these can include time spent in sports or even time spent watching television. Belief is simply the moral value the youth has in obeying the law.

Wu et al. (2015) applied these bonds to police perceptions using the 1999 data from the Evaluation of the Gang Resistance Education and Training Program. Measures of attachment included attachment to both the juvenile's mother and father. Commitment was assessed by measuring their commitment to school, and involvement was assessed by asking respondents the number of hours they spent in school, on religious activities, and on working/employment. Belief was measured by asking respondents how guilty they would feel if they engaged in several criminal behaviors.

The researchers found that race significantly impacted perceptions of the police. Black and Latino juveniles had significantly less favorable perceptions of the police than White juveniles, with Black juveniles having the most negative perceptions of the police. For social bonds, they found that greater attachment to father, involvement and belief significantly increased juveniles' positive perceptions of the police. Involvement in non-deviant activities and attachment to mother did not significantly impact perceptions. Social bonds were unable, however, to explain the difference in Black, White, and Latino juveniles' perceptions of the police. Therefore, some racial and ethnic differences in perceptions likely stem from other causes.

Other Factors Associated with Youths' Attitudes about the Police

Research has further found that juveniles who engage in acts of delinquency have lower perceptions of the police (Leiber et al., 1998). Brick, Taylor, and Esbensen (2009) found that involvement in minor acts of delinquency resulted in more negative perceptions of the police, but involvement in serious acts of delinquency did not. Wu et al. (2015) conversely found that serious offending led to more negative perceptions, but minor offending was not significantly related to perceptions of police. They also found that prior arrests decreased positive perceptions for White and Black youths but not Hispanic youths. The impact of gang membership has been mixed with some studies finding no impact (Flexon, Lurigio & Greenleaf, 2009; Wu et al., 2015) and other studies found that gang members hold more negative views of the police (Friedman, Lurigio, Greenleaf & Albertson, 2004; Jackson & McBride, 1985).

Additional research has suggested that geographical location can influence youths' attitudes toward the police. Taylor, Turner, Esbensen, and Winfree (2001) examined youths' attitudes of the police across 11 cities. They found that youths in larger cities held more negative views of the police, while juveniles in smaller and more rural cities held more positive views of the police. Hurst (2007) also found that rural youths seem to have better perceptions of the police. In addition, although she found that White youths did have better perceptions of police than Black youths, the difference was not statistically significant. More favorable perceptions of the police among rural youth might be due to police in urban areas conducting more field stops of juveniles, as research has found that officer-initiated police contact tends to lower peoples' perceptions of the police (Hurst, 2007; Ren, Cao, Lovrich & Gaffney, 2005). Despite only including large cities, however, Wu et al. (2015) also found differences across the cities examined in their study. Specifically, the youths in Phoenix, Arizona, held more positive perceptions of the police than youths in Lincoln, Nebraska; Omaha, Nebraska; Las Cruces, New Mexico; and Philadelphia, Pennsylvania. While it is possible that views across cities could also be explained by number of contacts that police make with juveniles, other differences in policing strategies should be explored as possible causes in across city variations.

Research has also revealed that fear of crime, gang membership, and past history of victimization might be connected to juveniles' perceptions of police. Wu et al. (2015) found that youths who were more fearful of crime had less positive perceptions of the police. This finding only held for Hispanic and Black juveniles; fear of crime did not appear to impact White juveniles' perceptions of police. In addition, past victimizations have also been shown to decrease juveniles' positive perceptions of the police (Brick et al., 2009; Hurst & Frank, 2000; Payne & Gainey, 2007; Wu et al. 2015). It has been speculated that this is likely due to victims feeling as though the police let them down by not preventing their victimization.

Case Study: The Trayvon Martin Case

On February 26, 2012, Trayvon Martin, a 17-year-old who had just been suspended from school, left his father's fiancée's house to purchase Skittles and iced tea. On his way back to the home, he was spotted by George

Zimmerman, the neighborhood watch captain of the gated community in which Trayvon's father's fiancée lived. The neighborhood watch committee had been constructed in response to burglaries and robberies that had occurred in the area. Zimmerman thought Trayvon looked suspicious so he called the police department to report a suspicious person. The police dispatcher advised Zimmerman not to follow or approach Martin. Although Zimmerman agreed not to approach Martin, after hanging up the phone, he did just that. During the altercation, the two engaged in a physical fight and Zimmerman shot Martin, who was unarmed, in the chest. Zimmerman was later charged with second-degree murder. The trial ended with Zimmerman being acquitted of all charges.

Although this case involved a watch captain and not a police officer, it and other highly publicized cases have worked to further fuel minority youths' distrust of police officers. Since his acquittal, George Zimmerman has remained in the news, being arrested for aggravated assault and domestic violence with a weapon (the weapon was a wine bottle) and for being shot at by another man who accused Zimmerman of pulling a gun on him first.

Sources:

http://www.cbsnews.com/feature/george-zimmerman-trial-trayvon-martin-case/

http://www.wesh.com/news/george-zimmerman-involved-in-shooting-in-lake-mary-police-say/32943828

http://www.cnn.com/2015/01/10/us/george-zimmerman-arrested/

Overall the research indicates that minorities tend to hold more negative attitudes toward police than White juveniles. Hispanic youths also have less favorable attitudes of the police, but they have more positive perceptions of the police than Black juveniles. Analyzing surveys of high school students, researchers have found Black youths tend to hold negative views of the police. However, some inconsistencies in the findings also exist. In addition to there being a theoretical explanation for the racial and ethnic disparities in perceptions, several other factors, such as engagement in delinquency, subcultural beliefs, and weakened social bonds are related to youths' negative perceptions of the police. These might also explain differences if they are unevenly distributed across races and ethnicities.

Programs to Improve Police Perceptions

Most of the effort that has been put into juvenile programs has focused on reducing or preventing juvenile offending. A few programs have been developed, however, that are aimed at improving juveniles' perceptions of the police. These programs try to increase the number of positive interactions between the police and youths in a hope that these interactions will have a positive effect on youths' perceptions of the police, similar to the manner in which negative interactions work to decrease perceptions. This can be difficult, however, as evidence suggests a negativity bias exists in the formation of perceptions of the police. This means that negative experiences tend to more heavily weigh on peoples' perceptions of the police than positive experiences (Skogan, 2006).

Police-Schools Liaison

Police-Schools Liaison (PSL) was developed to improve the image of police to youths and to develop juveniles' understanding of the police and the courts and probation services. The program was also intended to meet a number of other objectives such as prevent crime, develop youths into better citizens, and foster social responsibility. The PSL officers engaged in a number of activities in the school. They conducted patrols, helped with disciplinary issues, aided in investigations of crimes that occurred at school, and supervised special classes and activities. The intent of the program was to allow youths to interact with a police officer in a setting other than the street in hopes that this would result in the youths developing a different view of the police. The youths did not, however, always have direct exposure to the officers. Despite this it was expected that simply knowing the officers were present in the school and hearing about the officers engagement in activities in the school would foster positive perceptions.

Hopkins, Hewston, and Hantzi (1992) evaluated PSL's ability to improve juveniles' attitudes of the police. Comparisons of youths in the schools with PSLs and schools without PSLs indicated that youths in schools with PSLs did not hold significantly different attitudes of the police than those in schools without PSLs. For both groups, these attitudes grew more negative over time as would be expected with youths of this age. It appears, therefore, that the PSL program was not effective in improving youths' perceptions of the police.

DARE

The DARE program was created to prevent adolescents from using drugs and alcohol. DARE was a school-based educational program created by the

Los Angeles Police Department in partnership with the school district. For this program, a uniformed police officer delivered a highly structured curriculum that is uniform across schools. DARE was typically taught to fifth or sixth graders for one hour a week for seventeen weeks. Although DARE was highly popular among the public, evaluations of its effectiveness to reduce adolescent drug and alcohol use were disappointing. Despite these findings, other research has indicated that DARE might be effective in improving youths' perceptions of the police.

Schuck (2013) examined data from 24 schools in Illinois, 12 of which received DARE and 12 of which did not receive DARE. Data was collected on youths' perceptions of the police at seven different times. The study began when the youths were in fifth or sixth grade and ended when they were in eleventh or twelfth grade. Schuck found that youths began the study with positive perceptions of the police but that those perceptions declined over the course of years. By the end of the study this decrease began to either decelerate or stabilize. This trend was to be expected given the age of the youths, as we tend to see young children begin with positive attitudes of the police and then see those attitudes decrease as juveniles become teenagers. Once juveniles approach adulthood, attitudes of the police then improve.

Comparisons of the youths' perceptions who received DARE with those who did not receive DARE indicated that immediately after DARE, participants had slightly more positive perceptions of the police than non-participants. The difference, however, was not statistically significant. As time went on, the difference between the two groups grew larger. Those who received DARE did not experience the same decline in perceptions of the police that the youths who did not receive DARE experienced. When examining Black youths' perceptions separately, they found that Black youths who lived in predominately White neighborhoods experienced large declines in favorable perceptions of the police, unless they received DARE. If they received DARE, their perceptions of the police did not decline.

Police/Juvenile Community Engagement

In Connecticut, seven communities were given funds to develop programs that engaged police and juveniles in community activities. The programs implemented in the seven communities were not uniform but shared several requirements such as involved juvenile and police engagement in non-law enforcement activities, had a team-building component, included leadership opportunities, involved a community service project, served some at-risk juveniles, and did not use existing programs in which police served a teaching role (e.g., DARE).

Pre- and post-tests of 119 juveniles who participated in the programs indicated that the juveniles' attitudes toward the police were significantly more positive after the program. When examining the police officers' perceptions of the youths, however, there was no significant improvement from the program. Both the juveniles and the police, however, reported that they enjoyed the program. While it appears that these programs were successful in improving juveniles' perceptions of the police, the youths served by the program did not match the demographics of those youths who hold the most negative views of the police. For this initiative, most of the youths were White (75%), did not receive reduced or free lunch at school (91%), received mostly As and Bs in school (93%), and already had been involved with a police-youth program (76%). It is unknown, therefore, whether the initiative would have been as successful with juveniles who hold more negative views of the police (Goodrich, Anderson & LaMotte, 2015).

Students Talking it Over with Police

In Milwaukee, Wisconsin, the Milwaukee Police Department has implemented a program aimed at improving juveniles' perceptions of the police. The program, called Students Talking It Over with Police (STOP), is an in-school program that meets one-hour-a-week for seven weeks. The program utilizes a standardized curriculum that is facilitated by two uniformed officers to a group of about 12 juveniles. STOP teaches juveniles why the police stop people on the street, what to do if they are stopped by a police officer, and what they should expect the police officer to do during a police stop. The program also teaches juveniles about why police officers make the decisions that they make and what to do if they ever encounter a "bad" police officer.

STOP has been evaluated in private, charter and public schools across the city using an experimental design. The majority of the juveniles who participated in STOP were Black, followed by multi-racial, Hispanic, and White. Most were also from the inner city. The results of the evaluations found that the youths who completed the STOP program had increased general knowledge of the police, increased knowledge of what to do during a police stop, and increased general perceptions of the police. These youths also indicated that they were more likely to cooperate with the police and reported improved perceptions of procedural fairness (Freiburger, 2014).

Overall it appears that programs aimed at increasing positive police-juvenile contacts can be effective at improving juveniles' perceptions of the police. These programs appear to be effective for juveniles regardless of race and ethnicity. Programs that utilized police in a more traditional law enforcement role, such as the PSL program, do not appear to have the same success. Therefore, close, face-to-face interactions seem to be an integral component of program success.

Youths' Perceptions of the Juvenile System

In addition to youths' views of police, it is important to look at juveniles' views of other areas of the criminal justice system. Although perceptions of the police pertain to all youths, how juveniles perceive the rest of the juvenile justice system is often limited to those juveniles who actually enter the system. Fewer studies have examined youths' perceptions of the courts and no studies were located that examined juveniles' views of the correctional system.

Piquero et al. (2005) examined youths' perceptions of procedural justice and legal cynicism as they moved through the youth court over an 18-month period. Their analysis found a great deal of stability in perceptions of procedural justice and legal cynicism over the 18 months. They also found, however, that differences in perceptions of procedural justice and legal cynicism were related to certain factors. For legal cynicism Hispanic youths and youths with prior convictions reported greater cynicism. Black youths and youths who were sentenced to detention had less positive perceptions of procedural justice. They further found that perceptions of the court actors and the police impacted juveniles overall perceptions of the law and the legal system.

In addition to feelings of fairness in treatment, Greene, Sprott, Madon and Jung (2010) also examined how the courtroom environment affected youths' perceptions of the court. Observations were conducted regarding how well organized the court was, time delays, unprofessional conduct and preparedness of court actors, and the presence of relevant personnel in a Canadian court. Interviews with the youths were conducted after their initial appearances; these interviews indicated that court atmosphere was in fact related to youths' perceptions of the legitimacy of the court, with those having a more positive courtroom atmosphere rating the court as more legitimate than those witnessing a more negative courtroom atmosphere. They also found that those who viewed the court actors as more procedurally fair viewed the court as more legitimate. In a later study, Sprott and Greene (2010) further found that court outcomes affected the youths' broader perceptions of legitimacy. Youths also cared more about the quality of treatment that they received from the court than they did about their case outcome.

Cavanagh and Cauffman's (2015) research examined how Latino youths whose mothers were undocumented viewed the juvenile justice system. Their study included data from interviews with 155 male, Latino, first-time offenders between the ages of 13 and 17 in southern California. The mothers of the boys were also interviewed. They found that boys with undocumented mothers viewed the police less favorably than boys with documented mothers. Youths who were themselves undocumented also had more negative perceptions of the police than the boys who were documented. When examining perceptions of judges, however, boys with documented mothers and boys with undocumented mothers did not differ in their views, nor did documented and undocumented boys. It appears, therefore, that documentation status only affects views of the police and does not affect the views of other parts of the juvenile justice system.

Conclusion

Research has found that a clear racial and ethnic divide exists in youths' perceptions of the police. With few exceptions, most research has found that Black juveniles hold more negative views of the police than White juveniles. Hispanic juveniles tend to hold more negative views than White juveniles but more positive views than Black juveniles. While adherence to a delinquent subculture and weakened social bonds can help explain why some youths have more negative views of the police, these explanations cannot fully explain the racial and ethnic disparities in perceptions.

It is important that police officers be cognizant of the manner in which youths perceive them. It is also imperative that police do not contribute to juveniles' negative perceptions by treating juveniles with disrespect and antagonism. Clearly police must do their jobs, and investigating or even citing and arresting juveniles is sometimes necessary; however, as found by Tyler (1990), the manner in which citizens are treated during a policing encounter can be more impactful than the outcome. Therefore, police officers should make an effort to be fair and respectful to juveniles and explain their reasoning when making decisions. In addition, a few programs have been developed to increase the positive encounters that juveniles have with police officers. These programs only appear to be successful, however, when juveniles have direct contact with the police.

Furthermore, it appears that juveniles may view the juvenile court system more favorably than they view the police. It is impossible, however, to draw any substantial conclusions given the lack of research in this area. Because police are the gatekeepers to the juvenile justice system and are the most visible aspect of the system, it is not surprising that juveniles' perceptions of the police has garnered more research. It is important, however, that further research examine youths' views of the court. If juveniles' views of procedural fairness are impacted by the juvenile court and the treatment programs and detention centers in which they are placed, then these entities can have a profound impact on juveniles' likelihood of subsequent offending.

Discussion Questions

1.   Think about a time when you had contact with the police. Was the encounter positive or negative? If the encounter was positive, what made it positive? If it was negative, what made it negative? How did it shape your overall view of the police?
2.   Many have argued that the news only reports on negative incidences involving the police and ignores stories that portray the police in a positive light. Do you agree with this? If this is true, how do you think perceptions of the police might be different if more positive stories of the police were reported?
3.   Few programs exist that address juveniles' negative perceptions of the police. Why do you think this issue has been overlooked? Should more effort be put into this issue? Why or why not?

References

Bittner, E. (1990). *Aspects of police work*. Northeastern University Press, Boston, MA.

Black, D. & Reiss, A.J., Jr. (1970). Police control of juveniles. *American Sociological Review, 35*, 63–77.

Blumer, H. (1958). Race prejudice as a sense of group position. *The Pacific Sociological Review, 1*(1), 3–7.

Brick, B.T., Taylor, T.J. & Esbensen, F. (2009). Juvenile attitudes towards the police: The importance of subcultural involvement and community ties. *Journal of Criminal Justice, 37*, 499–495.

Brunson, R.K. & Weitzer, R. (2009). Police relations with Black and White youths in different urban neighborhoods. *Urban Affairs Review, 44*(6), 858–885.

Carr, P.J., Napolitano, L. & Keating, J. (2007). We never call the cops and here is why: A qualitative examination of legal cynicism in three Philadelphia neighborhoods. *Criminology, 45*(2), 445–480.

Carter, D. (1985). Hispanic perception of police performance: An empirical assessment. *Journal of Criminal Justice, 13*, 487–500.

Cavanagh, C. & Cauffman, E. (2015). The land of the free: Undocumented families in the juvenile justice system. *Law and Human Behavior, 39*(2), 152–161.

Eschholz, S., Blackwell, B., Gertz, M. & Chiricos, T. (2002). Race and attitudes toward the police: Assessing the effects of watching 'reality' police programs. *Journal of Criminal Justice, 30*, 327–41.

Fagan, J. & Tyler, T.R. (2005). Legal socialization of children and adolescents. *Social Justice Research, 18*(3), 217–242.

Flexon, J.L., Lurigio, A.J. & Greenleaf, R.G. (2009). Exploring the dimensions of trust in the police among Chicago juveniles. *Journal of Criminal Justice, 37*, 180–189.

Freiburger, T.L. (2014). *STOP Evaluation 2013–2014: Final Report* [Executive Summary Report submitted to Community Oriented Policing Services (COPS), United States Department of Justice].

Friedman, W., Lurigio, A., Greenleaf, R. & Albertson, S. (2004). Encounters between police and youth: Social costs of disrespect. *Journal of Crime and Justice, 27*, 1–25.

Goodrich, S.A., Anderson, S.A. & LaMotte, V. (2015). Evaluation of a program designed to promote positive police and youth interactions. *Journal of Juvenile Justice, 3*(2), 55–71.

Greene, C., Sprott J.B. Madon, N.S., Jung, M. (2010). Punishing Proccesses in Youth Court: Procedural Justice, Court Atmosphere and Youths' Views of the Legitimacy of the Justice System. *Canadian Journal of Criminology and Criminal Justice 52*(5), 527–544.

Hagan, J., Shedd, C. & Payne, M.R. (2005). Race, ethnicity, and youth perceptions of criminal injustice. *American Sociological Review, 70*, 381–407.

Hirschi, T. (1969). *Causes of delinquency.* Berkeley, CA: University of California Press.

Hopkins, N., Hewston, M. & Hantzi, A. (1992). Police-Schools Liaison and young people's image of the police: An intervention evaluation. *British Journal of Psychology, 83*, 203–220.

Hurst, Y. (2007). Juvenile attitudes toward the police: An examination of rural youth. *Criminal Justice Review, 32*, 121–141.

Hurst, Y.G. & Frank, J. (2000). How kids view cops: The nature of juvenile attitudes toward the police. *Journal of Criminal Justice, 28*, 189–202.

Hurst, Y.G., Frank, J. & Browning, S.L. (2000). The attitudes of juveniles toward the police: A comparison of black and white youth. *Policing: An International Journal of Police Strategies & Management, 23*(1), 37–53.

Hurst, Y.G., McDermott, M.J. & Thomas, D.L. (2005). The attitudes of girls toward the police: Differences by race. *Policing: An International Journal of Policing Strategies & Management, 28*(4), 578–593.

Jackson, R.K., and McBride, W.D. 1985. *Understanding Street Gangs*. Plackerville, CA: Custom Publishing.

Jones-Brown, D.D. (2000). Debunking the myth of officer friendly: How African American males experience community policing. *Journal of Contemporary Criminal Justice, 16*(2), 209–229.

Lee, J.M., Steinberg, L., Piquero, A.R. & Knight, G.P. (2011). Identity-linked perceptions of the police among African American juvenile offenders: A developmental perspective. *Journal of Youth Adolescence, 40,* 23–37.

Leiber, M., Nalla, M. & Farnworth, M, (1998). Explaining juveniles' attitudes toward the police. *Justice Quarterly, 15*(1), 151–173.

Ludman, R.J., Sykes, R.E. & Clark, J.P. (1978). Police control of juveniles: A replication. *Journal of Research in Crime and Delinquency, 15*(1), 74–91.

Payne, B. & Gainey, R. (2007). Attitudes about police and neighborhood safety in disadvantaged neighborhoods: The influence of criminal victimization and perceptions of drug problems. *Criminal Justice Review, 32,* 142–155.

Piquero, A.R. Fagan, J., Mulvey, E.P., Steinberg, L., & Odgers, C. (2005). Developmental trajectories of legal socialization among serious adolescent offenders. *Journal of Criminal Law & Criminology, 96*(1), 267–298.

Ren, L., Cao, L., Lovrich, N. & Gaffney, M. (2005). Linking confidence in the police with the performance of the police: Community policing can make a difference. *Journal of Criminal Justice, 33,* 55–66.

Schuck, A.M. (2013). A life-course perspective on adolescents' attitudes to police: DARE, delinquency, and residential segregation. *Journal of Research in Crime and Delinquency, 50*(4), 679–607.

Skogan, W. G. (2006). Asymmetry in the impact of encounters with police. *Policing & Society, 16,* 99–126.

Sprott, J.B. & Greene, C. (2010). Trust and confidence in the courts: Does the quality of treatment young offenders receive affect their views of the courts? *Crime & Delinquency, 56,* 269–289. http://dx.doi.org/10.1177/00111287 07308176.

Sunshine, J. & Tyler, T.R. (2003). The role of procedural justice and legitimacy in shaping public support for policing. *Law and Society Review, 37*(3), 555–589.

Snyder, H. & Sickmund, M. (1996). *Juvenile offenders and victims: A national report,* US Department of Justice, Washington, D.C.

Taylor, T., Turner, K., Esbensen, F. & Winfree, L., Jr. (2001). Coppin' an attitude: Attitudinal differences among juveniles toward police. *Journal of Criminal Justice, 29*, 501–521.

Tyler, T. (1990). *Why people obey the law.* New Haven: Yale University Press.

Tyler, T. & Huo, Y. (2002). *Trust in the law.* New York: Russell Sage.

Tyler, T.R. (2004). Enhancing police legitimacy. *The ANNALS of the American Academy of Police and Social Science, 593*, 84–99.

Tyler, T.R. (2006). Legitimacy and legitimation. *Annual Review of Psychology, 57*, 375–400.

Weitzer, R. & Tuch, S.A. (2004). Race and perceptions of police misconduct. *Social Problems, 51*(3), 305–325.

Wu, Y., Lake, R. & Cao, L. (2015). Race, social bonds, and juvenile attitudes toward the police. *Justice Quarterly, 32*(3), 445–470.

Chapter 6

Minorities and the Juvenile Court Process

Goals of the Chapter

The purpose of this chapter is to examine the role of race/ethnicity in juvenile court outcomes, specifically intake, detention, petition, adjudication, and disposition. Each of these decisions is unique, but earlier decisions often influence subsequent ones. In this chapter, we explore the effect of race and ethnicity in each one of these salient decisions. We also provide a thorough discussion of the leading research in this area. Finally, we discuss the theoretical reasons that can help explain the observed relationships.

After reading this chapter, you will be able to do the following:

1. Explain whether race/ethnicity has a direct and/or indirect effect on juvenile court outcomes;
2. Understand the advantages and disadvantages of examining each decision point separately, without regard to all of them as a whole; and
3. Explain how the impact of race on juvenile court outcomes is cumulative as youth continue through the judicial process.

In examining juvenile court outcomes, there are key decision points that are the focus in the empirical research. Each of these decisions is important because it is an opportunity for a court officer (e.g., prosecutors and judges) to make a formal decision as to what happens with a juvenile. The decision points are intake, detention, petition, adjudication, and placement. We will discuss each of these decisions at depth throughout the chapter. As mentioned in other chapters, the federal government has taken an interest in these specific court outcomes, because of the disproportionate percentage of minority youth who were either confined or had contact with the juvenile justice system (DMC). As identified in the introduction to the DMC Technical Assistance Manual:

As states have undertaken efforts to reduce disproportionate minority confinement for youth, they have found evidence that disproportionality occurs at every contact point within the juvenile justice system, from arrest to cases transferred to criminal court and not just at detention and correction. Moreover, what happens to youthful offenders during their initial contacts with the juvenile justice system influences their outcomes at the later stages, leading to a commonly observed amplification phenomenon (i.e., the extent of minority overrepresentation amplifies as minority youth penetrate deeper into the juvenile justice system). Therefore, to both understand the mechanisms that lead to DMC (which hereafter stands for disproportionate minority contact) and design appropriate intervention strategies to address these specific contributing mechanisms, one must first examine all contact points throughout the juvenile justice system from arrest to transfer to adult court and then target intervention at the relevant and selected priority contact points. (Hsia, 2009, Intro 1–2)

Not only is each decision point worthy of separate examination in assessing the influence of race on that particular outcome, but early court decisions have been shown to influence subsequent court decisions. Therefore, in order to have a solid understanding of the race/ethnic effects, all of the key juvenile court outcomes should be included. We organized the chapter by discussing each decision point separately, and then presenting the empirical literature relevant to the specific court outcome.

Intake

When youth are taken into custody, they go through an intake process. During this process, the intake officers (or whoever in that jurisdiction is given this authority) make the decision on whether formal proceedings will take place. During this phase, juveniles can be released, referred to a diversion programming, or referred to the court for formal proceedings. Multiple stakeholders are consulted at this stage, including police, prosecutors, school officials, social service agencies, and victims (Bishop, Leiber, & Johnson, 2010). Factors that are assumed to be considered at this stage are offense severity, prior record, and age. More serious and repeat offenders are presumed to be more likely to continue through formal processing. In addition, older youth are likely to go through formal processing because the juvenile court has limited time for jurisdiction. Many times, intake officers use assessment instruments to identify youths' risk. The assessment instruments list both risk and protective factors for criminal/delinquent behavior, and the intake officers use those forms as a guide to decision-making.

Figures 6.1 and 6.2 demonstrate the relative rate indexes for several different offenses during intake decisions. Figure 6.1 provides a visual for looking at whether disproportionate minority contact is an issue when intake staff make the decision to refer a juvenile to the court. Keeping in mind that a RRI more than 1.0 represents over-representation, Black youth are slightly over-represented, under-represented, and proportionate to White youth, depending on the offense. American Indian/Alaskan Native youth are mostly disproportionately over-represented for burglary offenses, while Asian/Hawaiian/Pacific Islander youth are most over-represented among robbery offenses.

Figure 6.1. Relative Rate Index and Referrals, 2012

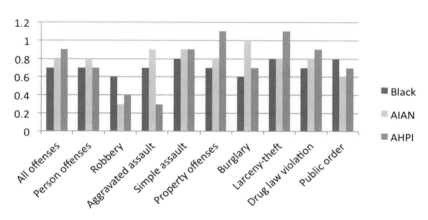

Office of Juvenile Justice and Delinquency Prevention (Puzzanchera & Hockenberry, 2015)

Figure 6.2 provides another aspect of decisions during the intake process. As opposed to just looking at referrals to the juvenile court, we can also examine the decision to refer youth to diversion programs, instead of the juvenile court. RRIs less than 1.0 mean those groups are disproportionately under-represented, meaning they are less likely than Whites to be referred to diversion programs. From the figure, it can be seen that all minority groups are under-represented with diversion referrals for almost all offenses. While the data presented in Figures 6.1 and 6.2 do not automatically translate into discrimination, some of the the disparities and patterns are worthy of additional discussion.

Figure 6.2. Relative Rate Index and Diversions, 2012

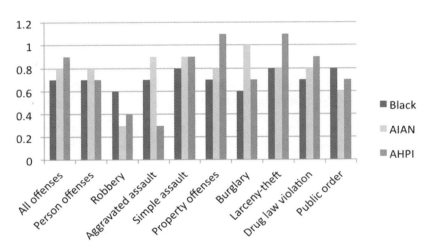

Office of Juvenile Justice and Delinquency Prevention (Puzzanchera & Hockenberry, 2015)

It should be noted that national RRIs are very useful, but must be examined in proper context. The Office of Juvenile Justice and Delinquency Prevention (OJJDP) measures race in four different categories: White, Black, Asian/Hawaiian/Pacific Islander, and American Indian/Alaskan Native. These are very broad categories and do not include a category for the largest non-White minority group: Hispanic/Latino. The FBI measures race in the same categories for its Uniform Crime Reporting program and many criticisms have been expressed in research (Gabbidon & Taylor Greene, 2013) regarding this measure, including a misrepresentation of the racial element of criminal court because Hispanics are likely grouped in with Whites. The National RRIs are just a snapshot of possible over-representation of minorities across the United States. Individual states and counties are not accounted for in that data.

As an example, the national RRIs report slight over-representation for Blacks regarding the referral decision. However, county data in Florida reports something more troubling than the national RRIs suggest. In that state, they include a separate category for Hispanics, clearly because Hispanics make up a fairly significant percentage of the population. In Miami-Dade county, for instance, the referral RRI for Hispanics during 2009-2010 was 2.3, while during this same time the RRI for Blacks was an astounding 6.1 (Florida Department of Juvenile Justice, 2011). The point is that RRI should be interpreted with caution.

Empirical Research on Intake

In early research, Bishop and Frazier (1988) examined delinquency cases in Florida between 1979 and 1981. They focused on slightly more than 54,000 Black and White youth. When examining the intake decision, they found that Black juveniles were more likely to be referred for formal prosecution than White youth. Research in Pennsylvania had similar findings. Leonard and Sontheimer (1995) found that Black and Hispanic youth had a greater likelihood of formal referral than White youth.

Another study by Bishop and Frazier (1996), they focused on approximately 137,000 delinquency cases in Florida from 1985 to 1987. The sample included only White and Black youth. They examined multiple decision points, including formal processing. When looking at the proportion of youth who were processed, Black youth were more likely to be processed than Whites. This relationship held when other legal and extralegal factors were statistically controlled for in the model.

Using juvenile court data from Pennsylvania during 1990, DeJong and Jackson (1998) examined the intake decision for over 4,600 youth. They found that Blacks were more likely to be referred to the juvenile court at the intake stage as compared to Whites. However, there was no significant difference between Hispanics and Whites. An interesting set of results were revealed with additional analyses. Age interacted with race for Whites, but not Blacks; older Whites were more likely to be referred to juvenile court. Also, White youth who resided with both parents had a lower probability of referral than those who lived with their mother only. However, living with both parents had no favorable impact for Black youth. The sample size for Hispanic youth was too small for similar types of follow-up analyses.

In Texas, Tracy (2002, 2005) found that within the three counties included in his study, there was no race or ethnicity effect on the decision to refer cases to the prosecutor in one urban county. When gender was examined separately, though, he found that Hispanic females were less likely to have their cases referred than both Blacks and Whites. He also found that Blacks, Hispanics, and Whites were treated similarly with this decision in another urban county and in the one the rural county included in this study.

In a Northwestern state during 2002 and 2003, Leiber, Johnson, Fox, and Lacks (2007) found that Blacks were more likely than White youth to be released during intake, though Asian youth had a lower probability of release. They also found that Blacks and Native Americans were less likely to receive a diversion. Being an older Native American also lowered the probability of being diverted from the juvenile system. In terms of the actual decision to formally refer youth to the juvenile system during the intake stage, individual races had similar likelihoods. However, upon further analysis, Black youth with more charges had an increased chance of having a petition filed, while older Native Americans had a higher probability.

Research in Iowa showed that Black youth were more likely than Whites to receive either the harshest sanction at intake (i.e., referral to juvenile court) or the most lenient (i.e., release), as compared to being provided a diversion opportunity (Leiber & Johnson, 2008). When looking at race and age, they found that young Whites had the lowest probability of being referred to the juvenile court, while Black youth (regardless of age) had an increased chance of court referral.

Bishop, Leiber, and Johnson (2010) examined approximately 5,700 youth in one county from a Midwestern state. The sample included only Black and White youth from 1980-2000. They found that Black youth were more likely to be referred to the court for formal processing as compared to being diverted from further prosecution. Further, race interacted with multiple other factors: Black females had an increased probability of being referred to the juvenile court, along with Black youth from single-parent households. Finally, White youth charged with a drug offense were less likely to be formally referred to the court.

Detention

Preventive detention in juvenile court is similar to bail in the criminal court system. One key difference between the adult and juvenile systems is that the youth in the juvenile court does not have a U.S. Constitutional right to bail (*Schall v. Martin* 1984). In Schall v. Martin, the Court declared that preventive detention is constitutional. Several states, however, have provided juveniles a right to bail under their respective state constitutions. The detention hearing is the first stage of the process where judges (as opposed to prosecutors and intake workers) are making formal decisions on youth accused of particular offenses. During this stage of the process, juvenile court judges make the decision on whether to release juveniles prior to their adjudication hearing (i.e., trial). In the Supreme Court decision, *Schall v. Martin*, the justices indicated that detention is allowed because it was not punishment and the juvenile court should have wide latitude in protecting juveniles from themselves and the community. This rationale can be grounded in the founding doctrine of *parens patriae* ("state as parent"), which allows the juvenile court discretion to intervene in the lives of juveniles and to engage in certain actions because it is thought to be in the "best interest of the child."

In Figure 6.3, RRIs are presented regarding the preadjudication detention decision. Similar to other decision points, RRIs above 1.0 indicates an over-

Figure 6.3. Relative Rate Index and Preadjudication Detentions, 2012

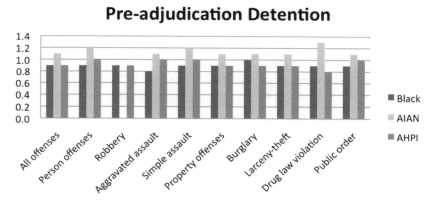

Office of Juvenile Justice and Delinquency Prevention (Puzzanchera & Hockenberry, 2015)

representation of minorities who are held in detention. The figure indicates that American Indians/Alaskan Natives are over-represented the most. Blacks and Asians/Hawaiians/Pacific Islanders are not over-represented as much in the detention decision.

Empirical Research on Detention

An early study by Wordes, Bynum, and Corley (1994), examined juveniles from five counties in one state. They focused on three different detention points: arrest, intake, and preliminary hearing. They found that both Blacks and Hispanics were more likely than Whites to be detained prior to adjudication across all of the detention decisions. Additional support was also found by Feld (1995). Using data from 1996, he examined the detention decision in one Minnesota county. Net the effects of legal factors, Feld found that both Blacks and Native Americans had a higher likelihood of detention than White youth.

Similar findings were found in Pennsylvania. Leonard and Sontheimer (1995) examined the pre-adjudication detention decision across a random stratified sample of 1,797 cases during 1986. They found that both Black and Hispanic youth were more likely to be detained than White youth. In research by Bishop and Frazier (1996), they found that Blacks were more likely to be held in detention than Whites, though their earlier research did not find a race effect (Bishop & Frazier, 1988). Similar results were found by Leiber and Fox (2005). They examined 21 years of juvenile court data from Iowa (1980-2000). The sample consisted of over 5000 juveniles, with about 70% being comprised of White youth and the remaining 30% being Black juveniles. Regarding detention, they found that Black youth were more likely to be detained than White youth. They also found that race interacted with offense type, as Black youth charged with drug offenses had an increased likelihood of being held in predisposition detention.

Other research focused on youth in Nebraska (Secret & Johnson, 1997). In this study, the authors examined approximately 25,000 juveniles from 1988-1993. The sample was comprised of Black and White youth, with Whites making up about 86% of the sample. They found that Blacks were more likely to be detained than Whites. However, another study included two research sites where Hispanics constituted a sizeable majority of the counties' populations (Maupin & Bond-Maupin, 1999). The researcher examined approximately 2,400 Hispanic and White juveniles who went through intake during 1994. In the results, they found that there was not a significant difference in pre-adjudication detention between the two racial/ethnic groups.

Tracy (2002, 2005) examined the detention decision in three Texas counties from 1993 to 1994. Counties 1 and 2 were urban areas, while County 3 was a rural area. From Counties 1 and 2, he included a sample of 2,000 from each. County 3 included 386 youth, but 763 total referrals. Each youth averaged approximately two referrals. In County 1, he found that Whites and Blacks were treated similarly with the detention decision, but Hispanics had a significantly higher probability of being detained. For County 2, Tracy found that race and ethnicity did not significantly impact the detention decision. However, when separated by gender, he found that Black males were more likely to be detained. However, Black and Hispanic females were *less* likely to be detained than White females. In the rural County 3, race and ethnicity were not significant in the detention decision.

Research conducted by Armstrong and Rodriguez (2005) examined over 8,000 youth who were referred to the juvenile court across 65 counties in a Northeastern state in 1990. They included juveniles who were referred for matters of delinquency, not matters of status offenses. Based on the results from their multilevel model, they found that both Blacks and Hispanics were more likely than Whites to be held in preventive detention. More specifically, Hispanics were more than two-and-one-half times as likely as Whites to be detained, while Blacks were almost one-half times more likely than White youth. Racial make-up at the county level was also significant. As the non-White population percentage increased in counties, the more likely youth were to be detained. The authors indicated that "[a] perceived threat of minority juveniles, especially those who lived in counties with populations high in racial and ethnic composition, may place minority juveniles at increased risk of detention regardless of actual crime rates in those jurisdictions" (p. 534).

Rodriguez (2007) followed up with additional research on pre-adjudication detention by examining over 3,000 cases in Maricopa County, Arizona from 2000–2002. She found that Black youth were less likely to be detained than Whites, which is counter to her findings in other research, where she found no significant difference between Hispanics and Whites. (Armstrong & Rodriguez, 2005). However, she did find that in areas of disadvantage (i.e., unemployment and poverty), Hispanic youth had a higher probability of detention as compared to White youth. However, as those particular disadvantage indicators continued to increase, the likelihood of detention became more similar between White and Hispanic youth. Finally, she found that Hispanics who lived in higher-crime areas had a lower chance of detention than Hispanics who lived in lower-crime neighborhoods. In attempting to explain the finding of Blacks having a lower likelihood of detention, Rodriguez (2005) discusses the extreme over-representation of Blacks at the arrest stage of the process. For instance, the National RRI for Blacks at the arrest decision for robbery is 11.0 (Puzzanchera & Hockenberry, 2015), meaning Black youth are 11 times more likely than Whites to be arrested for that offense. Rodriguez explains that the detention decision may also be used as a way to "correct" for the over-representation done at the earlier stage of arrest, resulting in Black youth having a lower likelihood of detention than Whites.

Guevara, Boyd, Taylor, and Brown (2011) examined juvenile detention across two large counties (one urban and one suburban) in a Midwestern state. They examined over 2,400 cases. They found that non-White youth were more likely to be detained than White youth. While it is not ideal to include a generic "non-White" category, it appears that the results were robust enough to detect a significant race effect.

Petition

At this stage of the juvenile court process, the sole decision-maker is the prosecutor's office, unlike the intake stage, which has multiple different entities and people involved (Bishop et al., 2010). During this phase, prosecutors make the decision on whether to formally charge juveniles, along with what the charges will be against the youth. Given that this decision is solely prosecutorial, it is not subject to review and traditional juvenile rights and processes are not applicable at this stage (Leiber & Stairs, 1999; Freiburger & Jordan, 2011). Prosecutors generally consider offense severity, prior record of the juvenile, and strength of the evidence. However, other factors also enter into the decision. Prosecutors must account for protection of the community, meaning they are likely to file charges against youth who pose a perceived danger to the community and society at large.

The RRIs for formal petitions are presented in Figure 6.4. Black youth are over-represented for petitions as compared to Whites for every offense except robbery and aggravated assault. American Indians/Alaskan Natives are over-represented for all offenses except burglary and public orders offenses. There

Figure 6.4. Relative Rate Index and Petitions, 2012

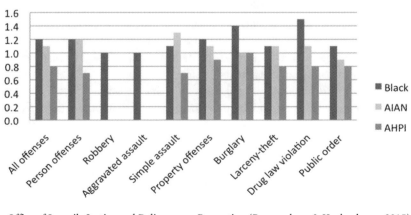

Office of Juvenile Justice and Delinquency Prevention (Puzzanchera & Hockenberry, 2015)

were not enough offenses to calculate a RRI for robbery and aggravated assaults.

Empirical Research on Petition

In an early study, it was found that Black youth were more likely to have their cases formally referred to the juvenile court by prosecutors (Bishop & Frazier, 1988). In addition, race interacted with detention status. White youth who were held in pre-adjudication detention and Whites who had a prior record were at an increased probability of having their cases referred to the juvenile court. Stated differently, in order for Whites to be referred to the juvenile court, they had to either have a prior record or have been detained prior to adjudication. Leonard and Sontheimer (1995) found that while Blacks were more likely to have a petition filed against them as compared to Whites, there was no significant difference between Hispanics and Whites.

Bishop and Frazier (1996) found that Black youth were more likely than White youth to have charges formally filed against them by prosecutors, though Leiber and Fox (2005) found no race effect. Leiber and Fox also examined the decision for youth to get a consent decree (usually a diversion) at this stage, which would then remove them from further juvenile court process. While race had no direct effect on this decision to grant a consent decree, it did become significant when interactions were considered. While individual Black youth were less likely to go through the initial appearance stage (as compared to getting a consent decree/diversion), Black youth with a prior record had an increased chance of going through the initial appearance.

In Texas, Tracy (2002, 2005) found that in County 1 (urban county), Blacks, Hispanics, and Whites were all treated similarly when prosecutors made the decision to formally file charges against youth. However, when each gender was examined separately, both Black and Hispanic males were at an increased likelihood of having charges filed. He also found that Blacks and Hispanics with prior records were actually *less* likely to be charged. In County 2 (also an urban area), he found that race/ethnicity had no effect on prosecutors' decisions to formally file charges against youth.

Other research found that race did not have a significant direct impact on the prosecutor's decision to formally file charges (Bishop et al., 2010). However, race did interact with the number of charges and offense severity. Blacks who were charged with felony offenses had an increased chance of formal prosecution, while Whites who had more charges were more likely to be prosecuted. The authors indicated that, "[t]he significant interaction between race and the number of charges suggests that prosecutors screen cases involving

Whites more carefully for evidentiary merit and apply lesser standards of pre-adjudicatory screening to cases involving non-Whites" (Bishop et al., 2010, p. 225).

Freiburger and Jordan (2011) examined slightly more than 3,000 youth from West Virginia during 2005. Similar to other studies, they included only Black and White youth. They found that there was no significant difference between Black and White youth in the likelihood of formal petitions being filed by prosecutors. They did, though, find that in areas of higher poverty, Black youth were more likely to have petitions formally filed against them.

Adjudication

The adjudication hearing is the equivalent of a trial in the adult criminal justice system. During this phase of the juvenile court process, many of the same protections are in place for juveniles as with adults (e.g., protection against self-incrimination, right to confront witnesses against them, right to counsel, beyond a reasonable doubt standard, etc.). One exception is a jury trial. In *McKeiver v. Pennsylvania* (1971), the U.S. Supreme Court declared that juveniles are not entitled to a jury trial. However, similar to preventive detention/ bail, a number of states do provide juveniles a right to a jury trial under their respective state constitutions. For the many states that do not have jury trials, the judge is the sole decision-maker in terms of adjudication. In other words, judges make the decision on whether or not youth are guilty of the charges. Theoretically, the decision to adjudicate youth as delinquent should be based on strength of the evidence and extra-legal factors such as race should have no impact on this decision.

Figure 6.5 provides the RRI for adjudications within the United States. From the figure, it shows that Black youth and those who are Asian/Hawaiian/Pacific Islander are either under-represented or proportionate for adjudications nationally. However, those who are American Indian/Alaskan Native are over-represented for most offenses. Another way to interpret this figure is that it *appears* that Whites are the group mostly disadvantaged. However, keep in mind that Hispanics are likely included in the White category, somewhat confounding the groupings. Nevertheless, the RRIs do provide a snapshot of what is going on nationally, recognizing the limitations of the race measures.

Figure 6.5. Relative Rate Index and Adjudication, 2012

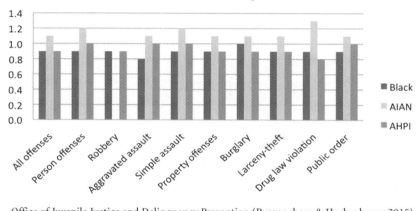

Office of Juvenile Justice and Delinquency Prevention (Puzzanchera & Hockenberry, 2015)

Empirical Research on Adjudication

In a study by Bishop and Frazier (1988), they found that Black youth were more likely to be adjudicated delinquent. White youth, however, were more likely to be adjudicated delinquent when combined with more serious offenses. This is concerning, as it implies that it requires a serious offense for juvenile court judges to impose guilty verdicts on White youth, while that same standard did not apply for Black youth. Other research, however, found that Blacks were less likely to be adjudicated delinquent (Secret & Johnson, 1997). Given that Blacks were more likely to be detained and those detained were more likely to be adjudicated delinquent, there may have been an indirect race effect on adjudication. Leonard and Sontheimer (1995) did not find a race/ethnicity effect, as it *appeared* that Blacks, Hispanics, and Whites were similar in the probability of adjudication. However, they also found that Blacks and Hispanics had a greater likelihood of pre-adjudication detention. Detention, then, increased the probability of adjudication. Therefore, the race and ethnicity effect may have been masked through the detention decision.

Leiber and Fox (2005) found that Black youth without counsel had a greater likelihood of being adjudicated delinquent, though Leiber et al. (2007) found no such race effect. Bishop et al. (2010) also found that race had no significant impact on the judicial decision to adjudicate youth as delinquent (i.e., conviction). However, in examining interactions, Black youth with more prior referrals were more likely to be adjudicated delinquent. "For minority youth, it appears that prior record becomes a self-fulfilling prophecy, reinforcing the stereotype of African Americans as likely to re-offend and increasing the probability of another conviction" (p. 225).

Disposition

At this disposition (sentencing) phase, judges make the decision of what to do with youth once they are adjudicated as a delinquent (Bishop et al., 2010). With the juvenile system, judges have fairly wide discretion on how to dispose of cases because of the *parens patriae* doctrine of the juvenile court. However, judges must also balance that against the protection of the community. In the adult system, the non-community options are generally jail and prison. However, with the juvenile system, there are a host of non-community options, such as training school, group home, residential facility, boot camp, etc. These options are available, in addition to community options (e.g., probation, restitution, fine, etc.).

There are usually no sentencing guidelines as one would find in the criminal justice system at the disposition hearing. Due to the juvenile court having a less punitive focus than the adult system, other entities enter into the disposition process. Probation officers, for instance, develop a predisposition report (similar to a presentence investigation report for adults), which includes reports from school officials, counselors, therapists, parents, etc. Juvenile probation officers often have conflicting roles, because they must juggle between treatment focus and offender accountability. Prosecutors and defense attorneys also provide disposition recommendations to judges at this phase. Given that these groups may have conflicting goals and beliefs, coupled with the lack of written disposition guidelines, it makes the final disposition of judges even more challenging.

Figure 6.6 highlights the RRIs for dispositions. More specifically, the disposition represents actual placements for youth who were adjudicated delinquent. Based on the figure, Black youth are over-represented among placements for most offenses. American Indians/Alaskan Natives are also over-represented for a number of offenses. Finally, the RRIs for Asian, Hawaiian, and Pacific Islander youth suggests they are under-represented across most offense categories.

Figure 6.6. Relative Rate Index and Disposition, 2012

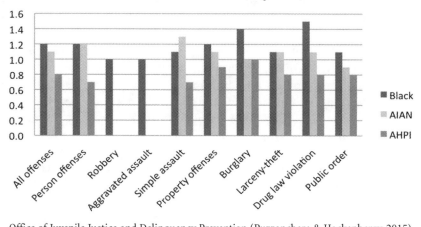

Office of Juvenile Justice and Delinquency Prevention (Puzzanchera & Hockenberry, 2015)

Empirical Research on Disposition

Multiple studies found that Black youth were more likely to be either incarcerated or transferred to the adult criminal justice system (Bishop & Frazier, 1988, 1996; Leiber & Fox, 2005). The issue, though, with these studies is the disposition measure. The authors combined being transferred to the adult system with being placed out of the home. Juveniles placed out of the home are comprised of youth with a guilt finding, while transferred youth are not yet convicted, since they are still being sent to the adult system for processing.

In Minnesota, Feld (1995) separated the disposition decision into two categories: out-of-home placement and secure confinement to an institution. The former could include such outcomes as placement in foster care and group homes, while the latter is formal commitment to a correctional institution. Feld found that Blacks and Native Americans were more likely to be sent to out-of-home placement, but there was no race effect regarding secure confinement decisions. Given that the bulk of research examining disposition focuses on out-of-home placement, Feld's study demonstrates the importance of developing a separate measure for secure confinement.

In Pennsylvania, researchers found that there was no race/ethnicity (Black, Hispanic, and White) effect on out-of-home placements (Leonard & Sontheimer, 1995). As mentioned earlier with this study and the adjudication decision, it cannot be automatically assumed there is no race/ethnicity effect. In this study, they found that Blacks and Hispanics had a higher probability of pre-adjudication detention. This study, then, found that being in detention increased the likelihood of out-of-home placement. Therefore, the effect of race/ethnicity may have been indirect through the detention decision.

In Nebraska, researchers found no race effect between Black and White youth on the decision to place youth outside of the home (Secret & Johnson, 1997). DeJong and Jackson (1998) also did not find a race effect in Pennsylvania, including between Hispanics and Whites. Further, they found that being convicted of a drug offense increased Blacks' probability of secured placement, while it had no effect with White youth. Also, living with both parents was a protective factor for White youth, reducing their probability of secured placement. However, parental circumstances played no role with Black youth. In other words, while certain factors insulated Whites from harsher outcomes, Blacks enjoyed no similar protections. Tracy (2002, 2005) found that there was no significant difference in placements between Blacks, Whites, and Hispanics in one urban county in Texas.

In an interesting study, MacDonald (2003) examined the role of ethnicity in the severity of outcomes in the state of Hawaii. According to MacDonald, there is no dominant race/ethnicity in the state, though native Hawaiians are a disadvantaged group. For this reason, examining the effect of being a native Hawaiian on severity of sanctions is particularly salient. In measuring severity, he developed an ordinal scale: dismissal, counsel and release, probation, and secure confinement. He found that native Hawaiians and Samoans suffered more severe sanctions than Whites. While interesting, this study suffers from attrition issues, as youth in the dismissal stage were not all captured at the confinement stage.

Two counties in a Midwestern state was the research site for Guevara, Spohn, and Herz (2004). They examined over 8,500 youth in this study. The purpose of this research was to examine severity of disposition once adjudicated as a delinquent. White youth received less severe sanctions than non-White youth, even after controlling for legally relevant factors.

In Missouri, researchers also focused on out-of-home placements (Bray, Sample & Leonard, 2005). They examined all delinquency cases in the state between 1992 and 1997. They only included Black and White offenders in their study. While the authors controlled for prior record, they did not control for offense (or offense seriousness or offense type). The authors found that not only were Blacks more likely than Whites to be placed out of the home, but the effect of race did not vary across the different court circuits in the state. Therefore, one could expect to find similar race effects, regardless of the specific circuit youth were processed.

In another study, a surprise finding was that White youth, not Black, were more likely to be placed either in a residential facility or transferred to the adult system (Bishop et al., 2010). One interaction effect found was that White youth charged with property offenses were less likely to be placed outside of the home or waived to the adult system.

In more recent research, researchers have examined the role of racial threat (percentage of Blacks in the population) on the ratio of Black-to-White out-of-home placements across 38 states in 1999 (Davis & Sorenson, 2013). The findings suggest that as the Black population increased, the ratio of Black-to-White placements also increased, but just missed statistical significance. On a broader issue, the placement rate for Black youth far outweighed that of White youth. According to Davis and Sorenson (2013), "Among the 38 states included in the current study, results showed that Black juveniles were placed in residential facilities almost 90% more often than White juveniles after controlling for arrest. This finding indicates that there remains, at least the possibility of, differential treatment within the juvenile justice system based on race" (p. 307). It then seems that the placement disparities in some states are so great, differential involvement in delinquency, alone, is not enough to explain away those differences. However, additional research by the same authors (Davis & Sorenson, 2012) found that since 1994, the Black-to-White ratio for out-of-home placement has been reduced by approximately 20%. This finding suggests some progress in DMC efforts to address this salient concern.

Related to out-of-home placements, the literature is somewhat underdeveloped on specific sentencing outcomes. The bulk of the literature measures the disposition decision as 1) out-of-home placements or not or 2) out-of-home placements/transfer to adult court or not. There are few notable exceptions (Feld, 1995; Davis & Sorenson, 2013). The juvenile justice system is unique in that it provides judges with a number of options that are typically not available for judges in the more punitive criminal justice system. Juvenile court judges can send youth to group homes, foster homes, training schools, to live with other relatives, correctional facilities, etc. The issue is that a generic "out-of-home placement" treats all of these options the same because each one of them does result in juveniles being sentenced away from his/her traditional home. Clearly some of these options are distinct from one another and treating them similarly can distort what is truly occurring to these youth during the disposition stage. We attempt to bring some clarity to this issue in Figures 6.7 and 6.8.

As can be seen in Figure 6.7, the rate of commitment to residential facilities for each race and ethnicity has been steadily decreasing over the past decade. However, Black youth continue to have the highest rates of commitment post-disposition, followed by American Indians, and then Hispanics. However, while the rate of commitment has been declining, the make-up of those who are committed has not changed. Figure 6.8 shows that while the percentage of White youth slightly decreased over time, the percentages for Blacks and Hispanics showed slight increases.

In 2011 (the last data point in Figures 6.7 and 6.8), the juvenile population in the United States was comprised of 55% Whites, 15.2% Blacks, 23.5% Hispanics, 5.2% Asians, and 1% American Indians. Based on Figure 6.8, it seems that of those sent to residential facilities after disposition, White and Asian youth are under-represented based on their make-up in the U.S. general population. Hispanic and American Indian youth appear to be fairly proportionate. However, Black youth are drastically over-represented among those who are in in residential facilities. Again, while making up 15% of the national juvenile population, they comprised approximately 40% of the youth in residential facilities.

Figure 6.7. National rates per 100,000 for delinquency commitments to residential facilities

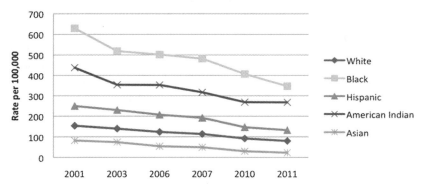

OJJDP's Census of Juveniles in Residential Placement (Sickmund, Sladky, Kang, & Puzzanchera).

Figure 6.8. Racial makeup of youth committed to residential facilities

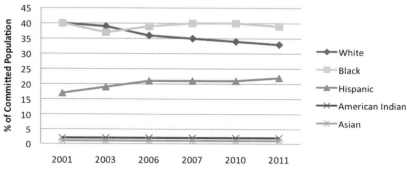

OJJDP's Census of Juveniles in Residential Placement

Case Study: "Kids for Cash"

In 2008, a scandal from the bench started unraveling in Luzerne County, Pennsylvania. The county's President Judge (Mark Ciavarella) and Senior Judge (Michael Conahan) pled guilty to federal fraud and tax charges. Both judges received kickbacks (payments) for sending juveniles to private detention facilities in the state. The judges were paid by the builders and owners of the correctional facilities for keeping them filled at capacity. Over a 5-year period, approximately 5,000 youth appeared before the judges. In total, the judges received more $2.6 million in payments. While it is not possible to know exactly how many of the 5,000 youth were sent to a detention center as part of this scheme, there are multiple examples that appear somewhat suspect. One child was sent away to a wilderness camp for mocking an assistant principal on social media. Another child was sentenced to detention and a boot camp for five months for stealing a CD from Wal-Mart. When interviewed, former Judge Ciavarella said, "Look, this was a finder's fee. I was always yelling at kids because that's what they needed because parents didn't know how to be parents and so forth. So what's the big deal now? I mean, everybody was celebrating me all these years and now they're not happy with me anymore just because I took this money?"

The RRI for Pennsylvania is presented on the next page:

	Arrest	Referral	Petition	Detention	Adjudication	Residential Placement
Black	3.27	1.14	1.17	2.46	1.22	1.37
Hispanic	1.37	1.39	1.07	1.50	0.99	N/A

1) Based on the RRI, were discriminatory practices occurring with the "kids for cash" scheme?
2) Even though the RRI for Black residential placement was 1.37, can the race effect within this corruptive operation actually be larger than the RRI suggests? How so?

Sources:
http://www.cnn.com/2009/CRIME/02/23/pennsylvania.corrupt.judges/index.html?eref=rss_us
http://www.npr.org/2014/03/08/287286626/kids-for-cash-captures-a-juvenile-justice-scandal-from-two-sides

Conclusion

The literature generally points to a relationship between race and court outcomes, mostly with Black youth receiving harsher outcomes, followed by Hispanics, and then Whites. There is also evidence that Native Americans are treated more harshly than Whites. While race and ethnicity appear to influence decision-making at every stage of the process, the effect appears more pronounced early in the process. "Minority youths are less often diverted, more often referred for formal processing, and more often held in secure detention than white youths who are legally similar" (Bishop, 2005, p. 62). Early decisions, most notably the pre-adjudication detention decision, have a significant impact on subsequent decisions (i.e., adjudication and disposition). Given that racial/ethnic minorities are treated less favorably early in the process and those early decisions then affect later outcomes, Blacks and Hispanics are more likely to have adjudications and be placed outside of the home. Although the results do not consistently point to similar findings, the body of literature suggests that there is enough research to warrant additional study.

Unfortunately, the racial/ethnicity effects serve as a problem. The federal government has charged states to address disproportionate minority contact in their respective jurisdictions and it still appears to be a concern. OJJDP developed a research summary of DMC issues (Pope & Feyerherm, 1995). In it, a few of the following recommendations are made regarding research:

1) Disaggregate data as much as possible, instead of on national, state, and county levels. Aggregate data will allow for subtle differences to be missed regarding the true effect of race/ethnicity on court outcomes.

2) Include multiple decision points in studies. Prior research has shown that Black youth are more likely to be detained. However, the research is fairly mixed regarding the race/ethnicity effect on subsequent decisions, such as adjudication and disposition. Studies, though, have shown that detention influences later outcomes. Therefore, the race effect may be masked through the detention decision.

3) Focus on racial groups other than only White and Black. At the very least, Hispanics should be incorporated in more research. While it has started to gain some attention, more is needed.

These recommendations were made approximately two decades ago, and some of the suggestions have not appeared more widely in the literature. In order to have a better understanding of race/ethnicity on court outcomes, they must be incorporated. In addition, subsequent research should focus more on dissecting the specific disposition outcome, instead of the generic "out-of-home" placement decision. It does not capture the true nuance of sanctions available and used by juvenile court judges when disposing of cases.

Discussion Questions

1. What is the relative rate index (RRI)? How important is it in explaining DMC within the juvenile justice system?

2. Are RRI scores more advantageous for policymakers at the national or state level?

3. Should empirical research focus on examining race/ethnicity at individual decision points or its cumulative effect throughout the court process?

4. At which juvenile court decision point does race/ethnicity play the strongest role?

References

Armstrong, G.S. & Rodriguez, N. (2005). Effects of individual and contextual characteristics on preadjudication detention of juvenile delinquents. *Justice Quarterly, 22*(4), 521–539.

Bishop, D.M. (2005). The role of race and ethnicity in juvenile justice processing. In D.F. Hawkins & K. Kempf-Leonard (Eds.), *Our children, their chlidren: Confronting racial and ethnic differences in American juvenile justice* (pp. 23–82). Chicago: The University of Chicago Press.

Bishop, D.M. & Frazier, C.E. (1988). The influence of race in juvenile justice processing. *Journal of Research in Crime and Delinquency, 25*(3), 242–263.

Bishop, D.M. & Frazier, C.E. (1996). Race effects in juvenile justice decision-making: Findings of a statewide analysis. *Criminology, 86*(2), 392–414.

Bishop, D.M., Leiber, M. & Johnson, J. (2010). Contexts of decision making in the juvenile justice system: An organizational approach to understanding minority overrepresentation. *Youth Violence and Juvenile Justice, 8*(3), 213–233.

Bray, T.M., Sample, L.L. & Kempf-Leonard, K. (2005). "Justice by geography": Racial disparity and juvenile courts. In D.F. Hawkins & K. Kempf-Leonard (Eds.), *Our children, their children: Confronting racial and ethnic diffrences in American juvenile justice* (pp. 270–299). Chicago: The University of Chicago Press.

Davis, J. & Sorensen, J.R. (2012). Disproportionate minority confinement of juveniles: A national examination of Black-White dispartity in placements, 1997–2006. *Crime & Delinquency, 59*(1), 115–139.

Davis, J. & Sorenson, J.R. (2013). Disproportionate juvenile minority confinement: A state-level assessment of racial threat. *Youth Violence and Juvenile Justice, 11*(4), 296–312.

DeJong, C. & Jackson, K.C. (1998). Putting race into context: Race, juvenile justice processing, and urbanization. *Justice Quarterly, 15*(3), 487–504.

Feld, B.C. (1995). The social context of juvenile justice administration: Racial disparities in an urban juvenile court. In K.K. Leonard, C.E. Pope & W.H. Feyerherm (Eds.), *Minorites in juvenile justice* (pp. 66–97). Thousand Oaks, CA: SAGE.

Florida Department of Juvenile Justice. (2011). Disproportionate Minority Contact Benchmark Reports. Retrieved from http://www.djj.state.fl.us/docs/research2/report2011_final.pdf?sFvrsn=0.

Freiburger, T.L. & Jordan, K.L. (2011). A multilevel analysis of race on the decision to petition a case in the juvenile court. *Race and Justice: An International Journal, 1*(2), 185–201.

Gabbidon, S.L. & Taylor Greene, H. (2013). *Race and crime* (3rd ed.). Thousand Oaks, CA: SAGE.

Guevara, L., Boyd, L.M., Taylor, A. P. & Brown, R.A. (2011). Racial disparities in juvenile court outcomes: A test of the liberation hypothesis. *Journal of Ethnicity in Criminal Justice, 9*(3), 200–217.

Guevara, L., Spohn, C. & Herz, D. (2004). Race, legal representation, and juvenile justice: Issues and concerns. *Crime & Delinquency, 50*(3), 344–371.

Hsia, H. (2009). DMC Technical Assistance Manual, Introduction (4th ed.). Washington, D.C.: U.S. Department of Justice.

Leiber, M.J. & Fox, K.C. (2005). Race and the impact of detention on juvenile justice decision making. *Crime & Delinquency, 51*(4), 470–497.

Leiber, M.J. & Johnson, J.J. (2008). Being young and Black: What are their effects on juvenile justice decision making? *Crime & Delinquency, 54*(4), 560–581.

Leiber, M.J., Johnson, J., Fox, K. & Lacks, R. (2007). Differentiating among racial/ethnic groups and its implications for understanding juvenile justice decision making. *Journal of Criminal Justice, 35*, 471–484.

Leiber, M.J. & Stairs, J.M. (1999). Race, contexts and the use of intake diversion. *Journal of Research in Crime and Delinquency, 36*(1), 56–86.

Leonard, K.K. & Sontheimer, H. (1995). The role of race in juvenile jusitce in Pennsylvania. In K.K. Leonard, C.E. Pope & W.H. Feyerherm (Eds.), *Minorities in juvenile justice* (pp. 98–127). Thousand Oaks, CA: SAGE.

MacDonald, J.M. (2003). The effect of ethnicity on juvenile decision making in Hawaii. *Youth & Society, 35*(2), 243–263.

Maupin, J.R. & Bond-Maupin, L.J. (1999). Detention decision-making in a predominantly Hispanic region: Rural and non-rural differences. *Juvenile & Family Court Journal, 50*(3), 11–23.

McKeiver v. Pennsylvania, 403 U.S 528 (1971).

Pope, C.E., & Peyerherm, W. (1995). Minorities in the Juvenile Justice System: Research Summary. Washington, DC: U.S. Department of Justice.

Puzzanchera, C. and Hockenberry, S. (2015). *National Disproportionate Minority Contact Databook.* Developed by the National Center for Juvenile Justice for the Office of Juvenile Justice and Delinquency Prevention. Online. Available: http://www.ojjdp.gov/ojstatbb/dmcdb/.

Rodriguez, N. (2007). Juvenile court context and detention decisions: Reconsidering the role of race, ethnicity, and community characteristics in juvenile court processes. *Justice Quarterly, 24*(4), 629–656.

Schall v. Martin, 467 U.S. 253 (1984).

Secret, P.E. & Johnson, J.B. (1997). The effect of race on juvenile justice decision making in Nebraska: Detention, adjudication, and disposition: 1988–1993. *Justice Quarterly, 14*(3), 445–478.

Sickmund, M., Sladky, T.J., Kang, W., and Puzzanchera, C. (2011) "Easy Access to the Census of Juveniles in Residen[al Placement." Available at http:// www.ojjdp.gov/ojstatbb/ezacjrp/.

Tracy, P.E. (2002). *Decision making and juvenile justice: An analysis of bias in case processing.* Westport, CT: Praeger.

Tracy, P.E. (2005). Race, ethnicity, and juvenile justice: Is there bias in postarrest decision making. In D. F. Hawkins & K. Kempf-Leonard (Eds.), *Our children, their children: Confronting racial and ethnic differences in American juvenile justice* (pp. 300–347). Chicago: The University of Chicago Press.

Wordes, M., Bynum, T.S. & Corley, C.J. (1994). Locking up youth: The impact of race on detention decisions. *Journal of Research in Crime and Delinquency, 31*(2), 149–165.

Chapter 7

Communities and the Punishment of Minority Juvenile Offenders

Goals of the Chapter

The purpose of this chapter is to examine how community factors differently affect the processing of juvenile offenders depending on a juvenile's race and ethnicity. In this chapter, we explore the theoretical explanations for why structural factors influence juvenile court processing decisions. The research examining these factors and their differing impacts on Black, White, and Hispanic juveniles is also reviewed. The chapter concludes with a discussion on the current state of research in this area.

After reading this chapter, you will be able to do the following:

1. Understand the theoretical reasoning suggesting that community effects vary by race and ethnicity;
2. Demonstrate an understanding of the empirical literature on the effect that race, ethnicity, and community factors have on the processing of juvenile offenders; and
3. Discuss the community characteristics that influence decision-making in the processing of juveniles of different races and ethnicities.

Much attention has been devoted to the effect that offender characteristics such as race, ethnicity, age, and gender have on juvenile court processing decisions. Also largely considered are the effects of offense characteristics such as severity of the offense, type of offense (e.g., property, drug, or personal), and number of charges. Until recently, less attention has been devoted to the possibility that the sanctions that juveniles receive might vary by community factors. Less research has also considered whether living in or being sentenced in areas of disadvantage results in the harsher treatment of juveniles, and whether juveniles of different races and ethnicities are treated differently in areas of disadvantage.

Prior to research considering differences in juvenile court processing across communities, it was recognized that findings on juvenile court decision-making varied across studies. Different results were yielded depending on the jurisdiction of the court and the time of the study. Although differences across courts are also found in the adult system, it is not surprising that it is even more prevalent in the juvenile court, as judges in the juvenile court have greater discretion than judges in the adult court. Unlike adult courts that are more focused on the punishment of the offense, juvenile courts are more concerned with the individual juvenile and the treatment needs of the juvenile. Focus, therefore, is not placed on applying the same sanction to every offense regardless of the offender and the offender's needs. Instead, sanctions are expected to vary by the offender. To accommodate this, practitioners have great latitude in the juvenile court when determining the most appropriate sanctions.

The possible effect of community factors on the processing of juvenile offenders is especially important as these differences often interact with racial and ethnic differences. Examining the division of social class by race and ethnicity shows that poverty is not equally distributed across racial and ethnic groups. According to the Forum on Child and Family Statistics, in 2012, 21.8% of children were living in poverty. As shown in Figure 7.1, for minority youth, rates were even higher with 38.4% of Black youth and 33.8% of Hispanic youth living in poverty. The rate of non-Hispanic White youths living in poverty was only 12.3%. The region with the highest percentage of children living in poverty was the South (24.2%), followed by the West (21.2%), the Midwest (19.9%), and Northeast (19.6%). Over 42% of the kids living in poverty were living in a female-headed household with no husband present. Due to the uneven distribution of minorities in disadvantaged communities, the harsher punishment of juvenile from disadvantaged communities will be expected to disproportionately affect Black and Hispanic youth.

Figure 7.1. Percentage of Youths Living in Poverty by Race

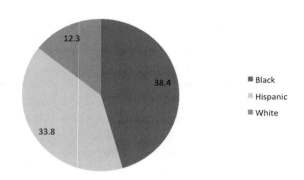

Case Study: Rich Kids versus Poor Kids

Karl Alexander, a sociologist at Johns Hopkins University, and his fellow researchers tracked 790 children who were born in Baltimore for 25 years. The study began in 1982 when the kids were three or four years of age and ended when they were 28 or 29. At the conclusion of the study, the researchers found that about one-half of the kids stayed in the same social economic status into which they were born. Only 33 children, out of the original 790, moved from the low-income bracket to the high-income bracket. The study also found that White men, who were born into families that were better-off social economically, had the highest rates of binge drinking, drug use, and chronic smoking. Despite this, however, they still experienced the most upward mobility. Among those with a criminal conviction from low income backgrounds, White men also fared better than Black men. Although rates of criminal convictions were similar (41% of White men versus 49% of Black men), White men with a criminal conviction were much more likely to be employed then the Black men with a criminal conviction (Alexander, Entwisle & Olson, 2014).

Other studies have also found unexpected differences in the drug use patterns of rich and poor kids. Data from California's Healthy Kids Survey found that kids in rich communities were more likely to use drugs and alcohol than kids in poorer communities. Given that youths from disadvantaged communities are more likely to be processed in the system for drug offenses, this raises questions regarding the fairness of the criminal justice system (Partnership for Drug-Free Kids, 2007 February 20).

The literature examining community structural factors and punishment decisions examines two levels of variables. The first level is referred to as individual-level variables. These variables consist of characteristics of individual juveniles, their offenses, and circumstances of each juvenile's case. Examples of individual-level variables are a juvenile's race, gender and age; the type (e.g., property, drug, or personal) and severity (e.g., status offense, misdemeanor or felony) of offense the juvenile allegedly committed; whether and what type of legal representation the juvenile had and whether the juvenile was detained prior to adjudication. The second level of variables is referred to as community-level variables. These variables represent aggregate information about the characteristics of geographical areas; data for these variables are often collected from the United States Census Bureau. Some examples of community-level variables are percentage of minorities residing in an area, percentage of female-headed households, and percentage of the population living in poverty. Most of the recent research examines both individual-level and community-level factors on juvenile processing.

While it is easy to understand why individual-level factors (e.g., race, gender, offense severity and prior record) are expected to influence juvenile court decision-making, it might be less clear how community-level factors can influence these decisions. This next section reviews the theoretical explanations for why and how characteristics of a community can influence decisions-makers' determinations of the most appropriate sanctions for juveniles.

Theoretical Perspectives

Unlike the consensus view that argues the law represents the collective interest of a society, conflict theory argues that the law is a tool used by the powerful to maintain their power. The law represents and protects the interest of the powerful, not the common interest of a society. Because the powerless members of a society could revolt, they pose a threat to the elites' power. In an effort to control them, they are subjected to harsh punishments and increased levels of social control. Conflict theory predicts, therefore, that punishment decisions will be more influenced by extralegal factors (e.g., race and social class) than by legal factors (e.g., severity of the offense, type of offense, prior record). Minorities, the poor, and the unemployed are viewed as threatening (Liska & Chamlin, 1984), and thus are subjected to disproportionately harsher punishments and higher rates of imprisonment.

Racial threat theory uses similar logic to explain disparities in the treatment of juveniles. According to Blalock's (1967) racial threat theory, as the number of minority citizens residing in an area increases, Whites' perceptions of the threat to their political, economic and social dominance increases. The threat is even more pronounced in areas where White and Black residents occupy the same jobs, as the competition for labor further threatens Whites' dominance in the economy. In order to preserve White ascendancy, minorities in these areas are subjected to increased levels of formal social control. This increased and punitive use of formal social control then decreases the possibility of social and political unrest in these areas. This occurs until the Black population becomes so large that it dominates the area. Once this occurs, the Black population accumulates political power and the amount of formal social control inflicted upon them is reduced. This theoretical perspective suggests, therefore, that in areas with almost equal percentages of Black and White residents, Black juveniles would be expected to be treated more harshly in the juvenile justice system.

It is difficult to imagine how poor and minority juveniles could pose a threat to the elite's position of power. Tittle and Curran (1988) provide an explanation as to how this can occur. They argue that decision makers do not actually view minority and poor juveniles as a direct threat to the power of the elite. Instead, there is a symbolic aspect to social threat, in which decision-makers feel uneasy about the behaviors and characteristics of these juveniles. Stereotypical images of poor and minority youths as dangerous, aggressive and undisciplined provoke fear and even jealousy into decision-makers who are unable to exhibit such behaviors as adults. Harsher punishments of juveniles, therefore, are actually a response to symbolic threat instead of a response to a real threat.

Sampson and Laub (1993) developed a macrostructural perspective to explain how the location of the court can affect decision-making in that court. To develop this perspective, they built on conflict theory and the symbolic threat thesis, expanding conflict theory to suggests that the elite are not the only group who feels threatened by minorities, the poor, and the unemployed. Instead, these groups appear threatening to the majority of Americans. Sampson and Laub also emphasized the use of stereotypes within the context of the war on drugs and the harsh treatment of drug offenses, arguing that the war on drugs has led to the portrayal of Black youths as drug-involved delinquents. Because of this portrayal, minority juveniles residing in geographical areas with high levels of racial inequality and a high percentage of the underclass population are often viewed as drug-involved and delinquent, resulting in the harsher treatment of these juveniles.

Case Study: Violent Suburban Youths

Prior to April, 20th 1999, juvenile violence was almost exclusively associated with minority urban youths. On that day, however, the face of the violent and dangerous juvenile changed when Dylan Klebold and Eric Harris entered the grounds of Columbine High School in Columbine, Colorado and began shooting their classmates. Dylan and Eric had planned the massacre for months. They had practiced making pipe bombs, schemed to purchase guns and bullets, and had practiced shooting for the big day. They also video recorded themselves discussing their plans in Dylan's basement (these infamous tapes later became known as the "basement tapes"). Their plan was to set off a pipe bomb across town to distract law enforcement so they would be occupied when Dylan and Eric shot their classmates. They also left homemade bombs in the cafeteria that were supposed to explode and kill the students who were running away trying to escape the shooting.

Luckily several of the events did not go as Dylan and Eric planned. The boys were late to school that day so many of the students had already left the campus for lunch. Also, their bombs in the high school cafeteria failed to detonate. Despite these failures, the boys killed 13 individuals in the school and injured many more with their gunfire.

Not only did this case have a devastating impact on the students at Columbine High School and on the surrounding community, but due to widespread national news coverage the case impacted the entire nation (Muschert, 2007). Many remember watching on television as the horrific events unfolded. They watched as law enforcement surrounded the school; kids held each other and cried; parents frantically searched for their children; and Patrick Ireland was pulled from a window of the library after being shot in the head. Suburban schools that were considered safe became feared. Kids who were previously considered to be harmlessly deviant by adhering to a gothic subculture were also suddenly feared, despite the fact that initial reports of Dylan and Eric as gothic outcasts were later debunked. The face of the dangerous offender changed from a minority boy from the inner-city to an awkward White boy from a middle-class suburb.

Attribution theory is also focused on how juveniles are viewed by court actors, but moves away from control theory arguments. Attribution theory focuses on internal and external attributes to explain why juveniles engage in delinquent behaviors and to determine which intervention is an appropriate response to these behaviors. Internal attributes are things like moral character and attitude. External attributes are things like a juvenile's family structure, peer associations, and neighborhood context. External attributes can lead to more lenient treatment for juveniles by shifting the blame away from the juvenile. They can also, however, lead to more severe punishments in some cases by indicating a greater likelihood of recidivating and lower likelihood of success in the community. In areas that are characterized as having high levels of poverty, unemployment and single-parent households, court officials may be concerned that prosocial models of behavior are not present and that the rewards for engaging in criminal activities are high. They may also be concerned that juveniles are not as well supervised in these areas (Anderson, 2002).

According to Shaw and McKay's (1969) theory of social disorganization, not all communities are able to effectively control the activities of their juvenile peer groups. This is especially problematic because juveniles tend to commit crimes in groups. Therefore, when a peer group forms in an area that is not equipped to monitor and control its behaviors, illegal activity often results. Because the area lacks communication and community ties due to issues with poverty, residential mobility and racial and ethnic heterogeneity, people are not willing to intervene and stop juvenile misbehaviors (Bursik & Grasmick, 1993). Higher numbers of single-parent households also leads to collectively fewer adults supervising children in those areas (Sampson, 1987). In addition, due to high rates of poverty the parents in those areas are often working several jobs, which greatly reduces their ability to be present to monitor their children's behaviors. High rates of poverty also result in fewer resources in the community to help monitor and supervise children (Kaplan, 2010; Lareau, 2001). A general sense of distrust in the community further makes parents weary of trusting others to help care for their children (Edin & Kefalas, 2005). This leaves parents in these areas with fewer forms of informal control to help monitor the behaviors of their children.

Given these issues, a judge might point to high levels of gang or drug activity in a juvenile's neighborhood and a lack of family supervision as reasons to detain the juvenile in order to prevent that juvenile from succumbing to criminal behavior. This can further have a disproportionately negative effect on Black juveniles, as they are most likely to reside in these areas. Black juveniles from these areas also fit the stereotypical image of a dangerous, violent, and chronic offender which can result in court personnel viewing them as more likely to recidivate and in need of formal social controls.

There is research that supports this idea that the area in which a juvenile resides can influence their likelihood of recidivating. One study examined the impact of community factors on the accuracy of the Youth Level of Service/Case Management Inventory (YLS/CMI). The YLS/CMI is the most common risk assessment tool used to predict juveniles' likelihoods of recidivating. Risk assessment tools calculate additive risks, meaning they add up all the risks factors present in a juvenile's life so that the more risks factors a juvenile has the higher risks score they receive. Using the eight subscales (offense history, family circumstances, education, peer group, substance abuse, leisure activity, attitude, and personality) that make up the YLS/CMI, juveniles' risks of recidivating is correctly predicted for two out of every three juveniles. Because the eight subscales only contain individual-level factors, Onifade, Peterson, Bynum and Davidson (2011) wanted to see if they could make the predictions more accurate by adding community-level factors.

The community-level data was collected from the U.S. Census Bureau for the census block group at which juveniles who were placed on probation resided. Three factors were examined that consisted of ten items. The first was household hardships; it consisted of measures for percentage of the population without a high school diploma, percentage of households receiving public assistance, percentage of households with more than one person per room. Household instability, the second factor, included measures of percentage of households in poverty, percentage of single-parent households, rate of vacant houses, and rate of rental properties. The last factor, labor capital, included measures for percentage of residents over 16 who were not employed, percentage of males over 16 who were not employed, and percentage of females over 16 who were not employed. Although the researchers did not find any of the three factors to have a direct effect on likelihood of recidivism, they did find that the household hardships of the block interacted with juveniles' YLS/CMI score. In areas with higher levels of household hardships, juveniles who rated high on the YLS/CMI were more likely to recidivate. Thus they were able to improve the predictions made with the YLS/CMI.

Theoretically, there appears to be good reason to expect the community in which a court is located to affect decision-making in that court. However, this was not explored in research until the early 1990s. Before that time, research almost exclusively focused on the effect of individual-level factors. Despite the fact that the findings of studies varied by place and time, empirical examinations into the community factors that influenced decision-making had not been conducted. Early research began by examining the level of "urbanization" of a county to determine differences in decision-making. Other research then began to explore the empirical validity of the threat perspectives and attribution theory. The next sections review the studies on how community factors affect juvenile court decisions and how they differently affect juveniles of different races and ethnicities.

Urbanization and Juvenile Processing

Feld (1991) first introduced the concept of "justice by geography" in a study that examined the judicial processing of juveniles in the Minnesota juvenile courts in 1986. He suggested that the geographical location of the court in which a juvenile is processed has an impact on the sanctions juveniles receive. In Minnesota, he identified two urban courts, eight suburban/small urban courts, and 77 rural courts. In regards to race, minority groups were located almost exclusively in the urban court jurisdictions. When examining the treatment of juveniles in these courts, Feld found that juveniles in urban courts were more likely to receive detention prior to adjudication and to receive more severe sanctions after disposition, due to the urban courts being more formal and bureaucratized than rural courts. He further found that urban courts had fewer informal control options (e.g., parental supervision and community support) available to them than the rural court, and subsequently had to rely more heavily on formal controls (e.g., probation and secure detention).

Additional research has suggested that the lack of informal controls in a community can result in families more heavily relying on the criminal justice system to regulate their children's behaviors. Richardson, Johnson, and Vil (2014) examined data from an ethnographic study conducted in Central Harlem in New York City. During interviews with parents, they found that Black parents often discussed problems due to a lack of resources available to them to aid in regulating their children's behaviors. To help fill these gaps, parents turned to the juvenile justice system to help control their boys' behaviors. One mother said this when discussing how the juvenile court helped her parent her son:

> If I need help or advice with my kids the only person I can rely on is the juvenile court social worker. I can rely on her more than my family and friends. I talk to her about everything really. She is the only person who really listens to me about things I'm going through with the kids. (Richardson et al., 2014 p. 509)

Other mothers spoke about the ability of the juvenile court to change their sons' behaviors.

> When I take him to court I gonna tell the judge I don't want him at my home anymore. He needs to grow up some. Maybe he'll grow up some and maybe if he stays up there (juvenile detention), he'll learn some discipline and maybe he'll learn to be a better person That's what I'm gonna pray happens. If I leave him on the streets any longer he will probably end up dead. (Richardson et al., 2014 p. 509)
>
> I hope Manny being locked up will shake him up a little. I want the judge to put something in his mind that is really going to scare him and make him think of going to school and being good. I hope he'll put him in a boot camp or a group home, the way I feel he needs to be punished a little. (Richardson et al., 2014 p. 510)

Given these findings, it might not just be judges who believe formal social controls are needed for urban youths as Feld's (1991) research suggests. It appears that parents residing in disadvantaged areas are also looking to the juvenile court to help control their youths.

Lack of resources in poor areas can also negatively affect juveniles, and can have a disproportionately negative effect on minority juveniles. Pullman and Heflinger (2009) examined the effect of community factors on the decision to refer juveniles to substance abuse treatment services in Tennessee for all juveniles who were processed in 1997. The results indicated that non-White youth were less likely than White youth to be referred to substance abuse treatment. They further found that youths in rural communities were less likely to receive substance abuse treatment than those in urban areas. When examining whether race and percentage minority in the county had a significant effect on substance abuse treatment referrals, the authors found a slight effect indicating that as the minority population increased the number of referrals in that county decreased. Therefore, it appeared that community factors might differently impact minority youths for referrals to substance abuse treatment, with referrals of minorities less likely in counties with higher minority populations. This finding was small, however, and referral decisions appeared to be more impacted by the availability of treatment services and the courts' connections to service providers (Pullman & Heflinger, 2009).

Using data from 1990 in Pennsylvania, DeJong and Jackson (1998) examined whether the level of urbanization of the county in which courts were located affected the decision to formally refer a juvenile to juvenile court and on the decision to place a juvenile in a secure detention facility after disposition. They also examined how urbanization affected Black, White, and Hispanic juveniles differently. The level of "urbanization" of a county was determined by measuring the population density of that county (higher population density signifies a more urban county).

Their results indicated that Hispanic juveniles were more likely to be referred than White juveniles. Black and White juveniles, however, did not differ significantly in their likelihood of being referred. Prior to accounting for urbanization, it appeared that Black youths were more likely to be referred than White youths, and that there was no significant difference between the referrals of White and Hispanic youths. This change indicates that what first appeared to be more severe treatment of Black youths was actually more severe treatment of urban youths, which can be explained by Feld's finding that urban courts tend to be more formal and utilize harsher sanctions more often than rural courts. The change in the finding for Hispanic youth might indicate that Hispanic youths were more likely to be processed in rural courts, and were more likely to receive harsher punishments than White youths in those rural courts.

When secure detention was examined, race was not significant. Black and Hispanic juveniles did not have significantly different likelihoods of being placed than White juveniles. The degree of urbanization in this model was also in the opposite direction. While juveniles processed in more urban counties were more likely to be referred, they were less likely to be placed in urban counties than in rural counties.

DeJong and Jackson (1998) also examined whether race affected the treatment of juveniles indirectly. To do this, they conducted additional analysis examining the factors that affected the decisions to refer and to place Black and White juveniles. Because there were too few Hispanic juveniles, they were not included in this analysis. The results indicated that White juveniles received preferential treatment in the decision to refer and in the decision to place juveniles in secure detention if they lived with both parents; Black juveniles did not receive this preferential treatment. For secure placement after disposition, Black youths were more likely to be placed if they committed a drug charge; this did not matter for White juveniles. Black youths were also more likely to be placed in counties that were less urban.

Minority Threat and Juvenile Processing

Another early study conducted by Sampson and Laub (1993) extended Feld's work and examined differences in urban, suburban, and rural courts to consider whether variations existed in the treatment of juveniles based on additional community characteristics. Using their macrostructural perspective, they hypothesized that due to the war on drugs creating a threatening image of dangerous urban youths, more disadvantaged areas would subject juveniles to harsher punishments. Furthermore, Black juveniles in these areas would be especially impacted, and would receive more punitive punishments than White juveniles. Drug offenders in these areas would also receive more punitive punishments than other offenders.

Level of structural disadvantage was measured through variables for underclass poverty, racial inequality, and the wealth and economic resources of a community. These measures were included as indirect measures of threat, assuming that court officials in areas with a larger underclass and with greater racial and economic inequality would be more threatened by Black juveniles. Hence juveniles in these communities would be processed more punitively. The outcomes examined were the rates of juveniles being petitioned to juvenile court, the number of juveniles receiving predisposition detention in petitioned and nonpetitioned cases, and the number of juveniles being placed out of the home. Sampson and Laub also examined the outcomes for different types of crimes (personal, property, drugs and public order) separately. Their analysis differs from more recent studies that examined both individual and community-level factors in that they only examine community-level factors. To do this, they examined each county as one unit of analysis; in newer studies, it is more common to examine the effect that community-level factors have on the individual.

Three hundred and twenty-two total counties were included, representing 21 different states across the county. The analysis revealed that racial inequality had the largest impact on the formal petitioning of cases for all crime types except drugs. For the detention of petitioned cases, greater racial inequality only resulted in higher rates of detention for personal crimes. For secure detention of nonpetitioned cases, greater racial inequality increased detention for personal and property crimes. Racial inequality was not related to rates of out-of-home placement. Higher rates of underclass resulted in increased detention in petitioned cases for drug offenses, in increased detention in nonpetitioned cases for property, drug and public order cases, and in out-of-home placements for personal and drug offenses. Underclass was not significantly related to number of petitioned cases. Higher wealth only increased secure detention for nonpetitioned personal and property cases.

When examining Black and White juveniles separately, Sampson and Laub found that as the size of the underclass increased the number of Black juveniles being detained for personal, property, and public order offenses, but did not significantly affect the detention of White juveniles. For out-of-home placement, underclass actually decreased the number of Whites being placed. For Black juveniles, the number of juveniles being placed increased for personal and drug offenses. Racial inequality increased the number of White juveniles being detained for personal and property offenses; it increased the rates of detention of Black juveniles for drug and property crimes. Racial inequality did not affect the number of White juveniles receiving out-of-home placement, but increased the number for Black juveniles for property crimes. Higher wealth was not significant for White juveniles, but increased detention for Black juveniles for personal, property, and drug offenses. Higher rates of wealth decreased out-of-home placement for White juveniles for property offenses, but increased the number of Black juveniles for drug offenses.

Overall, their findings indicated that areas with higher rates of underclass and greater racial inequality process their juveniles more formally. This effect also appears to be stronger for Black juveniles than for White juveniles. There did not appear to be a large difference in the handling of drug offenses relative to other offenses; instead, it appeared that the structural factors increased the formal handling of all cases. Wealth did not have as consistent of a relationship with processing decisions, indicating that presence of a larger underclass and of greater racial inequality are better indicators of symbolic threat.

Lieber and Stairs (1999) expanded on the work of Sampson and Laub (1993) to examine the structural factors of three courts in Iowa. Instead of including community structural factors as indirect measures of threat, their study directly measured decision-makers' perceptions and beliefs to determine what effect they had on the intake decisions. These perceptions and beliefs were examined by having court personnel respond on a five-point Likert scale (strongly disagree, disagree, neutral, agree, and strongly agree) to four statements about racial differences and four statements regarding retribution. An example of the racial differences statements was "Black youth have poorer attitudes than White youth," and an example of the retribution items is "The juvenile court is too lenient."

In addition, they included measures for the percentage of the population below the poverty level, the rate of unemployment, and percentage of the population with a high school diploma. Racial inequality was also included and measured with variables for the ratio of Black to White families below the poverty line and the percentage of minorities in poverty. Mortality and sexual promiscuity was also included. Sexual promiscuity was measured as the percentage of babies born out of wedlock to teenage mothers. Urbanization of the county was included as total population; percentage of citizens under 18, police expenditures per person in the county, and crime rate were also included.

The findings of their study indicated that Black youths were treated more harshly than White juveniles during intake. In jurisdictions with greater racial and social inequality, juveniles were subjected to harsher punishments. Juveniles were also treated more formally in jurisdictions where court personnel viewed Black juveniles more differently than White juveniles and where court personnel held more punitive attitudes. In these jurisdictions, Black juveniles were also treated more harshly than White juveniles. Their study did not, however, support Sampson and Laub's (1993) argument that race, drug offenses, and social control were related. In the counties where court personnel had increased beliefs of racial differences, Black youths from single-parent households were treated more harshly than other youth; family status did not have a significant impact on the intake decision for White youth.

In a more recent study, Freiburger and Jordan (2011) also used a symbolic threat perspective to examine the effect of community factors on the decision to petition youth to the juvenile court in West Virginia. Their data included all juveniles who were brought to the juvenile court in 2005. Unlike many other studies examining race and juvenile court processing, they did not find that race had an impact on petitioning decisions at the individual level. The community-level variables they examined, percentage poverty, percentage Black residents in the county, population density, and percentage of female-headed households, indicated that only percentage in poverty and percentage of female-headed households were significantly related to the decision to petition cases in the juvenile court. Increases in both of these variables led to decreased odds of juveniles having their cases petitioned. In other words, juveniles processed in courts that were located in areas that had high levels of poverty and a higher percentage of female-headed households were less likely to be petitioned than youths living in areas with less poverty and fewer female-headed households. An interaction term for percentage living in poverty and race was also significant. This indicated that Black youth were more likely to have their cases petitioned to the juvenile court if they were processed in a county with higher rates of poverty. This finding is consistent with the Sampson and Laub's symbolic threat, which suggests that the middle class is threatened by impoverished Black populations.

Rodriguez (2013) used data from Maricopa County, Arizona, to examine the effects of structural factors on the decision to detain juvenile offenders in a state institution at the disposition hearing. She also examined whether structural disadvantage could differently affect juveniles of different races and ethnicities. In addition to conducting a quantitative analysis on the 2,152 cases that resulted in a disposition in 2000, Rodriguez also conducted a qualitative content analysis of 50 cases that were randomly sampled from the original 2,152. She based her study on the logic of attribution theory. Her quantitative analysis provided an understanding of *what* impact community structural factors had on detention decisions, while the qualitative analysis provided insight into *how* community structural factors impacted detention decisions.

While the majority of studies have examined the effects of community factors by county, Rodriguez examined these impacts by juveniles' zip codes reported at intake. This differentiates her research in that it suggests that judges consider the community in which juveniles reside when determining the most appropriate sanction for a juvenile (in this case, whether to detain the juvenile or not), instead of focusing on how the community factors of the court location impact juvenile sentencing. To measure community context factors, data were then collected from the United States Census Bureau for the communities represented. Data for percent living in poverty, percent receiving public assistance, percent unemployed, percent with less than a high school education, and percent of female headed households with children under 18 years old were used to construct a concentrated disadvantage index.

Results of the quantitative analysis indicated that at the individual level, race and ethnicity had a substantial impact on the decision to detain juveniles, with Black youth having a 1.84 times greater likelihood of being confined than White youth. Hispanic youth were 2.05 times more likely to be detained than White youth. Rodriguez also found that structural disadvantage was significantly related to confinement decisions, with youths from communities with more structural disadvantage having a greater likelihood of being detained. Structural disadvantage did not significantly interact with race and ethnicity, however, meaning that being from a disadvantaged community had the same effect on minority youth as it did on White youth. Through her qualitative content analysis, she found that judges often cited concerns about drug activities in areas of structural disadvantage. They were also concerned about negative peer influences and gang behaviors in these neighborhoods.

Conclusion

Overall, race was not only found to have a direct effect on juvenile court processing in many studies, but several have also found race to have an indirect effect through family structural variables (DeJong & Jackson, 1998; Leiber & Stairs, 1999). Some studies further found support for Sampson and Laub's (1993) argument that the war on drugs has led to harsher treatment of Black juveniles and those living in disadvantage neighborhoods. DeJong and Jackson found that Black juveniles were more likely to be placed if they committed a drug offense. Rodriquez (2013) also found that court personnel voiced concerns about juveniles from disadvantaged communities being involved in drug activities.

In the majority of the studies, community structure appeared to have an impact on juvenile court processing (DeJong & Jackson 1998; Feld, 1991; Sampson & Laub, 1993). When examining whether the impact of community factors vary by race and ethnicity, however, the research is more mixed. Rodriquez (2013) found that community factors had the same impact on all juveniles, while other studies found that community factors had different impacts on Black (Freiburger & Jordan, 2011; Leiber & Stairs, 1999) or Hispanic juveniles (DeJong & Jackson, 1998) compared to White juveniles. With the exception of Leiber and Stairs (1999) studies examining racial threat relied on indirect structural variables to assess this threat and interpreted interactions of race and community factors to be indicators of this threat. In the future, more studies should take the approach of Lieber and Stairs, and utilize a direct measure of threat to determine the impact on juvenile court processing.

It was also found that community factors might impact treatment services, with juveniles having a decreased likelihood of receiving treatment in jurisdictions where programs are less abundant and where the counts have weaker connections to service providers (Pullman & Heflinger, 2009). Freiburger and Jordan (2010) also note that their finding that juveniles are more likely to have their cases petitioned to the court in areas with more poverty might be due to the accessibility of needed services. It is possible that because residents in these areas are less able to afford independent treatment services, court officials are more often relying on the juvenile court to provide these services.

Studies have varied in their approaches to examining the effects of community factors on juvenile court processing. Most studies (e.g., Freiburger & Jordan, 2011; Leiber & Stairs, 1999; Pullman & Heflinger, 2009) examined the community structure of the courts in which the juveniles were processed. Rodriguez (2013), on the other hand, examined the area in which the juvenile resided. Both have theoretically implications and are important examinations to understanding juvenile court decision-making. Theoretically, conflict theory and the symbolic threat perspective suggests that variations will be found across courts due to an effort by the court to suppress a threatening group, typically the underclass and minority population. The area in which the juvenile actually resides is also important as it can be an indicator to court personal as to juveniles' likelihoods of recidivating. Findings from both approaches suggest that community factors are important and that community factors have different effects for juveniles of different races and ethnicities. More research in both areas needs to be conducted, however, to really understand these effects.

Additional research should also consider possible variations across juvenile courts due to differences in state policies. Research conducted by Terry-McElrath,

Chriqui, Bates, and McBride (2014) examined this possibility for first time marijuana offenders. Their research focused on the decision making of the prosecutor. For their research, instead of analyzing judicial processing decisions in real juvenile cases, they presented prosecutors with scenarios of a juvenile offender and asked the prosecutors to indicate the appropriateness of various options to handle the case. In total, they analyzed 119 responses from 38 states plus Washington, DC. The results indicated that state statutory policy did influence juvenile court processing and diversion and transfer decisions. The researchers did not, however, examine whether prosecutorial decisions varied by the race and ethnicity of the juvenile. Additional research should be conducted to examine variations in punishment decisions across states, and assess what impact those variations have on minorities.

Discussion Questions

1. Part of Tittle and Curran's explanation for why minorities are treated more harshly by the court is because decision-makers are responding to a feeling of jealous toward these youths. They witness youths acting out aggressively and without discipline and feel resentment that they cannot exhibit those same behaviors. Do you agree with Tittle and Curran's position? Why or why not?

2. Given the research finding that community factors can be important in predicting juveniles' risks of recidivism, would you argue that the community in which a juvenile resides should be considered by juvenile court officials when making treatment and punishment decisions? Why or why not?

3. Consider the research conducted by Richardson et al. (2014) in Central Harlem, New York City, which found that Black parents living in social disadvantage communities find it necessary to rely on the juvenile justice system to regulate their children's behaviors. Come up with some policy or program options that do not involve the juvenile justice system that these parents could utilize.

4. Some states have recently legalized marijuana; although, marijuana possession still remains illegal in many states. Therefore, a person can engage in the exact same act (consume marijuana) in one state and it is legal, but in another state that same behavior subjects them to criminal sanctioning. Should the fact that a behavior is legal in other states affect how severely a state where the behavior is illegal punishes that behavior?

References

Alexander, K.L., Entwisle, D. & Olson, L. (2014). The long shadow: Family background disadvantaged urban youth, and the transition to adulthood. *(American Sociological Association's Rose Series in Sociology)*. New York: Russell Sage Foundation.

Anderson, A.M. (2002). Individual and contextual influences on delinquency: The role of the single-parent family. *Journal of Criminal Justice, 30*(6), 575–587.

Blalock, H.M., Jr. (1967). *Toward a theory of minority-group relations*. New York: Capricorn Books.

Bursik, R. & Grasmick, H.G. (1993). *Neighborhoods and crime: The dimensions of effective community control*. New York: Lexington Books.

DeJong, C. & Jackson, K.C. (1998). Putting race into context: Race, juvenile justice processing, and urbanization. *Justice Quarterly, 15*(3), 488–504.

Edin, K. & Kefalas, M. (2005). Promises I can keep: *Why poor women put motherhood before marriage*. Berkeley: University of California Press.

Feld, B.C. (1991). Justice by geography: Urban, suburban, and rural variations in juvenile justice administration. *The Journal of Criminal Law & Criminology, 82*(1), 156–201.

Forum on Child and Family Statistics. (2012). Retrieved from: http://www.childstats.gov/americaschildren/.

Freiburger, T.L. & Jordan, K.L. (2011). A multilevel analysis of race on the decision to prosecute in the juvenile court. Race and Justice: *An International Journal, 1*(2), 185–201.

Kaplan, E.B. (2010). Doing care on the run: Family strategies in the contested terrain of gender and institutional intransigence. *Journal of Contemporary Ethnography, 39*(6), 587–618.

Lareau, A. (2000). My wife can't tell me who I know: Methodological and conceptual problems in studying fathers. *Qualitative Sociology, 23*(4), 407–433.

Leiber, M.J. & Stairs, J.M. (1999). Race, contexts and the use of intake diversion. *Journal of Research in Crime and Delinquency, 36*(1), 56–86.

Liska, A.E. & Chamlin, M.B. (1984). Social structure and crime control among macro social units. *American Journal of Sociology, 90*, 383–395.

Muschert, G.W. (2007). The Columbine victims and the myth of the juvenile superpredator. *Youth Violence and Juvenile Justice. 5*(4), 351–366.

Onifade, E., Peterson, J., Bynum, T. & Davidson, W. (2011). Multilevel Recidivism Prediction: Incorporating Neighborhood Socioeconomic Ecology in jevenile Risk Assessment. *Criminal Justice and Behavior, 38* 840–854.

Partnership for Drug-Free Kids. (2007 February 20). Study finds rich kids more likely to use drugs than poor. Retrieved from: http://www.drugfree.org/ join-together/study-finds-rich-kids-more-likely-to-use-drugs-than-poor/.

Pullman, M.D. & Heflinger, C.A. (2009). Community determinants of substance abuse treatment referrals from juvenile courts: Do rural youths have equal access? *Journal of Child & Adolescent Substance Abuse, 18,* 359–378.

Richarson, J.B. Jr., Johnson, W.E. Jr., St. Vil, C. (2014). I want him locked up: Social capital, African American parenting strategies, and the juvenile court. *Journal of Contemporary Ethnography, 43*(4), 488–522.

Rodriguez, N. (2013). Concentrated disadvantage and the incarceration of youth: Examining how context affects juvenile justice. *Journal of Research in Crime and Delinquency, 50*(2), 189–215.

Sampson, R.J. (1987). Urban Black violence: The effect of male joblessness and family disruption. *American Journal of Sociology, 93,* 348–382.

Sampson, R. J. & Laub, J. H. (1993). Structural variations in juvenile court processing: Inequality, the underclass, and social control. *Law & Society Review, 27,* 285–311.

Shaw, C.R. & McKay, H.D. (1969). *Juvenile delinquency and urban areas: A study of rates of delinquency in relation to differential characteristics of local communities in American cities.* Chicago: University of Chicago Press.

Terry-McElrath, Y.M., Chriqui, J.F., Bates, H., McBride, D.C. (2014). Do State Policies Matter in Prosecutor Reported Juvenile Marijuana Case Disposition? *Crime and Delinquency,* 60(3), 402–442).

Tittle, C. & Curran, D. (1988). Contingencies for dispositional disparities in juvenile justice. *Social Forces, 67,* 23–53.

Chapter 8

Racial Disparities and Juveniles in the Adult Court

Goals of the Chapter

The purpose of this chapter is to examine the role of race/ethnicity in transferring juveniles to adult court. In this chapter, we explore the effect of race and ethnicity in the transfer decision, along with their role in sentencing among convicted offenders. The chapter ends with a discussion of the implications of transferring youth to the adult system, especially among historically overrepresented racial/ethnic groups.

After reading this chapter, you will be able to do the following:

1. Understand whether race plays a role in the decision to transfer youth to the adult system;
2. Discuss whether there are racial/ethnic disparities in populations of youth confined in adult correctional facilities; and
3. Explain the empirical literature that has explored the role of race/ethnicity in the legal practice of juvenile transfer.

Transferring (also called waiving or certifying) juvenile offenders to the adult criminal justice system is a practice that has been in place since the inception of the juvenile court in 1899 (Bernard & Kurlychek, 2010). Transferring youth to criminal court involves prosecuting juveniles in the criminal justice system as opposed to the juvenile court. Each state has a statutory age limit for juvenile court jurisdiction (e.g., age 17), but each state has provisions that allow for these youth be sent to adult court if predetermined criteria are met (e.g., age, offense, prior record, etc.).

Although transferring youth to criminal court has always been in place, it was dramatically expanded as a result of the youth violence increase that spanned between the mid-1980s to early 1990s (Myers, 2005; Jordan, 2006). Following the moral panic that resulted from the youth violence surge, almost every state expanded its transfer laws by making more youth eligible for criminal court processing based on age and offense criteria. Historically, juvenile court judges were responsible for the decision to transfer youth (i.e., judicial waiver). In making decisions, juvenile court judges would consider factors that extended beyond the traditional legal factors, such as school progress and participation of families in juveniles' treatment efforts. In other words, the juvenile court would focus on many aspects of the juvenile, instead of fairly limited considerations. The rationale was two-fold. First, the juvenile court needed to be distinct from the adult system, which focuses mainly on prior record and offense severity. Second, juvenile court judges generally believed that extra-legal factors helped provide a better knowledge of youth, resulting in a stronger case to be made regarding the appropriate disposition. Once state legislatures expanded their waiver laws, significant discretion was removed from the juvenile court judges and more youth were prosecuted in the adult system via prosecutors and state law mandates, focusing almost exclusively on age and offense characteristics.

As mentioned above, juvenile court judges were responsible for waiving the majority of youth to the adult system for criminal processing. This method of transfer is referred to as judicial waiver. However, after the moral panic of the juvenile "super-predator" (DiIulio, 1995), two additional types of waivers became more popular. Prosecutorial waiver, also called direct file, provides prosecutors with the ability to determine whether to file the case in either the juvenile or criminal system (Jordan, 2006). In these cases, both court systems exercise jurisdiction over the case, giving the prosecutor the final determination to file the case in the court s/he deems appropriate. The final method of transfer is legislative waiver. Under this method of transfer, youth bypass the juvenile court entirely and are processed in the criminal system. In several states, statutes exclude certain offenses (often in combination with age of youth and prior record) from juvenile court jurisdiction, meaning those youth are automatically in the adult system.

In almost one-half of the states, there are provisions that allow for initially transferred youth to be decertified or reverse-waived to the juvenile system for processing (Jordan & Myers, 2007). If juveniles can convince a criminal court judge (since they are in the adult system at the time) that it serves the public interest for them to be in the juvenile system, they can petition the court to be decertified. Criminal court judges are generally required to examine the factors that juvenile court judges consider when making the decision to actually transfer cases to the adult system (e.g., offense severity, prior record, victim injury, etc.). If juveniles are charged with less serious offenses and not have an extensive prior record, it increases their likelihood of decertification. Once decertification is granted, the case is processed through the juvenile court system the same as any other cases.

Characteristics of Transferred Youth

Data on the number of characteristics of transferred youth is mostly available only for those judicially waived to the adult system because systematic data are collected on youth in the juvenile system (although these youth are subsequently transferred). However, given that youth who are either direct filed or legislatively waived to the adult system bypass the juvenile court and begin in the adult system, there is no national database that captures the characteristics of those youth.

Given this limitation, as part of the State Court Processing Statistics series that captures data on felony defendants in criminal court, there is also a Juvenile Defendant in Criminal Court (JDCC) data set (U.S. Dept. of Justice, 2003). In this data, 40 of the nation's largest 75 counties are included from 1998 in order to identify characteristics of youth processed in the adult system. Limitations of the data set are that it is not representative of the entire United States and it only includes felony defendants, instead of felony and misdemeanors. However, it does provide a picture of how juvenile transfer looks in those 40 counties.

Among those 40 counties, approximately 7,100 juveniles were transferred to the adult system during 1998 for felony offenses. This number does not include misdemeanors or the other counties and states not captured in these data. Of those transferred, 35% were direct filed and 40% were legislatively waived, indicating that the smallest percentage of youth was judicially waived. In examining the characteristics of the youth, approximately 62% were Black, 16% were Hispanic, and 20% were White. While this is not a nationally representative sample, again, this does provide some insight into two areas: 1) direct files and legislative waivers are transferring a larger percentage of youth to the adult system, and 2) Blacks and Hispanics are likely over-represented among the population of waived youth.

In the latest year available at the time of this writing, 2012, there were 4,600 youth *judicially* waived to the adult system, which is less than 1% of the total number of juvenile arrests (Puzzanchera & Hockenberry, 2015). However, the racial breakdown of that number includes 2,400 White youth and 2,100 Black youth.[1] At first glance, it appears that White youth have a greater likelihood of being judicially waived to the adult system. However, based on the percentage of youth in the population, White youth have a lower risk of being waived.

---

1. Hispanic, as an ethnic group, is not captured in the data. They are classified mostly in either the White or Black races.

The Office of Juvenile Justice & Delinquency Prevention captures data on Disproportionate Minority Contact (DMC) with the juvenile justice system. As a measure of DMC, the agency reports the Relative Rate Index (RRI) of minority youth (Black, American Indian/Alaskan Native, and Asian/Hawaiian/Pacific Islander) as compared to White youth at multiple decision points in the juvenile system (Puzzanchera & Hockenberry, 2015).

Figure 8.1. Relative Rate Index and Judicial Waivers in 2012

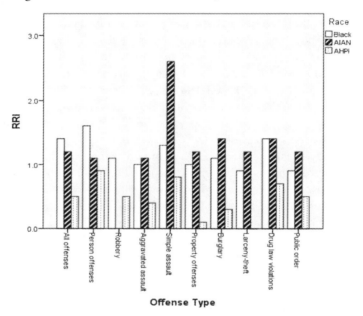

Office of Juvenile Justice and Delinquency Prevention (Puzzanchera & Hockenberry, 2015)

Figure 8.1 includes the RRI for 2012. A RRI less than 1.0 indicates the group is waived at a rate less proportionate to Whites, while a RRI greater than one indicates the group is waived disproportionately higher than Whites. A RRI of 1.0 means that the group is transferred at a rate proportionate to White youth. As can be seen in the figure, Black and American Indian/Alaskan Native youth are waived to adult court at disproportionately higher rates for almost every category of offense as compared to White youth.

Two main explanations have been advanced to explain DMC. First, minorities are disproportionately over-represented due to differential offending.

In other words, certain groups of minorities are more likely to be waived than White youth because those groups are more serious offenders, resulting in a greater likelihood of transfer. This explanation minimizes the discrimination argument because after legal factors (e.g., offense, prior record, etc.) are considered, the race effect disappears. The second explanation is discrimination. Whether intentional or unintentional, this position suggests that the laws and/or court actors (e.g., judges and prosecutors) are biased against minority youth. Due to this negative view of minority youth, harsher sanctions are more likely to occur, including the transferring of these youth to the adult system.

Case Study: Lionel Tate

In 1999, Lionel Tate was an 11-year-old African-American male living in Florida. Tate's mother was babysitting a 6-year-old girl (Tiffany Eunick), but she was upstairs while Lionel and Tiffany were downstairs playing. At some point, Lionel went upstairs to tell his mother that Tiffany was not breathing. According to Lionel, he and Tiffany were playing and practicing the wrestling moves he had seen on television. Lionel stated that he put Tiffany in a head lock and slammed her head into the table. Lionel was subsequently arrested for murder and charged in the adult criminal justice system.

During the court process, the prosecution offered Lionel a plea deal. The deal was that he would serve three years in a juvenile facility and then ten years on probation. Lionel's mother, a Florida Highway Patrol officer, rejected the deal in hopes of him getting acquitted. He was subsequently found guilty of second degree murder. During sentencing, the prosecution joined the defense in asking for leniency. The judge stated, "It not only casts the prosecutor in a light totally inconsistent with his role in the criminal justice system, but it makes the whole court process seem like a game, where if the results are unfavorable, they'll run to a higher source to seek a different result. A trial is not a test balloon, sent up to see what may happen. And if the results displease both sides, so be it: This is what our jury system is about." In making the argument that the prosecution sought a murder conviction, the judge then stated, "They got what they wanted. They now have to take responsibility for their actions in seeking it in the first place." Lionel was sentenced to a mandatory life sentence in prison at the conclusion of the trial; he was 13 years old at that point.

On appeal, his conviction was overturned because he was not mentally evaluated prior to his trial. Instead of going through another trial, a plea bargain on second degree murder was reached: one year of house arrest and 10 years on probation. During his first year of house arrest in 2004 (age 17), he was found with an 8-inch knife away from home; the judge added five years to his probation. The following year at age 18, he was convicted of robbing a pizza delivery driver. He was sentenced to prison until the year 2031.

Sources:

http://www.sun-sentinel.com/local/broward/sfl-tatesentencing-story.html#page=1

http://abcnews.go.com/US/story?id=93884

http://www.nytimes.com/2006/03/02/national/02tate.html?_r=0

Race and Transfer Decisions

In making the decision to transfer youth to juvenile court, legal factors are generally the strongest determinants. As offense seriousness and prior record increase, the greater the likelihood of being sent to the adult system. According to Jordan and Myers (2007), " … because our society believes that sentences should be predictable and nondiscriminatory, it is logical for offense seriousness and prior record to play a strong role in sentences" (p. 201). In other words, the strongest predictors of transfer are those factors that are legally relevant in the court process. These findings appear consistent with one goal of juvenile transfer, which is to waive the most serious offenders to the adult criminal system. At first glance, then, it seems that juvenile transfer is accomplishing its goal by focusing on a select group of chronic and/or violent offenders.

Early research provides evidence of non-Whites making up the largest percentage of youth who are transferred to the adult system. One of the first studies on juvenile transfer (Keiter, 1973) examined judicial waivers during 1970 in the nation's first juvenile court: Cook County, Illinois. Keiter found that 92% of those judicially waived were Black youth. What is more interesting is that he examined prior delinquent histories among transferred youth and found that

White youth had more extensive histories. In combination, these findings suggest that the minimum threshold for waiving Black youth is lower than Whites.

Thomas and Bilchik (1985) included cases from Dade County (Miami), Florida, during 1981 and found that 68% of the transferred cases were non-White. In this study, the authors did not rely on juvenile court data, as did Keiter (1973). They collected data from the criminal court; therefore, they captured data on all waived youth, regardless of the transfer mechanism for entering the adult system. Clement (1997) examined cases in Richmond, Virginia, from 1986-1991 and found similar results to Keiter (1973). He found that Blacks made up approximately 97% of those judicially waived to the adult system. From these early studies, then, it appears that minority youth, especially Black youth, were being highly disadvantaged regarding waiver decisions.

However, other research has found that when legal factors are statistically controlled for in the analyses, the direct race effect disappears (Fagan & Deschenes, 1990; Fagan, Forst, & Vivora, 1987; Poulos & Orchowsky, 1994). In other words, it appears as though the DMC at the transfer decision stage can be explained away through factors such as offense seriousness and prior record. Even researchers publishing in early studies cautioned people against this conclusion. According to Fagan et al. (1987), "There is a racial component to transfer, but it apparently is expressed through a variety of intervening characteristics, independent of offense-specific criteria. Reducing disparity in transfer decisions will require addressing not only judicial disposition decision behaviors, but also larger social policy issues on the fairness and equity of available rehabilitative services and economic opportunities" (p. 277). In other words, minority youth may commit offenses that are more likely to result in transfer to the adult system. In addition, judges may be more likely to follow through with their decision to transfer these youth because there are fewer legitimate resources in the community. Judges may view these lack of resources as one indication of having a higher probability for re-offending, resulting in a harsher punishment of transfer to the adult system. In addition, the lack of economic opportunities in minority areas may influence the decision to commit more serious offenses, which in turn, increases minority youths' probability of getting transferred to the adult system.

Case Study: Nathaniel Abraham

Nathaniel Abraham, an African-American juvenile, was eleven years old in 1997. He lived in Michigan. One day, he borrowed a .22-caliber rifle and subsequently shot a stranger exiting from a convenience store. He was later convicted of second degree murder. Abraham's attorney claimed that race played a role, indicating that the population of the county was only eight percent Black. The jury was made up of 12 people, with one juror being Black.

During sentencing, the judge had three options. First, he could sentence Abraham to an adult institution (with a lengthy adult sentence). Second, he could impose a blended sentence, which would have resulted in the incarceration of Abraham in a juvenile facility until the age of 21 and then the judge would have the option of imposing an adult sentence. The final option was to sentence Abraham as a juvenile only, which would result in his release at the age of 21, which is when the juvenile court loses jurisdiction. The judge opted for the third option, helping Abraham avoid an adult punishment altogether.

Following his release the day before his 21st birthday in January 2007, he was re-arrested in 2008 for selling ecstasy pills. He was convicted for the offense and sentenced to a 4–20 year sentence. While incarcerated for this offense, he was charged with and convicted of attacking a correctional officer. The judge sentenced him to five years of probation. At the time of this writing, he was still incarcerated in a Michigan state prison.

Sources

http://www.nytimes.com/1999/11/17/us/michigan-boy-who-killed-at-11-is-convicted-of-murder-as-adult.html

http://www.cnn.com/TRANSCRIPTS/0001/13/bn.01.html

http://www.foxnews.com/us/2012/06/19/probation-in-assault-case-for-man-who-killed-at-11/

Race and Sentencing among Transferred and Retained Youth

When examining sentencing among transferred youth, there are multiple bodies of literature. The first set of literature focuses on a comparison between youth who are transferred to the adult system and youth who are in the juvenile system. The general idea behind this research is to draw conclusions about the impact of transfer on sentencing decisions. Most of the research has included race as a control variable in the analyses. Though not the actual focus of the studies, the results do provide some indication of the role of race in sentencing among this group of serious offenders (both transferred and non-transferred youth).

Myers (2001, 2003) studied sentencing outcomes in Pennsylvania utilizing a sample of violent offenders. His sample included 378 juvenile offenders, of which almost one-third were transferred to the adult system. The findings were that non-Whites (almost all Black youth) were treated similarly to Whites regarding the incarceration decision and incarceration length. Myers findings suggest comparable treatment among his sample of violent offenders.

Pennsylvania was also the site for research conducted by Lemmon, Austin, Verrecchia, and Fetzer (2005). They examined almost 314 violent juvenile offenders who were transferred to the adult system during 1996. Approximately 120 of the offenders were decertified (i.e., reverse waived) to the juvenile system, while the remaining were retained in the adult criminal justice system. They found that non-Whites had a similar probability to Whites for both out-of-home placement (for decertified youth) and incarceration (for transferred youth).

Kupchik (2006) examined juvenile transfer in New York and New Jersey. His sample included almost 1,500 cases from 1992 and 1993 with approximately two-third of the youth coming from New York's adult criminal court and the remaining one-third coming from New Jersey's juvenile system. His findings suggest that African-Americans are more likely to be incarcerated than Whites. This result hints at disparate treatment among Black youth who are convicted. However, the race effect disappears once a series of interaction effects are included in the model.

Jordan and Myers (2011) examined violent youth who were initially transferred to adult court in three Pennsylvania counties during 1996. A small group of youth was reverse waived to the juvenile justice system for processing. They found that race was not significant in the incarceration decision, though significant regarding incarceration time. Non-Whites were sentenced to longer confinement than Whites.

Race and Sentencing among All Transferred Youth

The next set of research includes only juveniles who are transferred to the adult system. In contrast to the studies discussed previously, the research discussed here focuses only on transferred juveniles. The authors of these studies generally wanted to examine criminal sentencing among this group of offenders, often using race as the central or control variable in the analyses.

Utilizing a national sample of juveniles convicted in the adult system during 1998, one study examined the impact of race and ethnicity on criminal sentencing decisions among almost 4,000 youth (Jordan & Freiburger, 2010). More specifically, they compared sentencing decisions among Black, Hispanic, and White youth convicted in the adult criminal court. They found that Black youth were more likely than Whites to be sentenced to jail over probation, and more likely to be sentenced to prison over jail. Hispanics were also more likely than Whites to be sentenced to prison over jail.

Race also appeared to interact with other factors with sentencing. According to Jordan and Freiburger (2010), "It is interesting that having prior contact with the juvenile justice system and being Black increased the likelihood of receiving prison versus jail, and it decreased the likelihood of the same for Whites. These opposite findings could mean that judges view prior record differently for these racial groups, with prior record representing more dangerousness for Blacks (i.e., greater chance of prison) but not for Whites (i.e., lower chance of prison)." This finding is very salient in examining sentencing because it suggests that judges may, consciously or subconsciously, view factors differently based on the race of juvenile defendants. While prior record serves as a risk factor for Blacks by increasing punishments, it seems to serve as a protective factor for White youth by decreasing punishment.

Howell and Hutto (2012) utilized data from the Inter-University Consortium for Political and Social Research (ICPSR), examining sentencing outcomes of almost 2,000 convicted felony defendants transferred to the adult system in 1998. Unique to this study is that they excluded those with prison sentences and focused only on those who were sentenced to restitution, probation, and jail. The authors also excluded from the dataset those offenders who were sentenced to a combination of sentences (e.g., probation plus restitution) and only included those who were sentenced to a singular sentence outcome. As compared to Whites, Blacks were more likely to be sentenced to both probation and jail, while Hispanics were more likely than Whites be sentenced to jail. Race/ethnicity did not appear to impact the judicial decision to sentence offenders to restitution only. Given the finding regarding the jail decision, Howell and Hutto concluded that the results "further underscore the importance of increasing efforts to reduce rates of disproportionate minority confinement."

Race and Sentencing among Transferred Youth and Adults

The final set of studies draw comparisons between transferred juveniles and adults. These studies are meant to assess whether juveniles are, in fact, sentenced similarly to adults in the criminal system. In most of these studies, race and ethnicity were utilized as control variables in the analyses; they were not the focus of the research. However, we can examine the results of these studies to assess whether race and/or ethnicity were significant.

Kurlychek and Johnson (2004) examined approximately 35,000 convicted offenders in the adult criminal justice system, of which slightly more than 1,000 were juveniles. They focused on sentence severity among this group of offenders convicted between 1997 and 1999 in Pennsylvania. Among the full sample of juveniles and adults, Blacks and Whites were all sentenced similarly in terms of severity. Hispanics, however, were sentenced more harshly than Whites. However, when the authors split the sample between juveniles and adults, the finding disappeared. Blacks, Hispanics, and Whites were sentenced similarly.

Steiner (2005) examined 102 juveniles transferred to adult court over a five-year period (1995–1999) in Idaho. He focused on three separate sentencing options: probation, prison, and a juvenile boot-camp facility. Steiner also examined the amount of time served for these transferred youth. Although race was not a significant predictor for any of the outcomes, the measure of race was restricted to a non-White versus White comparison. Research suggests that measuring race in this manner obscures potential race effects in sentencing outcomes, especially if Hispanics, which is typically found to be a disadvantaged group, are included in the White measure.

Kurlychek and Johnson (2010) compared a sample of transferred juveniles and young adults in Maryland from 1999 through 2006. They examined over 18,500 offenders, with almost 2,400 of the sample being comprised of juveniles. Black offenders were sentenced more harshly than Whites across all models (10–20 years old, 16–19 years old, and 17–18 years old). Hispanics and other races (non-Black) were punished more harshly than Whites among those 16–19 years old and 17–18 years old. When examined across type of offense, the results suggested that all races were given similar sentence severity for drug offenses. However, regarding person offenses, Blacks and Hispanics/other races were punished more harshly than Whites. These findings suggest bias in sentencing among these racial/ethnic groups.

Finally, Jordan (2014) examined a national sample of over 35,000 offenders convicted in the adult system. A small portion (n=240) were juveniles. The sample included four years of data: 2000, 2002, 2004, and 2006. He found that Blacks and Hispanics were more likely than Whites to be incarcerated (both jail and prison). His findings also suggested that Blacks were given longer jail time than Whites, while Hispanics were sentenced to longer jail and prison time than Whites. These findings suggest that race and ethnicity may have a different impact on sentencing, depending on the specific outcome examined.

Figure 8.2 provides a visual of the racial and ethnic disparities in transferring youth in the adult system. Both sources of data included a weighting variable, allowing the results to be representative of the nation's state prisons and local jails. First in focusing on the number of youth incarcerated in state prisons across the United States, there were 2,561 in 2004. Almost one-half (48.7% or 1,247) were Black and another 30.5% (or 736) were Hispanic. Stated differently, approximately 80% of the state prison inmates under the age of 18 were youth

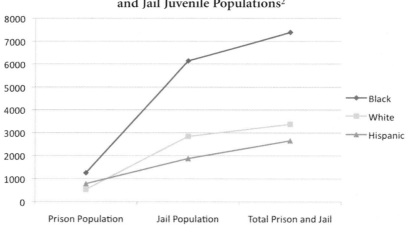

Figure 8.2. Racial/Ethnic Make-up of State Prison and Jail Juvenile Populations[2]

Survey of Inmates in Local Jails (U.S. Dept. of Justice, 2012) and Survey of Inmates in State and Federal Correctional Facilities (U.S. Dept. of Justice, 2007); both data sets downloaded and analyzed from the Inter-consortium for Political and Social Research.

---

2. Other races/ethnicities made up less than four percent of the juvenile population, so we did not include them in the figure.

of color, namely Black and Hispanic. White youth comprised the remaining 20.8% (or 532) of the state prison juvenile population.

The racial/ethnic disparities for local jails is equally (if not more) alarming, given the larger population. There were more than four times the number of youth confined in local jails in 2002 as compared to state prisons. In total, 10,849 juveniles were in local jails. The racial/ethnic breakdown was somewhat similar to prisons. Black youth still made up the largest percentage of jail inmates (56.6% or 6,137), followed by Whites (26.2% or 2,841), and then Hispanics (17.2% or 1,871).

These numbers are fairly disturbing because, combined, Blacks make up 55% of the juvenile population in adult correctional institutions, followed by Whites at 25.2%, and then Hispanics at 19.8%. However, in looking at the U.S. juvenile population during the time, Blacks and Hispanics made up approximately 15% each, while Whites made up approximately 64%. Whites are highly under-represented among the incarcerated juvenile population, while Blacks were severely over-represented. Hispanics were also over-represented, but not to the same degree as Black youth. While legal factors such as offense seriousness and prior record may explain some of this disparity, it should be noted that these are very stark differences that likely cannot be fully explained by Blacks and Hispanics committing more serious offenses.

Implications of Racial Effects in Juvenile Waivers

There are multiple implications regarding minority youth having a disproportionately higher likelihood of being represented among the transferred population, in addition to experiencing negative consequences once in the adult system. First, research has demonstrated that transferred youth are more likely to be victimized while confined in adult facilities (Beck & Harrison, 2008). The victimization they face, both physical and sexual, is at higher rates than their counterparts in juvenile facilities.

Transferred youth also have an increased probability of recidivism (Fagan, 1995; Bishop, Frazier, Lanza-Kaduce, & Winner 1996, Winner, Lanza-Kaduce, Bishop, & Frazier 1997; Podkopacz & Feld, 1996; Myers, 2003; Lanza-Kaduce Lane, Bishop, & Frazier 2005). Not only are transferred youth more likely to recidivate, but they do so more quickly than non-transferred youth and tend to commit more serious offenses. Therefore, waiving youth to the adult system appears to have the opposite effect of deterrence, since these youth are more likely to commit subsequent offenses and tend to commit more offenses after adult court punishment.

Therefore, because minority youth are more likely to be waived to the adult system and get more severe punishments, they have a greater likelihood of physical victimization, sexual victimization, and recidivism. All of these factors also increase the probability of subsequent violence and continuing further contact with the criminal justice system. Given most states have "once an adult, always an adult" provisions for waived juvenile offenders, meaning that all additional crimes committed by the juvenile will automatically be processed through the adult court instead of the juvenile court, any subsequent illegal infraction by these youth will result in additional criminal court procedures and punishments.

Theoretical Explanations to Explain Race/Ethnicity and Juvenile Transfer

Multiple theories can be used to explain the influence of race/ethnicity on juvenile transfer to criminal court.[3] One theory often used is focal concerns theory, which is applied to judicial decision-making. According to this theory, sentencing is influenced by three factors: 1) offender's blameworthiness, 2) protection of the community, and 3) practical constraints and consequences (Steffensmeier, Kramer & Streifel, 1993; Steffensmeier, Ulmer & Kramer, 1998; Johnson, Ulmer & Kramer, 2008). Given the disproportionate number of Black and Hispanic youth who are arrested, it is likely that these groups enter the juvenile court system (prior to judicial waiver hearing) with a perceived increased culpability for the offense. After adding the likely serious nature of the offense to a stigma of "criminality" based on race, the first criterion is met.

This results in a self-fulfilling prophecy, in which the prediction itself causes the outcome to be true. Transferred youth are more likely to recidivate. Given that Blacks and Hispanics are disproportionately more likely to be among the waived population, it is logical that those racial/ethnic groups are inadvertently then more likely to re-offend. Therefore, judges may feel as though they have to protect the community from these groups.

Finally, judges must consider practical constraints, such as community resources, parental supervision, ability to afford and/or attend treatment programs. Blacks and Hispanics have a larger likelihood of being in impoverished areas, resulting in fewer economic resources and social capital. According to

---

3. For a broader discussion of these theories, see Chapter 3.

the 2010 U.S. Census, 38% of Black children live in poverty, 35% of Hispanic children, and 12% of White children. Again, given the few resources available to these youth and families, judges may feel as though the "community" is not a proper place for these youth. Due to all of these issues, Blacks and Hispanics are likely to experience harsher outcomes, both in the transfer decision and sentencing once convicted.

A second theory that can help explain the racial/ethnic effect in juvenile transfer is attribution theory. Applying the theory directly to juvenile waiver, it focuses on causal reasons why crimes took place (Albonetti, 1991; Bridges & Steen, 1998; Rodriguez, 2013). More specifically, when judges are attributing perceived causes of behavior among these serious offenders, the factors are usually defined as either internal or external. Internal factors are those assumed to be within the individual, while external factors are environmental influences (e.g., schools, neighborhood, etc.). Perceived internal factors increase sentence severity, while perceived external factors decrease sentence severity.

When attributing "causes" of criminality, it opens to door for perceptions, true or false. If attribution theory is correct, according to Force (2008), "African American defendants in criminal trials are not being discriminated against solely on the basis of the color of their skin, but also on an assumption of social class that jurors associate with skin color" (pp. 7–8). Therefore, attribution theory presumes that social class carries a certain stigma that increases the perceived internal factors that are associated with criminality. Given that our nation's laws carry heavier sentences for "street-crimes" than "elite-crimes," and due to Black and Hispanic youth being over-represented in the lower socioeconomic status, those groups are more likely to be punished more harshly. In other words, the criminality by Blacks and Hispanics (via social class) may be thought to be caused by internal factors, thus increasing the likelihood of transfer to criminal court and tougher sanctions when convicted. Conversely, the criminality of White youth is viewed to be caused by external factors, resulting in a lower likelihood of waiver and less severe sanctions.

Conclusion

Juvenile transfer to adult court has received a significant amount of empirical attention, but the race and ethnic components have not generally garnered as much focus. From the work that has been done and the data from national statistics, Black and Hispanic juveniles have suffered in the transfer decision. Although the latest figures from judicial waivers suggest some DMC, those numbers are greatly exemplified once one considers the current incarcerated population based on racial/ethnic make-up. The judicial waivers results in some disproportionate minority contact, but it does not explain the number presented.

One explanation to help understand the numbers is that most states made transferring juveniles easier as a result of the "super predator" fear from the mid-1980s to mid-1990s. As a result of this moral panic, states expanded juvenile waiver laws and gave more authority to prosecutors in determining the court jurisdiction to prosecute the youth. Through this mechanism, based on focal concern and attribution theories, Black and Hispanic youth were likely perceived as more dangerous and ultimately waived to the adult system.

Although the body of knowledge is not fully developed at this time, the impact of race and ethnicity in this process cannot be ignored. Some research finds a race effect, while other research finds no effect. However, if taken in context of other factors which are associated with these sentencing outcomes (e.g., social class, offense severity, prior record), an argument can be made that the impact of race/ethnicity is either direct or indirect through these other elements. Regardless, it is clear that race and ethnicity are operating in some form in the decision to transfer these youth, and ultimately, in the sentence that is received once convicted.

Discussion Questions

1. Which explanation best describes the overrepresentation of Blacks in the number of juveniles who are transferred to adult court?
2. What role may direct file and legislative waiver play in the overrepresentation of Blacks and Hispanics among transferred youth?
3. What can be done to reduce the number of Blacks and Hispanics who are transferred to the adult criminal justice system?

References

Albonetti, C.A. (1991). An integration of theories to explain judicial discretion. *Social Problems, 38*, 247–266.

Beck, A. & Harrison, P.M. (2008). Sexual victimization in state and federal prisons reported by inmates, 2007. Washington, DC: U.S. Department of Justice, Office of Justice Programs, Bureau of Justice Statistics.

Bernard, T.J. & Kurlychek, M.C. (2010). The cycle of juvenile justice (2nd ed.). New York, NY: Oxford University Press.

Bishop, D.M., Frazier, C.E., Lanza-Kaduce, L. & Winner, L. (1996). The transfer of juveniles to criminal court: Does it make a difference? *Crime and Delinquency, 42*, 171–191.

Bridges, G.S. & Steen, S. (1998). Racial disparities in official assessments of juvenile offenders: Attributional stereotypes as mediating mechanisms. *American Sociological Review, 63*, 554–570.

Clement, M.J. (1997). A five-year study of juvenile waiver and adult sentences: Implications for policy. *Criminal Justice Policy Review, 8*(2/3), 201–219.

DiIulio, J.J. (1995). The coming of the super-predators. *The Weekly Standard, 1*, 23–28.

Fagan, J. (1995). Separating the Men From the Boys: The comparative advantage of juvenile versus criminal court sanctions on recidivism among adolescent felony offenders. In J. C. Howell, B. Krisberg, J. D. Hawkins & J.J. Wilson, *A sourcebook: Serious, violent, and chronic juvenile offenders* (pp. 238–260). Thousand Oaks, CA: SAGE.

Fagan, J. & Deschenes, E.P. (1990). Determinants of judicial waiver decisions for violent juvenile offenders. *Journal of Criminal Law and Criminology, 81*(2), 314–347.

Fagan, J., Forst, M. & Vivona, T.S. (1987). Racial determinants of the judicial transfer decision: Prosecuting violent youth in criminal court. *Crime & Delinquency, 33*(2), 259–286.

Force, N. (2008). Factors influencing juror sentencing decisions: Race, social economic status, attorney credibility and the relevance of stereotype attribution theory. Boca Raton, FL: University Publishers.

Howell, R.J. & Hutto, T.S. (2012). Sentencing convicted juvenile felony offenders in the adult court: The direct effects of race. *Behavioral Sciences and the Law,30*(6), 782–799.

Johnson, B., Ulmer, J.T. & Kramer, J. (2008). The social context of guideline circumvention: The case of federal district courts. *Criminology, 46*, 737–783.

Jordan, K.L. (2006). *Violent youth in adult court; The decertification of transferred offender.* New York: LFB Scholarly.

Jordan, K.L. (2014). Juvenile status and sentencing: Does it matter in the adult system? *Youth Violence and Juvenile Justice, 12*, 315–331.

Jordan, K.L. & Freiburger, T.L. (2010). Examining the impact of race and ethnicity on the sentencing of juveniles in the adult court. *Criminal Justice Policy Review, 21*(2), 185–201.

Jordan, K.L. & Myers, D.L. (2007). The decertification of transferred youth: Examining the determinants of reverse waiver. *Youth Violence and Juvenile Justice*, 188–206.

Jordan, K.L. & Myers, D.L. (2011). Juvenile transfer and deterrence: Re-examining the effectiveness of a 'get tough' policy. *Crime and Delinquency*, 57, 247–270.

Keiter, R.B. (1973). Criminal or delinquent? A study of juvenile cases transferred to the criminal court. *Crime & Delinquency*, 19, 528–538.

Kupchik, A. (2006). The decision to incarcerate in juvenile and criminal courts. Criminal Justice Review, 31, 309–336.

Kurlycheck, M.C. & Johnson, B.D. (2010). Juvenility and punishment: Sentencing juveniles in adult criminal court. *Criminology*, 48, 725–758.

Kurlychek, M.C. & Johnson, B.D. (2004). The juvenile penalty: A comparison of juvenile and young adult sentencing outcomes in criminal court. *Criminology*, 42, 485–517.

Lanza-Kaduce, L., Lane, J., Bishop, D.M. & Frazier, C.E. (2005). Juvenile offenders and adult felony recidivism: The impact of transfer. Journal of Crime and Justice, 28, 59–77.

Lemmon, J.H., Austin, T.L., Verrecchia, P.J. & Fetzer, M. (2005). The effect of legal and extralegal factors on statutory exclusion of juvenile offenders. *Youth Violence and Juvenile Justice*, 3, 214–234.

Myers, D.L. (2001). *Excluding violent youths from juvenile court: The effectiveness of legislative waiver*. New York: LFB Scholarly Publishing.

Myers, D. (2003). The recidivism of violent youths in juvenile and adult court: A consideration of selection bias. *Youth Violence and Juvenile Justice*, 1, 79–101.

Myers, D.L. (2005). *Boys among men: Trying and sentencing juveniles as adults*. Westport, CT: Praeger.

Podkopacz, M.R. & Feld, B.C. (1996). The end of the line: An empirical study of judicial waiver. *Journal of Criminal Law and Criminology*, 86(2), 449–492.

Poulos, T.M. & Orchowsky, S. (1994). Serious juvenile offenders: Predicting the probability of transfer to criminal court. *Crime & Delinquency*, 40(1), 3–17.

Puzzanchera, C. and Hockenberry, S. (2015). National Disproportionate Minority Contact Databook. *Developed by the National Center for Juvenile Justice for the Office of Juvenile Justice and Delinquency Prevention. Online.* Available:http://www.ojjdp.gov/ojstatbb/dmcdb/.

Rodriguez, N. (2013). Concentrated disadvantage and the incarceration of youth: Examining how context affects juvenile justice. *Journal of Research in Crime and Delinquency*, 50, 189–215.

Steffensmeier, D., Kramer, J. & Streifel, C. (1993). Gender and imprisonment decisions. *Criminology, 31*, 411–446.

Steffensmeier, D., Ulmer, J. & Kramer, J. (1998). The interaction of race, gender, and age in criminal sentencing: The punishment of being young, Black, and male. *Criminology, 36*, 763–797.

Steiner, B. (2005). Predicting sentencing outcomes and time served for juveniles transferred to criminal court in a rural northwestern state. *Journal of Criminal Justice, 33*, 601–610.

Thomas, C.W. & Bilchik, S. (1985). Prosecuting juveniles in criminal courts: A legal and empirical analysis. *Journal of Criminal Law and Criminology, 76*(2), 439–479.

U.S. Department of Justice. Bureau of Justice Statistics. (2003). Juvenile Defendants in Criminal Courts (JDCC): Survey of 40 Counties in the United States, 1998. ICPSR03750-vl. Ann Arbor, MI: Inter-university Consortium for Political and Social Research.

U.S. Department of Justice. Bureau of Justice Statistics. (2007). Survey of Inmates in State and Federal Correctional Facilities, 2004. ICPSR04572-v2. Ann Arbor, MI: Inter-university Consortium for Political and Social Research.

U.S. Department of Justice. Office of Justice Programs. Bureau of Justice Statistics. (2012). Survey of Inmates in Local Jails, 2002. ICPSR04359-v2. Ann Arbor, MI: Inter-university Consortium for Political and Social Research [distributor], 2012-08-22.

Winner, L., Lanza-Kaduce, L., Bishop, D.M. & Frazier, C.E. (1997). The transfer of juveniles to criminal court: Reexamining recidivism over the long term. Crime and Delinquency, 43, 548–563.

Chapter 9

Girls in the Juvenile Justice System

Goals of the Chapter

The purpose of this chapter is to examine racial and ethnic issues relating to female juvenile delinquents. This chapter first provides an overview of girls' arrests statistics and risk factors for delinquency. Next, the intersectionality perspective is explained as well as differences in the offending patterns of girls and boys. How gender affects the arrest and juvenile court processing decisions for girls of different races and ethnicities is also discussed. The chapter concludes with a discussion of the program and treatment needs of girls.

After reading this chapter, you will be able to do the following:

1. Understand the risks factors associated with girls' offending and how these are similar and different from boys;
2. Demonstrate an understanding of the intersectionality perspective;
3. Critically assess the empirical literature on the effect that race and ethnicity have on the processing of girls; and
4. Understand the unique treatment and program needs of girls.

Relative to boys, girls commit fewer acts of delinquency. In fact, girls only account for about 29% of the total juveniles arrested (Zahn, Day, Mihalics & Tichavsky 2010). The underrepresentation of girls in juvenile offending is found across most types of offenses. According to the Office of Juvenile Justice and Delinquency Prevention, the rate of juvenile arrests for violent index one crimes was four times greater for boys than for girls in 2012. For property crimes, males' rates were double those of females. Females comprised especially small portions of arrests for the most serious violent offenses, accounting for only 9% of murders, 2% of rapes and 20% of robberies in 2012 (OJJDP, n.d.). Among violent offenses, girls were most represented in simple (35%) and aggravated assaults (25%) (Zahn et al., 2008). Females, however, made up over half (55%) of all juveniles arrested for running away (OJJDP, n.d.).

Comparisons of male and female delinquents find that they both face similar risks factors that lead them into the juvenile justice system. According to a report by the Office of Juvenile Justice and Delinquency Prevention, delinquents often come from families with poor and inconsistent parenting and families with parental deviance. They also tend to have deviant peers, be from disadvantaged schools and communities, and lack involvement in prosocial activities (e.g., participation in school activites). Girls and boys who engage in delinquent behaviors also have higher rates of experiencing physical abuse than their non-offending counterparts, with male and female delinquents experiencing physical abuse at approximately the same rate (Lederman, Dakof, Larrea & Li, 2004; Shelton, 2004; Wood, Foy, Goguen, Pyoos & James, 2002).

Despite these similarities, boys and girls differ in some important ways. When examining sexual abuse, research finds that girls are more likely than boys to experience sexual abuse and rape (Hennessey, Ford, Mahoney, Ko & Siegfried, 2004; Smith, Leve & Chamberlain, 2006; Snyder, 2000), with some studies reporting rates of sexual abuse among detained girls as high as 72% (Zahn et al., 2010). This is especially problematic as histories of sexual abuse are strongly linked to future engagement in criminal activities (Widom, 1995; Widom & Maxfield, 2001) and aggressive behaviors (Swanston, Parkinson, O'Tool, Plunkett, Shrimpton & Oats, 2003). Research conducted by Conrad, Tolou-Shams, Rizzo, Placella, and Brown (2014) confirmed that histories of abuse impacted girls more than boys in their sample of juveniles from the Northeast. Their research found that, for girls, histories of childhood sexual abuse led to a greater likelihood of recidivating. In fact, girls who had histories of childhood sexual abuse were five times more likely to recidivate during the 12 month follow-up period than girls who did not have histories of childhood sexual abuse. For boys, past histories of childhood sexual abuse did not significantly impact their likelihood of recidivating.

Research also finds that many girls who are chronic runaways have experienced sexual and physical abuse in the past. For these girls, running away can be an escape from the abuse, and signify more serious problems than their minor criminal behavior suggests (Feitel, Margetson, Chamas & Lipman, 1992; Welsh, Archambault, Janus & Brown, 1995). Moore (1991) found that victimizations that happens within the family can lead girls to join a gang for protection after running away from home. This ends up being a catch twenty-two; however, as the gangs save girls from being victimized at home but make girls more vulnerable to being victimized as they enter into a risky lifestyle. In fact, researchers have documented that girls in gangs have a high risk of being sexually victimized by boyfriends and male peers (Miller, 2001; Moore, 1991; Valdz, 2007). These victimizations can further lead to mental health issues and posttraumatic stress disorder. In fact, incarcerated girls have been found to be 50% more likely to be suffering from posttraumatic stress disorder than boys (Hennesse, Ford, Mahoney, Ku, & Seigfried, 2004). Other mental health problems are also more common among girls than among boys. Kirkpatrick and Saunders (2009) found that among high school students 36.3% of females and 25.1% of males suffered from depression and 17.5% of females compared to 9.7% of males considered suicide.

In addition to different risks factors, there is also evidence that boys and girls might differ in the way that they respond to the juvenile justice system. Labeling theory argues that bringing juveniles into the system and formally handling their behaviors could actually produce the very behavior the system is intended to prevent. This perspective distinguishes between delinquent behavior that juveniles engage in before entering into the system, which is referred to as primary deviance, and the delinquent behavior juveniles engage in after entering the system, referred to as secondary deviance. It further stipulates that once primary deviance is labeled as delinquent, it can actually cause secondary deviance, if the juvenile associates with the deviant label and considers himself or herself a juvenile delinquent (Lemert, 1972). According to Braithwaite (1989), this is more likely to occur if the juvenile experiences "stigmatized" shaming versus "reintegrative" shaming. Stigmatized shaming rejects the juvenile's actions and condemns the juvenile while reintegrative shaming only condemns the delinquent act and not the juvenile. If juveniles are stigmatized by the system, their involvement in the system will actually increase the likelihood that they will engage in subsequent delinquent activities. Punishment that is reintegrative, on the other hand, will not lead to future criminal involvement (i.e., secondary deviance).

McGrath (2010) examined the possibility that girls are differently affected by stigmatization than boys. His findings indicated that for girls, feeling more stigmatized increased the likelihood that they would be arrested for a subsequent offense. Stigmatization did not have the same effect on boys. Boys who felt more stigmatized were not more likely to offend. In fact, for boys who had more extensive criminal histories, stigmatization was actually associated with a decreased likelihood of offending. McGrath (2010) speculated that girls might be more affected by stigmatization because they are subjected to greater pressures to conform than boys or because girls might be more emotionally acute than boys.

Case Study: Violent Girls

In the summer of 2009, a 13-year-old girl was arrested for stabbing her 48-year-old step-grandfather in Milwaukee, Wisconsin. The two had gotten in an argument over milk. The man had poured enough milk for the baby in the house and then poured the rest down the sink even though he knew that the 13-year-old wanted it for her cereal. According to the girl's reports, the two argued and the step-grandfather began to strangle her. In response, the girl grabbed a paring knife and stabbed her step-grandfather in the neck. The man died. Although the case began in the adult court, a judge moved the case back to the juvenile court. If processed in the adult court, the girl would have been sentenced to a mandatory life sentence. Because she was processed through the juvenile court, however, she was sentenced to a minimum of one year in detention and a maximum of 12 years detention, or until she reaches the age of 25.

Similar to other cases in which girls engage in extreme acts of violence, the girl in this case had familial problems in the past. According to reports, county officials were involved in other incidences that occurred at the house. Neighbors also reported that the girl had a lot of problems and had not received the help that she needed (Girl, 13, Stabbed Grandfather, 2011 March 9; Associate Press, 2011 March 8).

Race, Ethnicity, Gender and Juvenile Offending

When examining the treatment of girls in the juvenile justice system, considering gender alone is not enough to fully understand the experiences of girls. It is important to consider the intersection of gender with race and ethnicity. The intersectionality perspective identifies certain groups as being more socially advantaged than others. For gender, males are considered more socially advantaged than females. For race and ethnicity, Whites are considered more socially advantaged than Blacks and Hispanics. White males hold a position of advantage in both areas, while White females hold a position of advantage in race but a position of disadvantage in gender. Black and Hispanic males are advantaged in gender but disadvantaged in race, and Black and Hispanic females suffer social disadvantage in both gender and race. Social position is further influenced by economic class. Those in the lower economic classes are more disadvantaged than those in the middle and upper classes. Economic class also has an effect on a person's social position depending on their race, ethnicity and gender. Again, White males of middle or upper class are considered the most advantaged and minority women of lower economic classes are considered to be the most disadvantaged. For each of these groups, girls' roles and expectations in the family also vary. Even within racial and ethnic groups the expectation of girls can be different in different social classes.

As the intersectionality perspective suggests, gender does not have the same meaning for all girls. Thinking that all girls' experiences are the same is called essentialism. Essentialism simplifies the experiences of all girls into one common experience that is often only truly representative of a White middle-class female (Hurtado, 1989; Spelman, 1988). The intersectional framework recognizes that girls' experiences will vary by their race and ethnicity and that being female can have different meanings for girls of different races and ethnicities. Instead of clumping all girls' experiences together, it recognizes that the experiences of White girls will be different than the experiences of Black girls and Hispanic girls, and what it means to be a girl will be different for White girls, Black girls, and Hispanic girls.

Along with the intersectionality perspective, the stereotypical images of girls have been found to vary for girls of different races and ethnicities. White girls are typically viewed as being more passive, nonthreatening, and responsive to rehabilitation (Franklin & Fearn, 2008; Gaarder, Rodriguez & Zatz, 2004). Black girls are stereotyped as being more independent, aggressive, crime-prone, and less feminine. They are also considered to be rude, pushy, and loud. Hispanic women are often stereotyped as sexually subordinate to males and family-oriented.

Gaarder et al. (2004) examined the attitudes of juvenile probation officers, psychologists and other individuals in the juvenile court to assess the views that these practitioners had of juvenile girls in the courts. Gaarder et al.'s data were derived from delinquent girls' case files and included narrative reports written by probation officers about the girls, psychological reports of the girls, narrative information about the girls' family members, and the treatment recommendations made by the probation officers. In addition to these data, they conducted fourteen interviews with juvenile probation officers. The researchers found that a gap existed in court officials' views of girls and the realities of the girls' lives. They also found that the treatment programs recommended for girls were often inadequate to meet the actual needs of the girls. For example, many court officials documented issues associated with pregnancy and being a young mother; however, they rarely recommended treatment programs to help the girls deal with these issues.

The girls were often perceived as whiners, liars and manipulators who were promiscuous. Although many of the probation officers believed that most of the girls were victims of abuse, they also believed that the girls often fabricated reports of abuse. The probation officers did not recognize the tie between manipulative behaviors and histories of abuse. Instead, they viewed them as two separate and unrelated issues. Therefore, treatment programs were not recommended to address these issues.

The officers also reported girls as difficult to work with because they had too many issues and were too needy. One probation officer interviewed reported that he groaned whenever a girl was placed on his caseload. Views of the girls' families were also littered with negative images. The officers often described the girls' mothers as sluts or commented on their clothing, appearance, and poor parenting skills. Similar comments were never made about the girls' fathers. Most of the girls and their families were also living in poverty. For Hispanic girls, problems also stemmed from probation officers inability to communicate with many of the girls' family members due to those family members not speaking English.

Given the different expectations and stereotypes placed on girls and boys of different races and ethnicities, it is important to consider the possibility that the offending patterns of boys and girls might also vary by their race and ethnicities. Simpson and Elis (1995) examined the offending patterns of boys and girls using the National Longitudinal Survey of Youth to identify whether various factors such as parental attitudes, parental influence, peer influence, peer aspirations, juveniles' attitudes and experiences with education, and the characteristics of the schools the juveniles attended, had different effects on the frequency at which Black and White boys and girls engage in property and violent offenses. Their findings suggested that stronger parental influence reduced violent offending for Black boys. They also found that White boys were more strongly influenced by peers than Black boys. For property offenses, peers influenced White girls more than Black girls. Low peer aspirations measured as to whether their peers planned to finish high school and attend college, increased offending for White girls and Black and White boys. School environment also had a greater effect on girls than boys. Overall, this research indicates that factors do differently affect the likelihood of a juvenile engaging in delinquent behavior. It should not be assumed, therefore, that addressing the same risks factors for boys and girls of different races and ethnicities will have the same preventive effect for all juvenile groups.

Juvenile Girls in Gangs

Gang involvement is an important aspect of juvenile delinquency, as gang-involved youth tend to have higher rates of offending. In fact, research has found that 90% of male and female gang members have engaged in a violent act within the past year (Esbensen, Peterson, Taylor & Freng, 2010). Membership in gangs is largely considered to be an issue with boys. In fact, research and policing responses to gangs often ignores girls. Law enforcement commonly considers girls to be "accessories" or "appendages" to male gang activity (Curry & Decker, 1998). This is likely due to the fact that many sources show that the majority of gang members are male. The 1996 National Youth Gang Survey indicated that only about 10% of gang members were female. In 2010 that estimate was even lower, with the National Gang Center reporting that only about 7.4% of gang members were female (National Youth Gang Center, 2000).

Percentages of female gang involvement are higher, however, when examining self-report data. Examination of the Denver Youth Survey found that females made up between 20% and 46% of gang members (Esbensen & Huizinga, 1993; Esbensen, Huizinga & Weiher, 1993). Research by Pyrooz (2014) found that in self-report studies girls made up about 30% of gang members who were age 13. For gang members age 20, girls made up about 13%, indicating that girls are more involved in gangs when they are young and tend to drift out of the gang as they get older. Ebensen and Carson (2012) examined data from the second National Evaluation of the Gang Resistance Education and Training (G.R.E.A.T.) program. G.R.E.A.T. is a school-based gang prevention program facilitated by law enforcement. The program is intended to prevent youths from joining gangs and from engaging in delinquent behavior. The data used by Ebensen and Carson was collected as part of a larger evaluation of the G.R.E.A.T. program. They included the data from seven major cities in the United States. Similar to Pyrooz (2014), they concluded that girls tended to be more involved in gangs when they were younger than when they got older, with females comprising 45% of gang members at age 11.5 and 31% at age 15.5. One reason that girls tended to leave gangs as they get older was pregnancy. Fleisher and Krienert (2004) studied 74 female gang members in an all-Black neighborhood with high levels of poverty and disorder located in Champaign, Illinois, and also found that girls' gang activities decreased once they become pregnant and had children.

Despite their small numbers, research has found that gang-involved girls engage in five times more criminal activities than non-gang-involved boys. In addition, girls involved with gangs are found to engage in criminal activities at about the same rate as gang-involved boys (Ebensen & Carson, 2012; Fleisher & Krienert, 2004). Ebensen et al. (2010) also found that 75% of girls reported being involved with gang fights and 37% reported that they had attacked someone with a weapon. Therefore, while girls make up a minority of gang members, research indicates that the girls who are involved with gangs engage in a significant amount of violent and criminal behavior.

To determine the best response to gang activity, it is important to examine whether different factors lead girls and boys to join gangs. If the same factors are associated with boys and girls' gang activities, then programs aimed at gang prevention can be the same for boys and girls. If these factors are different, however, than programs should be "gender-specific" so they meet the needs of girls and boys. Furthermore, it is important to determine whether factors differ by race and ethnicity in order to determine if programming should be racial and ethnic specific in addition to being gender specific.

Walker-Barnes and Mason (2001) examined the factors that led girls to join gangs. Their study involved interviews with 26 African American, two Jamaican American, and three Hispanic girls from an alternative school located in a high crime urban neighborhood. All the girls interviewed were considered to be high risks for becoming involved with gangs. During the interviews, the girls were presented with four broad categories that contained risk factors for gang involvement. The four categories were family, neighborhood, friends, and self. When presented with these categories, the girls were asked to choose the category that they felt had the strongest influence on female gang involvement and to list additional specific reasons, related to that category, as to why a girl would join a gang. The girls were also asked by the interviewer to consider the importance of several additional predetermined specific factors. For each specific factor (both those presented by the girls and by the researchers), the girls were then asked to rate each from 0 to 4, with 0 representing "doesn't matter" and 4 representing "matters a lot." Overall the girls ranked all the specific factors and the four broad categories. They also provided qualitative insight into why they believed each factor mattered or did not matter. The girls were also asked to rate these items for why boys join gangs so the researchers could determine whether the reasons for joining a gang differed for boys and girls.

The results of their study indicated that the most influential factor in African American and Hispanic girls' decisions to join gangs was friends. The other factors in order of importance were neighborhoods, family, and self. Many of the girls believed that girls join gangs in an effort to keep their friendships, in response to peer pressure, and as a way to fit in. The girls also viewed the excitement a gang provided and the opportunity to make money as important factors that caused girls to join gangs. In the neighborhood category, exposure to violence was considered to have the strongest impact on a girl's likelihood to join a gang. Being exposed to violence in their neighborhoods desensitized girls and provided them with behavior to mimic. Safety was also rated as an influential factor, as being in a gang provided girls with protection from being victimized in their neighborhoods. For family, the girls identified the lack of parental concern and involvement in girls' lives, fighting and arguing in the family, and the absence of a father to be causes of gang involvement. In regards to self, the girls indicated that this influenced gang involvement by making girls feel important and feared among their peers, which translated into respect.

Walker-Barnes and Mason (2001) further found that the factors that mattered for girls also mattered for boys. For the four broad categories (friends, neighborhoods, family, and self), there were no significant differences in the way the girls rated these factors for boys and girls. Using a nationally representative sample, Bell (2009) similarly found few differences in the factors that affected girls and boys likelihood of being involved with gangs. He found that parental social control, attachment and involvement to conventional activities and individuals, school safety, peer fighting, age, and race had similar influences on male and female gang behaviors.

Other researchers, however, have found important differences in male and female gang members. Campbell (1991) found that female gang members came from more disadvantaged backgrounds than male gang members. She also found that female gang members were more likely to come from broken and unemployed homes, and have a history of family violence and parental drug use. Fleisher and Krienert (2004) similarly found that most of the girls they studied had experienced a childhood victimization, had come from single-family households without a father present, had parents who had been arrested and incarcerated in the past, and had parents who used drugs and alcohol.

Case Study: Female Gang Members

According to Moore and Hagedorn (2001) most female gang members are African American or Latina. Females' roles in gangs appear to vary by race and ethnicity. Research suggests that African American female gang members are more frequently equal to male gang members and engage in similar criminal activities as the males (Brown, 1977; Fishman, 1998; Taylor, 1993). Latina females, on the other hand, are more often found to be auxilliaries to male gangs (Moore & Hagedorn, 2001). Latina female gang members, refered to as "cholas," have generated the most public attention and research. Cholas are girls who are members of a Mexican gang subculture located in Los Angeles. Most of these girls are girlfriends or sisters of male gang members. The attention given to cholas has largely centered around their physical appearance. They dress in white tank tops or flannel shirts, men's Dickie pants, and sneakers. They often wear gold jewelry with crosses and other religious symbols. Their makeup is also a trademark, with penciled-in eyebrows, dark lined lips with lighter lipstick, and brightly painted fingernails. Cholas are also characterized by their gelled or moussed "crunchy" hairstyles, high bangs, and high ponytails. Their look has been copied by several famous celebrities such as Sandra Bullock, Gwen Stefani, and Selena Gomez.

While the rates of violence among girl gang members are noteworthy, other scholars argue that violent girls are still rare. Chesney-Lind and Irwin (2008) warn that the violent female gang member is largely a fragment of 1990s media hype. While the face of the female gang member presented by the media is a Black or Hispanic girl who is equally as violent as her male gang member counterpart, Chesney-Lind and Irwin (2008) argue that female gang members are often the victims of violence at the hands of male gang members and often do not have the same lucrative criminal opportunities available to them that are available to male gang members.

Case Study: Slender Man Case

Other rare cases of girls committing acts of violence have generated large amounts of media attention. During the summer of 2014, a pair of 12-year-old girls were arrested in Waukesha, Wisconsin, a suburb fewer than 20 miles west of Milwaukee. The girls were arrested for allegedly attempting to murder their friend, another 12-year-old girl. They had stabbed their friend 19 times, coming less than a millimeter away from a major artery in the girl's heart.

During police questioning, the girls claimed they had tried to kill their friend to please Slender Man, a fictional character from the Internet who is believed to lurk in the background and to murder children. The girls reported that they believed that if they killed their friend, Slender Man would take them to live with him in his mansion in the woods.

In Wisconsin, first degree attempted murder cases are automatically filed under the jurisdiction of the adult court when the perpetrator is age 10 or older. Although the girls' attorneys requested that the court move the case to juvenile court, a judge ruled that the case would remain in the adult court. The girls now face a possible sentence of 65 years (Sanchick & Searns, 2015 March 13).

Several aspects of this case have sparked national attention. This attention has led many to conclude that these types of cases, in which young girls commit extreme acts of violence, are becoming increasingly common. This is not the case, and it is important to remember that these types of cases are extremely rare, especially those that involve perpetrators without familial problems and from communities that are not socially and economically disadvantaged.

Changing Rates of Girls and Delinquency

While the number of boys who engage in criminal behavior is still larger than the number of girls, the gap between juvenile boys' and girls' violent offending appears to be narrowing. While violent offenses committed by juveniles have decreased overall, the number of girls being arrested for these offenses has either increased or decreased at a lower rate than boys (Zahn et al., 2008). For all crimes, male rates of arrest have decreased by 35%; for females, rates have only decreased by 32% (OJJDP, n.d.). From 1996 to 2005, the number of boys arrested for aggregated assault decreased 28%, while the rate for girls only decreased by 5%. For simple assault, girls experienced a 24% increase while boys experienced a decrease (Zahn et al., 2008). Rates at which girls are being brought into the juvenile court show similar patterns. In 2009, 30% of the 1.5 million cases in the juvenile courts involved girls. Over the past 25 years, the number of cases in the juvenile courts involving girls has increased 86%, while the number of cases involving boys has only increased 17% (Puzzanchera, Adams & Hockenberry, 2012).

Two theoretical explanations can explain changes in arrest rates. The first is normative theory. This theoretical explanation argues that increases in arrests are the product of an increase in criminal behavior. Under this explanation, girls are being arrested more often because they are committing more crimes. The constructionist theory, on the other hand, asserts that arrests rates can increase due to a change in the way criminal justice decision makers handle certain criminal behavior (Rosenfeld, 2007). Under this explanation, the increase in girls' arrest rates is due to a change in the handling of girls' criminal behavior. Specifically, the increased tendency to treat minor offenses more formally in the juvenile justice system, may have led to an increase in girls being arrested and processed through the system. According to Feld (2009), the increase in simple and aggravated assaults is partially due to girls' greater likelihood of committing acts of violence against family members instead of an acquaintance or a stranger. Specifically, the new "get tough" stance on domestic violence and in-school violence cases has led to girls being arrested for assault instead of being processed as status offenders as had been the practice in the past.

These two divergent explanations have led to research examining the reason for the narrowing of the gender gap for juvenile offending. Steffensmeier, Schwartz, Zhong and Ackerman (2005) compared official data collected from Uniform Crime Reports (UCR) to the self-report data from the National Crime Victimization Survey, the Monitoring the Future data and the National Youth Risk Behavior Survey to determine whether this decrease is due to an increase in female offending rates or to changes in the official responses to girls' offending. Using trend analysis, they were able to examine the gender gap in offending for all four datasets. The UCR data examined whether changes had occurred over time in the arrest rates for males and females. Data from the National Crime Victimization Survey allowed the researchers to determine whether changes occurred in the rate at which victims reported being victimized by a male or female offender. Lastly, Monitoring the Future data and the National Youth Risk Behavior Survey data showed whether any changes occurred in the rate at which males and females self-reported criminal behavior.

The findings of their research indicated that when examining the Uniform Crime Reports data, the rate of females being arrested for violent crimes had increased. When examining the victimization survey data, however, there did not appear to be a change in the rate at which individuals reported being victimized by girls versus boys. Similarly, the self-report datasets did not show a change or a narrowing of the gender gap in the rate at which boys and girls self-reported criminal behavior. In fact, the National Youth Risk Behavior Survey indicated that females were actually becoming increasingly less violent than boys. Overall, therefore, their research indicated that while the rate in girls being arrested increased more than boys, female rates of offending were not increasing at a rate greater than that of males. Because the UCR is the only data examined that is influenced by criminal justice decision makers, their findings suggest that the rise in violent offenses committed by girls is likely due to police reclassifying female offenders who used to be considered status offenders as violent offenders, supporting the constructionist theory.

Additional research by Stevens, Morash and Chesney-Lind (2011) similarly examined whether girls were engaging in more criminal activity or if the treatment of girls in the system has led to the increase in girls being arrested. Unlike Steffensmeier et al.'s (2005) study that looked at aggregate rates of boys and girls offending and their arrests patterns, Stevens et al. examined individual level data to determine whether changes occurred in girls' likelihood of being convicted, charged and being placed (i.e., institutionalized) in 1980 than in 2000 relative to boys. They also examined whether assault cases were being handled differently in the two time periods.

Their findings indicated that the likelihood of girls entering the juvenile justice system was greater in 2000 than it was in 1980. In fact, girls were twice as likely to be charged with a crime in 2000 than in 1980. This increased likelihood was especially large for African American girls. In addition, girls who self-reported engagement in more acts of violence were more likely to be charged than girls in 1980. While increasing the number of past assaults led to sharp increases in the likelihood of being charged for girls in 2000, it made little difference for girls in 1980. In 2000, girls with a high number of previous assaults had a three-in-four chance of being charged, while girls in 1980 with a high number of previous assaults had a one in four chance of being charged. Again, this effect was greater for African American girls. African American girls with a high number of past assaults in 2000 were almost seven times more likely to be charged than their 1980 counterparts. For boys, only African American boys were more likely to be charged with a crime in 2000 than in 1980; White and Hispanic boys did not have significantly different likelihoods of being charged across the two time periods. When examining rates of conviction and placement, girls in 2000 did not have higher rates than girls in 1980.

Overall, their results also indicate that girls were not becoming more violent than they were in the past. Instead, the treatment of girls' criminal behavior has changed, with girls having a greater likelihood of being brought into the juvenile justice system than they had in the past. This was especially true for African American girls and girls who engaged in more acts of violence. It appears, therefore, that tolerance has decreased for girls who engage in criminal behavior with the least amount of tolerance prescribed to African American girls, and to girls with more extensive records of engaging in violent behavior. Again, the findings of this study support the constructionist theory. Given these results, it is important to consider the treatment of girls in the system to get a better understanding of the extent to which they are entering the juvenile justice system.

Girls and Arrests

Although girls are found to be more likely to have referrals from entities other than the police, such as parents, schools, and social service agencies (Chesney-Lind & Sheldon, 1998), the majority of juveniles entering the juvenile justice system do so through police contact (Puzzanchera, Adams & Hockenberry, 2012). How gender affects the decision to arrest has received little attention in research. An older study conducted by Chesney-Lind (1973) concluded that police had less tolerance for girls who engaged in minor offenses than boys who engaged in these same offenses. Girls who engaged in these behaviors were considered deviant and were being arrested for sexual activity, while these behaviors were tolerated among boys. Another early conducted by Visher (1983) is the most thorough and comprehensive examination of the effects of race and gender on arrest decisions. This study included the analysis of researcher observations of 785 police-suspect encounters in three cities (St. Louis, MO, Rochester, NY, and Tampa-St. Petersburg, FL). Of the 785 encounters, 142 involved a female suspect; 20% of the encounters with males resulted in an arrest and 16% of the encounters with females resulted in an arrest. Similar to Chesney-Lind (1973), Visher found that the race of girls impacted arrest decisions, and that race actually had a stronger impact in the decision to arrest girls than in the decision to arrest boys. Police officers held chivalrous attitudes toward White girls but not Black girls, resulting in more preferential treatment of White girls (Visher, 1983). In fact, Black girls were equally as likely to be arrested as White males. Age also impacted the likelihood of arrest for females, with younger girls having a greater likelihood of arrest than older females. Age did not have a significant impact on arrests for boys. For males, arrests decisions were more influenced by situational factors such as having a relationship with the victim, whether bystanders were present and whether the victim was a business establishment.

In a recent study, Strom, Warner, Tichavsky, and Zahn (2014) examined gender disparities in the decision to arrest girls and boys for acts of domestic violence. The authors used data from the Nation Incident Based Reporting System (NIBRS) from 2000 to 2004 to determine whether girls were more likely to be arrested in cases in which the most serious charge was aggravated assault, simple assault or intimidation in which a parent or caregiver was the victim. Of the qualifying offenses, 40% involved a female perpetrator. In almost 83%

of the incidences in which a girl was the offender, the victim was the girl's mother or grandmother. The boy's mother or grandmother was also the most common victim in cases with a male offender (67.49%), but was not as common as with female offenders. Cases involving girls were also more likely to have resulted in an injury than cases involving boys (42% versus 35.4%).

The rate at which girls and boys were arrested for these offenses were fairly similar (approximately 56% of girls arrested compared to 55% of boys), and no significant difference was found in the likelihood of girls and boys being arrested. The authors did find, however, that over the five years of data examined, the likelihood of arrest for girls increased at a rate greater than that of boys (about 22% versus 9%, respectively). This may indicate that the way police handle domestic violence cases with a female offender have changed, with police being more likely to arrest girls, and this may be part of the cause for the narrowing of the gender gap in arrests. For boys and girls, those who assaulted their mother or grandmother were more likely to be arrested than those who assaulted their father or grandfather. This is an important detail as girls assaulted their mothers and grandmothers more often than boys. Race did not affect the likelihood of arrest for girls; however, White boys were more likely than Black boys to be arrested.

Despite the limited amount of research on the treatment of girls during the decision to arrest, the research that has been conducted suggests that race and ethnicity might differently affect boys and girls. Although, it is not clear how it influences the decision to arrests girls. Earlier studies found that minority girls were more likely to be arrested than White girls, while a recent study on arrest decisions in domestic violence cases found no race effect. It is possible that these differences exists simply because of the time period examined. It might also be the case that the difference is due to the different setting in which arrests decisions were examined. Visher's (1983) examination included many street arrests for any offense, while Strom et al. (2014) limited their examination to arrests for acts of domestic violence. It is possible that race and ethnicity have a greater impact on arrest for other offenses, especially given the media attention devoted to minority gang members as dangerous.

Racial Issues and Girls in the Juvenile Court System

Regardless of the reason for more girls being arrested, more arrests of girls are leading to more girls entering into the juvenile court. In the juvenile court, girls are often more likely than boys to be handled formally and detained for minor offenses. As discussed in Chapter 6, there are several decision points in the juvenile court at which disparity can occur. Research on the treatment of girls and boys of different racial and ethnic backgrounds has focused on these various points.

Research by Freiburger and Burke (2010) examined the treatment of Black girls and boys, White girls and boys, Hispanic girls and boys, and Native American girls and boys in the juvenile court in Arizona on the decision to adjudicate juveniles. Their study indicated that Native American and Hispanic boys had the highest odds of adjudication. Hispanic and Native American girls were more likely to be adjudicated than Black and White girls. When comparing the treatment of all the groups of girls to White boys, Hispanic, Native American, and Black girls did not have significantly different odds of adjudication than White boys. White girls, however, were less likely than White boys to be adjudicated. Boys and girls were not treated significantly different within the other ethnic groups. Their results are similar to earlier findings from Bishop and Fraizer (1996), who found that White females were less likely to be detained than White boys, while non-White girls did not have significantly different likelihoods of being detained than their male counterparts. Cochran and Mears (2015) examined the treatment of juveniles in the Florida juvenile justice system and also found that White girls were the most likely to receive rehabilitative programming and the least likely to receive punitive punishments. Black boys, on the other hand, were the least likely to receive rehabilitative program and the most likely to receive punitive punishments.

Examining the several decision points in the juvenile court processing of boys and girls in the Iowa juvenile court, Leiber and Mack (2003) also found that Black girls and boys were not treated significantly different. Additionally, they found that Black girls and boys are often treated more harshly than their White counterparts. Their results differed from the previous works discussed, however, when it came to White youths. Instead of finding leniency for White girls, they found that White boys were treated more leniently at intake than White girls and all the other groups examined. In addition to examining race and gender, they also examined the effects of family status for boys and girls. Their findings indicated that family status had little effect on the treatment of Black youths. For Whites, however, coming from a single-parent household often resulted in leniency for girls compared to the other gender and racial groups. For White males, coming from a single-parent household also resulted in greater leniency than those from two-parent households.

Overall, it appears that minority girls are not being treated as leniently as their White counterparts during the juvenile court process. This might be explained by the chivalry and paternalism perspectives. According to these ideas, court actors subject females to more lenient treatment than males because they view women as more fragile and in need of protection. In an effort to protect girls from the harshness of the juvenile justice system, therefore, court officials are less likely to subject them to formal processing. In order to receive this leniency, however, it is essential for girls to prescribe to traditional female expectations. If girls do not act according to these expectations, by being aggressive, rude, loud, disrespectful, or masculine, then they are not afforded leniency and may even be treated more harshly than boys. It is possible that adhering to traditional female expectations might be associated more with White girls than for some minority girls. These minority girls, therefore, may not receive the same lenient treatment as White girls.

Programming Needs and the Treatment of Girls

When Congress reauthorized the Juvenile Justice and Delinquency Prevention (JJDP) Act in 1992 it added a requirement that states must examine the adequacy of their programming for female juvenile delinquents. With this requirement, many states were prompted to develop new programs for girls that were gender-specific and could better meet girls' needs and could recognize the developmental differences between girls and boys. The Office of Juvenile Justice and Delinquency Prevention defines gender-specific programs as "designed to address needs unique to the gender of the individual to whom such services are provided" (1992, 42 USC 5603 sec. 1[c][20]). Gender-specific programs are also often referred to as "gender-responsive" (Hubbard & Matthews, 2008), and consider all the differences in offending rates, risks and protective factors, needs, and histories of girls and boys. In addition to programs being gender-specific some argue that programs should also be specific to the race and ethnicity of girls.

The Reaffirming Young Sisters' Excellence (RYSE) program is an example of a gender specific program for delinquent girls. It was developed in Alameda County, California, as an alternative to probation. RYSE mixed traditional probation programs with gender and culturally specific programming. Probation officers for the RYSE program had small caseloads and worked closely with the girls and the girls' families. Programming for girls was determined through individual assessments of the girls to improve their social, academic and vocational competencies, as well as to address risks of getting pregnant and the need for parenting training. An evaluation of the RYSE program found that the program was more successful than traditional probation in reducing recidivism for African American girls but not for Hispanic, Asian or White girls (Le, Arifuku & Nunez, 2003). This was largely due, however, to the fact that African American girls did so poorly in traditional probation. In fact, the African American girls did even worse than White girls in the RYSE program (Wolf, Graziano & Hartney, 2009).

Given that many juvenile delinquents have a history of maltreatment, the child welfare system has a valuable opportunity to intervene in young peoples' lives and to target the specific needs of girls and boys to prevent the progression into delinquency. Goodkind, Shook, Kim, Pohlg, and Herring (2013) examined how involvement in the child welfare system affected later delinquency for White and minority girls and boys. They examined data from Allegheny County (Pittsburgh and the surrounding suburban area), Pennsylvania and found that boys were four times more likely to become involved with the juvenile justice system than girls. African American youth were also twice as likely as White youth to be detained in a juvenile detention center or residential facility. They also found that being placed in out-of-the home care by the child welfare system had a more significant effect on girls than on boys in increasing the likelihood that they would be involved with the juvenile justice system. In addition, the type of placement mattered differently for boys and girls. Girls who were placed in congregate care, meaning that they were placed in a group home or residential treatment facility instead of a foster home were more likely to be involved in the juvenile justice system. Placement in congregate care, however, did not have an impact on non-White and males' likelihood of juvenile justice involvement. They further found that the substance abuse treatment needs of African American boys and all girls appeared to be going undetected in the social welfare system.

When thinking about gender and gender-specific programs, it is important to remember that boys are also influenced by their gender. It is common for discussions of gender-specific program to focus only on girls and leave out boys. However, it is important that gender-specific programs meet the specific needs of girls as well as the specific needs of boys. Day, Zahn, and Tichavsky (2015) examined the effectiveness of a gender responsive program for girls and boys who were detained in a secure facility in Connecticut. While previous studies have examined the effectiveness of these programs on girls (Hipwell & Loeber, 2006; Zahn et al., 2009), their study is the first to examine whether gender response program is effective for both girls *and boys*. To evaluate the program, Day et al., used propensity score matching to compare boys and girls, who received the gender-response program, to boys and girls who received traditional behavioral response therapy. Propensity score matching is a statistical technique that is used to create a comparison group that is similar to a treatment group (i.e., the group who received the program that is being assessed). The authors found that of those girls who completed the gender-response program 51% recidivated within 12 months, while 53% of the girls who received the traditional behavioral response therapy recidivated. For boys, 64% of those in the gender response sample recidivated within 12 months compared to only 53% in the behavioral response sample. The differences in the rates of recidivism for the two groups were not statistically significant for either boys or girls.

Although these differences seem to indicate that gender response therapy is not better than traditional therapy, the authors conducted additional analysis to determine whether gender-response programming works better for girls with more gender-specific risks factors than for girls with fewer gender-specific risks factors. The gender-specific risks factors considered for girls were trauma, depression/anxiety, alcohol and drug problems, anger and irritability and somatic complaints. This analysis confirmed that girls who displayed more of these risks factors had significantly lower rates of recidivism if they were in the gender-response program instead of the traditional behavioral response program. Girls who had none of these risks, on the other hand, actually did better in the traditional behavioral response program than the gender-response program. These findings indicate that gender-response programs were only effective for girls who exhibited gender-specific risks, and that all girls cannot be treated the same. Regardless of risks factors, boys did not benefit from the gender-response program.

Despite the fact that girls make up 30% of juveniles in the system and the attention that has been given to gender-specific programming, Lipsey's (2009) review of juvenile justice programs found that only 4% were programs for girls, while 87% served all or mostly all boys. Therefore, it appears that the majority of programming for girls is the same that is being used for boys. Evaluations of some of these programs, however, have also indicated that they can be successful for boys and girls of different races and ethnicities.

Multisystemic Therapy (MST) for Juvenile Offenders has been found to be effective with boys and girls of various racial and ethnic backgrounds. MST operates through the community, school and family to increase protective factors that can prevent involvement in delinquency. Participation in the program usually consists of multiple therapy visits lasting four months. Evaluations of MST have found that it is effective in reducing delinquency among girls and boys and among serious and violent juvenile offenders (Borduin et al., 1995; Schaeffer & Borduin, 2005).

Brief Strategic Family Therapy (BSFT) is another gender-neutral program that has been found to be successful for girls as well as for boys. It was originally designed for Hispanic families but has also been used with African American families, and is aimed at preventing delinquency. BSFT targets juveniles aged eight to 17 who demonstrate behavioral problems and substance abuse issues. The program consists of sessions with the families aimed at changing how the family functions by prompting positive parenting, parental monitoring, effective discipline strategies, and family cohesion. Several evaluations have been conducted examining the effectiveness of BSFT. Santisteban et al. (2003) utilized an experimental design to determine whether BSFT was effective with a sample of Hispanic youths. They found that the kids who participated in BSFT had lower rates of conduct problems and delinquency. Additional research also found that BSFT was successful in reducing recidivism for African American youths (Santisteban, Coatsworth, Perez-Vidal, Mitrani, Jean-Gilles, & Szapocznik, 1997) and juvenile girls engaged in bullying (Nickel, Luley, Krawczyk, Nickel, Widerman, Lahmann, et. al., 2006).

Overall it appears that gender-specific programming can be effective in treating delinquent youths. There are also gender-neutral programs that have been effective for both boys and girls of various races and ethnicities. It should not be assumed, however, that all girls have had the same experiences and carry the same risks. It is further possible that gender-specific programs work better for girls and boys of certain racial and ethnic backgrounds or it may be the case that differences exists within gender and race/ethnicity groups the same as they do across gender groups. It also appears that the most effective programs are those that are able to individualize treatment to each juvenile. It is possible; therefore, that the most important aspect of programming might be that it meets the specific risks and needs of all juveniles. If a program is not flexible enough to respond to specific needs, it is unlikely that it will be effective for juveniles of all genders, races, and ethnicities.

Conclusion

Boys have received the greatest amount of attention in the juvenile justice system. This has largely been due to the fact that offending is more common among boys than girls. When examining risks factors for girls and boys it appears that many of the same risks factors affect their likelihoods of juvenile offending. These factors may, however, have different impacts for girls and boys, and might also differently impact girls and boys of different races and ethnicities.

Despite the fact that delinquent behavior is still more common among boys than girls, the number of girls entering the system is increasing. There is debate about whether this increase is due to an increase in girls' offending or to a change in the way girls' acts of deviance are handled by juvenile justice officials. The possibility that this increase is due to changes in the treatment of girls' actions is especially concerning for minority girls as research indicates that they are not treated as leniently as their White counterparts during arrests and during the juvenile court process.

Regardless of the reason for the increased number of girls in the system, girls are now accounting for an increasing percentage of juvenile offenders, making it especially important that the system responds to the treatment needs of these girls. Research suggests, however, that the system is not always meeting these girls' needs. Bright, Kohl and Jonson-Reid (2014) examined the profiles of 700 girls involved with the juvenile justice system and found that the girls who were the most in need of juvenile court services were also the least likely to receive those services, with only three percent receiving them. These girls were also the most likely to recidivate as juveniles and to engage in adult crime later in life. The girls in this group were also more likely to be African American and to be from the poorest neighborhoods.

It is important that the juvenile system address the specific needs of girls to prevent future offending. While consideration has been given to the argument that many gender-neutral programs are really designed for boys and should not be expected to be equally effective for girls, less consideration has been devoted to the stance that gender-specific programs might not be equally effective for girls of all races and ethnicities. There is a further lack of understanding as to what gender- and race/ethnic-specific programs should encompass. This is concerning as research has also indicated that programs are not equally effective for marginalized groups of girls.

Discussion Questions

1. How do you think media reports of incidences like the Slender Man case have shaped the public's view of female-perpetrated violence and the "typical" female offender? Do you think the media attention of the case would differ if the girls were minorities? Why or why not?
2. What advantages or disadvantages do you see to the more severe handling of juvenile girls' deviant activities by the police and the juvenile justice system?
3. Do you agree with the paternalism perspective that court actors are trying to protect girls? Where do you think this instinct to protect girls comes from?
4. Should the juvenile justice system focus on gender- and race-specific programming? Why or why not?

References

Archer, L. & Grascia, A.M. (2006). Girls, gangs, and crime: A profile of the young female offender. *Journal of Gang Research, 13*, 37–49.

Associate Press. (2011 March 8). Milwaukee teen Admits to killing step-grandfather over spilt milk. *FOX News*. Retrieved on June 14, 2014 from: http://www.foxnews.com/us/2011/03/08/milwaukee-teen-admits-killing-step-grandfather-spilt-milk/.

Bell, K.E. (2009). Gender and gangs: A quantitative comparison. *Crime & Delinquency, 55*(3), 363–387.

Bishop, D.M. & Frazier, C.E. (1996). Race effects in juvenile justice decision making: Findings of a statewide analysis. *Journal of Criminal Law and Criminology, 86*(2), 392–414.

Borduin, C.M., Mann, B J., Cone, L.T., Henggeler, S. W., Fucci, B. R., Blaske, D.M., et al. (1995). Multisystemic treatment of serious juvenile offenders: Long-term prevention of criminality and violence. *Journal of Consulting and Clinical Psychology, 63*(4), 569–578.

Braithwaite, J. (1989). *Crime, shame, and reintegration*. Cambridge, UL: Cambridge University Press.

Bright, C.L., Kohl, P.L., Jonson-Reid, M. (2014). Females in the juvenile justice system: Who are they and how do they fare? *Crime & Delinquency, 60*(1), 106–125.

Brown, W.K. (1977). Black female gangs in Philadelphia. *International Journal of Offender Therapy and Comparative Criminology, 21*, 221–228.

Campbell, A. (1991). *Girls in the gang* (2nd ed.). Cambridge, MA: Basil Blackwell.

Chesney-Lind, M. (1973). Judicial enforcement of the female sex role *Issues in Criminology, 8*, 51–70.

Chesney-Lind, M. & Irwin, K. (2008). *Beyond bad girls: Gender, violence, and hype*. New York: Routledge.

Chesney-Lind, M. & Shelden, R.G. (1998). Girls, delinquency, and juvenile justice 2nd Ed. Pacific Grove, CA: Brooks/Cole.

Cochran, J.C. & Mears, D.P. (2015). Race, ethnic, and gender divides in juvenile court sanctioning and rehabilitative intervention. *Journal of Research in Crime & Delinquency, 52*(2), 181–212.

Conrad, S.M., Tolou-Shams, M., Rizzo, C.J., Placella, N. & Brown, L.K. (2014). Gender differences in recidivism rates for juvenile justice youth: The impact of sexual abuse. *Law and Human Behavior, 38*(4), 305–314.

Curry, D. & Decker, S. (1998). *Confronting gangs*. Los Angeles, CA: Roxbury.

Day, J.C., Zahn, M.A., Tichavsky, L.P. (2015). What works for whom? The effects of genderresponsive programming on girls and boys in secure detention. *Journal of Research in Crime and Delinquency, 52*(1), 92–129.

Dennis, J.P. (2012). Girls will be girls: Childhood gender polarization and delinquency. *Feminist Criminology, 7*(3), 220–233.

Esbensen, F. & Carson, D.C. (2012). Who are the gangsters? An examination of the age, race/ethnicity, sex, and immigration status of self-reported gang members in a seven-city study of American youth. *Journal of Contemporary Criminal Justice, 28*(4), 465–481.

Esbensen, F. & Huizinga, D. (1993). Gangs, drugs, and delinquency in a survey of urban youth. *Criminology, 31*, 565–589.

Esbensen, F. & Huizinga, D. & Weiher, A.W. (1993). Gang and non-gang youth: Differences in explanatory variables. *Journal of Contemporary Criminal Justice, 9*, 94–116.

Esbensen, F. & Huizinga, D. & Winfree, L.T. (1999). Differences between gang girls and gang boys: Results from a multisite survey. *Youth & Society, 31*(1), 27–53.

Esbensen, F., Peterson, D., Taylor, T.J., Freng, A. (2010). *Youth violence: Sex and race differences in offending, victimization, and gang membership.* Philadelphia, PA: Temple University Press.

Feld, B.C. (2009). Violent girls or relabeled status offenders? *Crime & Delinquency, 55*(2), 241–265.

Feitel, B., Margetson, N., Chamas, J. & Lipman, C. (1992). Psychosocial background and behavioral and emotional disorders of homeless and runaway youth. *Hospital and Community Psychiatry, 43*, 155–159.

Fishman, L. (1998). Black female gang behavior: An historical and ethnographic perspective. In *Female Gangs in America*, M. Chesney-Lind and J. Hagedorn (Editors). Chicago, IL: Lakeview Press.

Fleisher, M. (1998). *Dead end kids: Gang girls and the boys they know.* Madison: University of Wisconsin Press.

Fleisher, M.S. & Krienert, J.L. (2004). Life-course events, social networks, and the emergence of violence among female gang members. *Journal of Community Psychology, 32*(5), 607–622.

Franklin, C.A. & Fearn, N.E. (2008). Gender, race, and formal court decision-making outcomes: Chivalry/paternalism, conflict theory or gender conflict. *Journal of Criminal Justice, 36*, 279–290.

Freiburger, T.L. & Burke, A.S. (2010). Adjudication decision of Black, White, Hispanic, and Native American youth in juvenile court. *Journal of Ethnicity in Criminal Justice, 8*(4), 231–247.

Gaarder, E., Rodriguez, N. & Zatz, M.S. (2004). Criers, liars, and manipulators: Probation officers' views of girls. *Justice Quarterly, 21*(3), 547–578.

Girl, 13, Stabs Grandfather to Death after He Poured Milk Down the Drain. *Daily Mail.* Retrieved on June 14, 2014 from: http://www.dailymail.co.uk/news/article-1364444/Milwaukee-girl-13-stabbed-grandfather-dead-pouring-milk-away-jailed-year.html.

Goodkind, S., Shook, J.J., Kim, K.H., Pohlg, R.T & Herring, D.J. (2013). From child welfare to juvenile justice: Race, gender, and system experiences. *Youth Violence and Juvenile Justice, 11*(3), 249–272.

Hennessey, M., Ford, J.D., Mahoney, K., Ko, S.J. & Siegfried, C.B. (2004). *Trauma among girls in the juvenile justice system.* Los Angeles, CA: National Child Traumatic Stress Network.

Hipwell, A.E., Loeber, R. (2006). Do we know which interventions are effective for disruptive and delinquent girls? *Clinical Child and Family Psychology Review, 9,* 221–255.

Hubbard, D.J. & Matthews, B. (2008). Reconciling the differences between the 'Gender-Responsive' and the 'What Works' literature to improve services for girls. *Crime & Delinquency, 54,* 225–258.

Hurtado, A. (1989). Relating to privilege: Seduction and rejection in the subordination of White women and women of color. *Signs, 14,* 833–855.

Juvenile Justice and Delinquency Prevention Act. (1992). 42 USC 5603 sec. 1[c][20].

Kirkpatrick, D.G. & Saunders, B. (2009). *National survey of adolescents in the United States, 1995,* Ann Arbor, MI: ICPSR.

Le, T., Arifuku, I. & Nunez, M. (2003). Girls and culture in delinquency intervention: A case study of RYSE. *Juvenile and Family Court Journal, 54,* 25–34.

Lederman, C.S., Dakof, G.A., Larrea, M.A., Li, H. (2004). Characteristics of adolescent females in juvenile detention. *International Journal of Law and Psychiatry, 27,* 321–337.

Leiber, M. & Mack, K. (2003). The individual and joint effects of race, gender, and family status on juvenile justice decision-making. *Journal of Research in Crime & Delinquency, 41*(1), 34–70.

Lemert, E.M. (1972). *Human deviance, social problems, and social control.* Englewood Cliffs, NJ: Prentice Hall.

Lipsey, M. 2009. The primary factors that characterized effective interventions with juvenile offenders: A meta-analytic overview. *Victims & Offenders: An International Journal of Evidence-based Research, Policy, and Practice. 4(2)* 124–147.

McGrath, A.J. (2010). The subjective impact of contact with the criminal justice system: The role of gender and stigmatization. *Crime & Delinquency, 60*(6), 884–908.

Miller, J.A. (2001). *One of the guys: Girls, gangs, and gender.* New York, NY: Oxford University Press.

Moore, J.W. (1991). *Going down to the barrio: Homeboys and homegirls in change.* Philadelphia, PA: Temple University Press.

Moore, J. & Hagedorn, J. (2001). (2008). *Female gangs: A focus on research.* Washington, D.C.: Office of Juvenile Justice and Delinquency Prevention, Office of Justice Programs, U.S. Department of Justice.

National Youth Gang Center. (2000). *1998 National Youth Gang Survey.* Washington, DC: U.S. Department of Justice, Office of Justice Programs, Office of Juvenile Justice and Delinquency Prevention.

Nickel, M., Luley, J., Krawczyk, J., Nickel, C., Widermann, C., Lahmann, C., et al. (2006). Bullying girls—Changes after Brief Strategic Family Therapy: A randomized, prospective, controlled trial with one-year follow-up. *Psychotherapy and Psychosomatics, 75*(1), 47–55.

Office of Juvenile Justice and Delinquency Prevention (OJJPD). (n.d.). Retrieved from http://www.ojjdp.gov/ojstatbb/crime/jar.asp.

Office of Juvenile Justice and Delinquency Prevention, Office of Justice Programs, U.S. Department of Justice.

Puzzanchera, C. Adams, B. & Hockenberry, S. (2012). *Juvenile Court Statistics 2009.* Pittsburgh, PA: National Center for Juvenile Justice.

Pyrooz, D.C. (2014). "From your first cigarette to your last dyin' day": The patterning of gang membership in the life-course. *Journal of Quantitative Criminology, 30,* 349–372.

Rosenfeld, R. (2007). Explaining the divergence between UCR and NCVS aggravated assault trends. In J.P. Lynch & L.A. Addington (Eds.), *Understanding crime statistics: Revisiting the divergence of the NCVS and UCR* (pp. 251–268). New York: Cambridge University Press.

Sanchick, M. & Sears, A. (2015 March 13). Girls accused of stabbing a classmate will remain in the adult court ... for now. *FOX6 Now.* Retrieved from: http://fox6now.com/2015/03/13/judge-set-to-rule-on-whether-slenderman-stabbing-case-should-proceed-in-adult-court/.

Santisteban, D.A., Coatsworth, J. D., Perez-Vidal, A., Mitrani, V., Jean-Gilles, M. & Szapocznik, J. (1997). Brief Structural/Strategic Family Therapy with African American and Hispanic high-risk youth. *Journal of Community Psychology, 25*(5), 453–471.

Santisteban, D.A., Szapocznik, J., Perez-Vidal, A., Kurtines, W.M., Murray, E.J. & LaPerriere, A. (1996). Efficacy of intervention for engaging youth and families into treatment and some variables that may contribute to differential effectiveness. *Journal of Family Psychology, 10,* 35–44.

Schaeffer, C.M. & Borduin, C. M. (2005). Long-term follow-up to a randomized clinical trial of Multisystemic Therapy with serious and violent juvenile offenders. *Journal of Consulting and Clinical Psychology, 73*(3), 445–453.

Shelton, D. (2004). Experiences of detained young offenders in need of mental health care. *Journal of Nursing Scholarship, 36*, 129–133.

Simpson, S. & Ellis, L. (1995). Doing gender: Sorting out the caste and crime conundrum. *Criminology, 33*, 47–77.

Smith, D.K., Leve, L.D. & Chamberlian, P. (2006). Adolescent girls' offending and health-risking sexual behavior: The predictive role of trauma. *Child Maltreatment, 11*, 346–353.

Snyder, H. (2000). *Sexual assault of young children as reported to law enforcement: Victim,* incident, and offender characteristics report. Washington, DC: U.S. Department of Justice, Office of Justice Programs, Bureau of Justice Statistics.

Spelman, E.V. (1988). *Inessential women.* Boston, MA: Beacon.

Steffensmeier, Schwartz, J., Zhong, S.H., Ackerman, J. (2005). An assessment of recent trends in girls' violence using diverse longitudinal sources: Is the gender gap closing? *Criminology, 43*, 355–405.

Stevens, T. Morash, M. & Chesney-Lind, M. (2011). Are girls getting tougher, or are we tougher on girls? Probability of arrest and juvenile court oversight in 1980 and 2000. *Justice Quarterly, 28*(5), 719–744.

Strom, K.J., Warner, T.D., Tichavsky, L. & Zahn, M.A. (2014). Policing juveniles: Domestic violence arrest policies, gender, and police response to child-parent violence. *Crime and Delinquency, 60*(3), 427–450.

Swanston, H., Parkinson, P., O'Tool, B., Plunkett, A., Shrimpton, S. & Oats, R. (2003). Juvenile crime, aggression and delinquency after sexual abuse: A longitudinal study. *British Journal of Criminology, 43*, 729–749.

Taylor, C. (1993). *Girls, gangs, women and drugs.* East Lansing, MI: Michigan State University Press.

U.S. Department of Justice, Office of Juvenile Justice and Delinquency Prevention. (1998). Highlights of the 1996 national youth gang survey. Washington, DC: Government Printing Office.

Valdez, A. (2007). *Mexican American girls and gang violence: Beyond Risk.* New York, NY: Palgrave Macmillan.

Visher, C.A. (1983). Gender, police arrest decisions, and notions of chivalry. *Criminology, 21*, 5–28.

Walker-Barnes, C.J. & Mason, C.A. (2001). Perceptions of risk factors for female gang involvement among African American and Hispanic women. *Youth & Society, 32*(3), 303–336.

Welsh, L.A., Archambault, F.X., Janus, M.D. & Brown, S.W. (1995). *Running for their lives: Physical and sexual abuse of runaway adolescents.* New York, NY: Garland.

Widom, C. (1995). *Victims of childhood sexual abuse: Later criminal consequences.* Washington, DC: National Institute of Justice.

Widom, C. & Maxfield, M. (2001). *An update of the "cycle of violence."* Washington. DC: Department of Justice, Office of Justice Programs.

Wolf, A.M., Graziano, J. & Hartney, C. (2009). The provision and completion of gender-specific variation by race and ethnicity. *Crime & Delinquency, 55*(2), 294–312.

Wood, J., Foy, D., Goguen, C., Pynoos, R. & James, C. (2002). Violence exposure and PTSD among delinquent girls. *Journal of Aggression, Maltreatment and Trauma, 6,* 109–126.

Zahn, M.A., Agnew, R., Fishbein, D., Miller, S., Winn, D., Dakoff, G., Kruttschnitt, C., Giordano, P., Gottfreson, D.C., Payne, A.A., Feld, B.C. & Chesney-Lind, M. (2010). *Causes and correlates of girls' delinquency.* Washington, DC: Office of Juvenile Justice and Delinquency Prevention.

Zahn, M.A., Brumbaugh, S., Steffensmeier, D., Feld. B.C., Morash, M., Chesney-Lind, M., Miller, J., Payne, A.A., Gottfredson, D. & Kruttschnitt, C. (2008). *Violence by teenage girls: trends and context.* Washington, D.C.: Office of Juvenile Justice and Delinquency Prevention, Office of Justice Programs, U.S. Department of Justice.

Zahn, M.A., Day, J.C., Mihalic, S.F., Tichavsky, L. (2009). Determining what works for girls in the juvenile justice system: A summary of evaluation evidence. *Crime & Delinquency, 55,* 266–293.

Chapter 10

Status Offenders

Goals of the Chapter

The purpose of this chapter is to examine status offenders and the processing of status offenders in the juvenile justice system, paying special attention to racial and ethnic issues relating to these offenders. This chapter provides an overview of status offender characteristics, and racial and ethnic divisions of status offenders. The research examining the argument that status offenders escalate into more serious offenders is also assessed. Theoretical explanations and the empirical research examining the effects of race and ethnicity in the processing of status offenders in the juvenile court are also reviewed. The chapter concludes with an overview of the experiences of three states in adopting alternative strategies to handle status offenders.

After reading this chapter, you will be able to do the following:

1. Understand who is arrested for status offenses;
2. Critically assess the relationship between status offending and criminal offending; and
3. Demonstrate an understanding of the empirical literature on the effect that race, ethnicity, and community factors have on the processing of status offenders.

In addition to juveniles who engage in criminal behaviors, the juvenile court oversees juveniles who engage in status offenses. Status offenses are acts that are legal for adults to engage in but are prohibited for juveniles. Therefore, the age of the offender determines whether the act is illegal. Examples of status offenses are running away, using tobacco, being incorrigible (i.e., ungovernable or unmanageable), alcohol consumption, and truancy.

Status offenses make up less of the juvenile courts' caseloads than criminal offenses. In 2010, the juvenile courts formally processed almost 137,000 status offense cases, making up about 16% of the cases in the juvenile court. Table 10.1 presents the breakdown of status offenses for 2010 according to the 2014

National Center for Juvenile Justice Report. As shown in Table 10.1, the majority of these cases were for truancy, followed by liquor law violations, ungovernable cases, runaway cases, curfew violations, and other cases (e.g., tobacco use and court order violations) (Hockenberry & Puzzanchera, 2014).

Table 10.1. Status Offense Cases in 2010

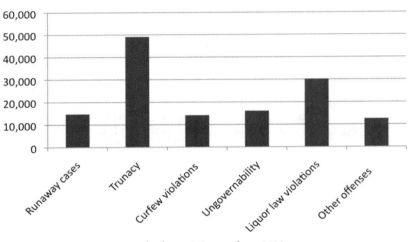

Hockenberry & Puzzanchera, 2014

When examining who commits the majority of status offenses, females, who only make up 28% of delinquency cases, account for 43% of status offenses. Although females account for a higher percentage of status offense cases than delinquency cases (28%), males still outnumber females for truancy (54% versus 46%), curfew violations (67% versus 33%), incorrigibility (58% versus 42%), and liquor violations (61% versus 39%). For running away, however, females account for a higher majority (58%) than males (42%).

As shown in Figure 10.1, the most common offense for White, Black and Asian status offenders in 2011 was truancy. For American Indian status offenders, liquor law violations were the most common offenses. Liquor law violations were more prevalent among American Indian and White youth than among Black youth, running away was more common among Black and Asian youth than among White and American Indian youths.

Hispanics were not separated from the other groups in these estimates (most were included in the White juvenile category). An idea of status offending among Hispanics can be gathered, however, from the Office of Juvenile Justice

Figure 10.1. Most Common Status Offenses by Race

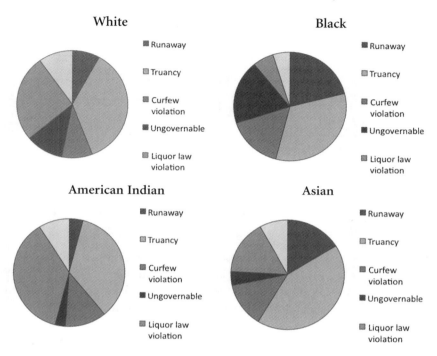

and Delinquency Prevention's Statistical Briefing Book, which reports statistics for liquor law violations, curfew and running away. As show in Table 2, 7.8% of Hispanic juveniles arrested were arrested for running away, 4.2% for curfew violations, and 5.9% for liquor law violations. When compared to the other groups, as displayed in Table 10.2, we see that running away and curfew violations were most common for Hispanic and American Indian groups. Hispanics had higher rates of running away than Whites, Blacks, American Indians and Asians. For curfew violations, Hispanics and American Indians were tied for the highest rates. For liquor law violations, Hispanics were second to last after Blacks for the lowest rates (Hockenberry & Puzzanchera, 2014). Statistics for ungovernable and truancy were not reported.

Table 10.2. Percentage of Hispanic Youth Status Offenses
Compared to Other Youths

	Hispanic	White	Black	Native American	Asian
Runaway	7.8	4.7	5.0	7.2	6.7
Curfew	4.2	3.6	3.5	4.2	3.6
Liquor Law Violations	5.9	9.8	1.4	16.0	7.1

Office of Juvenile Justice and Delinquency Prevention Statistical Briefing Book, http://www.ojjdp.gov/ojstatbb/special_topics/qa10503.asp?qaDate=2012.

Status Offenders and Crime Escalation

There have been conflicted opinions on whether status offenders are actually different juveniles than the juveniles who commit criminal acts. In other words, is there such thing as a juvenile who only engages in status offenses? Maxson and Klein (1997) argue that they are very rare. Few offenders only engage in status offenses and not in criminal behavior. Instead, most of the juveniles who commit status offenses are also committing crimes.

There are additional concerns that status offenses are "gateway" acts of deviance that lead to later criminal activity. Juveniles begin as minor offenders, committing status offenses, but later escalate to more serious criminal behavior. Although some research has found that juveniles, whose first appearance before the court was for a status offense, were less likely to recidivate than those juveniles whose first appearance was for a felony or misdemeanor crime (e.g., Kelley, 1983), other studies have found that status offenses have been linked to later delinquency.

Sheldon, Horvath, and Tracy (1989) examined court records for 863 youths referred to the juvenile court in Las Vegas for a status or criminal offense to determine if status offenders "escalate" to more serious offending. They found that while 67.5% of status offenders returned to the court for the same offenses or a less serious offense (e.g., status offense, administrative or public order offenses), only 32.5% returned for a more serious crime (e.g., personal, property or drug crime). Juveniles referred to the court for running away or being incorrigible had even lower rates (19.6%) of returning to the court for more serious offenses, than those referred for curfew, liquor law violations, and truancy.

When comparing males and females, more males (40.5%) returned for a more serious offense than females (18.4%). More females (59.5%), however, returned for an offense that was the same level of seriousness or less serious than did males. When looking at the different types of status offenses, the difference was even greater for juveniles referred for running away (3.2% of females returned for a more serious offense compared to 21.4% of males; 96.8% of females returned for a same or less serious offenses compared to 78.6% of males) and being incorrigible (8.2% of females returned for a more serious offense compared to 35.9% of males; 91.8% of females returned for a same or less serious offenses compared to 64.1% of males). Similar gender patterns were found for liquor law violations and truancy. For curfew, however, girls (56.3%) were more likely than boys (28%) to return for more serious offenses. Additional comparisons of status offenders and criminal offenders showed that status offenders were more likely to return to the court, but not for more serious offenses. This indicates that, when comparing the likelihood of a juvenile who committed a status offense committing another status offense to the likelihood of a juvenile who committed a crime committing another crime, the status offender is more likely to commit another status offense. These status offenders, however, do not typically commit a more serious offense.

There are several reasons why involvement in status offenses may lead to later criminal behaviors. It is very likely that some status offenses can lead to the destruction of social bonds in a child's life. These destroyed bonds can then lead to subsequent criminal behaviors. For example, children who are chronically truant are likely to feel less committed to school the more days they miss. They fall behind in their school work and cannot keep up with the lessons that the other students are learning. School becomes even more frustrating the further behind they get. They might also face disciplinary sanctions at the school for unexcused absences, making them feel more alienated and resentful toward school teachers and administrators.

Truancy, therefore, links to many additional problems. Juveniles who are truant are more likely to do poorly in school and to drop out (Heck & Mahoe, 2006; Heilbrunn, 2007). They are also more likely to become involved with the juvenile justice system (Newsome, Anderson-Butcher, Fink, Hall & Huffer, 2008) and to engage in substance use (Henry & Thornberry, 2010). Flannery, Frank, and Kato (2012) examined the most common disciplinary actions proscribed to truant juveniles. Across 193 public high schools, they found that punitive exclusionary sanctions (e.g., suspension) were the most commonly used. Preventive and mentoring programs were seldom used. Examining the truancy records of ninth graders who skipped at least one class period, they found that making juveniles attend school on a Saturday resulted in a greater likelihood of subsequent truancy. Out-of-school suspension also resulted in a short-term reduction in truancy. Long-term out-of-school suspensions, however, resulted in a greater likelihood of truancies. It appears, therefore, that a longer out-of-school suspension has a negative effect when used for chronic truancy cases. It is easy to see how these types of punishments could be viewed as a reward for juveniles who are trying to avoid school. In addition, as discussed above, these types of punishments can sever the already weak bonds these juveniles have to school, exacerbating the problem.

Case Study: Should Parents Pay When Kids Skip School?

A new way to deal with kids' truancy is to punish their parents. In Adrian, Michigan, parents can receive a $500 fine and go to jail for up to 90 days if their child does not go to school. In Illinois, parents can be charged with a misdemeanor for which they can be fined $1,500 and serve up to 30 days in jail (Sheeby, August 2012). In Delaware, it is a $1,000 fine and six months in jail (Parents Could Face Charges, 2009).

Most states now have laws that hold parents accountable if their children miss too many days of school. Prosecutors are exercising these laws and judges are holding parents accountable. In one West Virginia court, a woman was sentenced to 20 days in jail for each of her three children who were truant. When asked by the judge why she did not comply with an early order to get her kids to school, she said this, "I have them sometimes," she said. "One refused to go, skipping school, doctor's appointments and I didn't have excuses. Their father keeps them, too. And he's not in trouble" (Caswell, 2012 May 23). Her statement brings up a couple of important considerations. First, is it fair to hold parents responsible? Do these practices disadvantage single parents? Is it fair to target one parent or should both parents be equally held responsible? Concerns have also arisen that the laws unfairly target minorities and those of lower social economic status. Single parents who are experiencing financial hardships are often forced to work multiple jobs, making it difficult to monitor their children during school hours. When judges impose fines or parenting classes, it can be impossible for these parents to pay the fines or get away from work to attend parenting classes. This can increase their likelihood of ultimately being placed in jail.

Additional research conducted by Monahan, VanDerhei, Bechtold, and Cauffman (2014) raise concerns about the use of out-of-school suspensions and school expulsions. Their study examined data from 1,354 juvenile offenders in two major metropolitan areas. For the study, juveniles self-reported involvement in delinquent activities and any school suspensions or expulsions during interviews with the researchers. The researchers found that during months when juveniles were suspended or expelled from school, they were more likely to be arrested. The risks of being arrested were highest for youth who did not have a history of behavioral problems and for youth who did not associate with delinquent peers. This study indicates, therefore, that suspension and expulsions can have especially detrimental effects on lower risks juveniles, leading them into juvenile delinquency. This effect was present for Black, Hispanic, and White juveniles.

The use of harsh punishments in schools is part of the zero tolerance movement, aimed at punitively addressing even minor acts of misconduct by juveniles. Zero tolerance policies were enacted in an effort to make schools safer and to prevent problematic juveniles from interrupting a school environment conducive to learning. These polices have led to the increased use of harsh punishments in schools. Unfortunately, however, these harsh punishments can then lead to criminal behavior, as demonstrated by Monahan et al. (2014). This sequence of events has been termed the school-to-prison pipeline. Even more problematic, it appears that the school-to prison pipeline is working to further exacerbate minority overrepresentation in the juvenile justice system, as males and minorities (Aud, KewalRamani & Fronlich, 2011; Skiba, Michael, Nardo & Peterson, 2002) and juveniles of low social economic status (Wu, Pink, Crain & Moles, 1982) are more likely to receive school punishments. In fact, data collected by the Department of Education's Office of Civil Rights found that Black students comprised 46% of school suspensions, 39% of expulsions, and 36% of arrests on school grounds nationally during the 2009–2010 school year (Civil Rights Data Collection, n.d.).

Case Study: Zero Tolerance in Schools

In Ohio, a 10-year-old boy was suspended from school for pointing his finger like a gun and putting his hand to his friend's head and saying "boom" (Cuevas, 2014 March 4). In Washington State, elementary school kids were suspended for playing with Nerf guns at school, even though the students claimed their teacher had approved it prior (Golgowski, 2013 June 5). In an article for the *Washington Post*, Tunette Powell writes about her sons who have been suspended a combined total of eight times. The oldest had already been suspended three times, twice for throwing a chair and once for spitting on another student. He was four years old. The younger boy was three and had been suspended five times. Through conversations with other parents, Tunette Powell learned that White kids had committed similar, and sometimes more serious, acts and had not been suspended (Powell, 2014 July 24). Cases like these have led people to argue that zero tolerance policies have gone too far. In addition, the American Civil Liberties Union (ACLU) has made challenging these laws a priority (ACLU, n.d.).

Punitive punishments are also not successful in combating truancy because truancy is often a sign of other problems within the home. These punitive programs do not address those problems. Other programs that take a more comprehensive approach to helping kids return to school appear more promising. The Truancy Intervention Program (TIP) was developed in Atlanta, Georgia. TIP assigns truant juveniles with an adult mentor who, in addition to providing mentorship, helps the family secure needed public and private community resources. The mentor also serves as an advocate for the child in court proceedings, and works with school officials and the juvenile's social worker and probation officer. All of the mentors are community volunteers, with most being attorneys. In Georgia, the child is petitioned to the court for truancy if he or she is age 12 or older. If a juvenile is under 12, the child's parents are petitioned. TIP includes both of these cases (when a child or parent is the one being petitioned), and also operates as an early intervention program, meaning they identify juveniles who are in danger of reaching the threshold for court intervention and bring those juveniles into the program. Although the TIP program has not been formally evaluated, of the 877 cases in the TIP program from 2009-2010, 80% of the truancy cases and 90% of the early intervention cases did not commit another offense or reenter the juvenile justice system (Skola & Williamson, 2012).

Running away has also been found to create future problems in a child's life. Shaffer and Caton (1984) found that out of the 118 homeless and runaway youths they studied in New York, over half had been charged with a criminal offenses. Kaufman and Widom (1999) also found that those who ran away as juveniles were more likely to be arrested. When children are on the street they are often unable to find legitimate employment and have no means to support themselves. These juveniles are often reluctant to reach out for help through shelters and other community organizations out of fear of being sent back home or being arrested. Their need to survive on the streets can then lead them to engage in subsequent delinquent acts, such as stealing and prostitution (Baron & Hartnagel, 1998; Hagan & McCarthy, 1997). The Justice Department estimates that one-third of all the teenagers on the street will be approached by a pimp within 48 hours of leaving home. With nowhere to sleep and no means of support, these juveniles are vulnerable to adults looking to take advantage of them. Pimps are nice to them, buy them things and give them a place to stay. Once they are lured in, pimps will often use mental and physical abuse and threats to keep these juveniles under their control.

Case Study: Sex Trafficking of Runaways

Nicole Clark's story is a familiar one. She ran away from home at the age of 14. After sleeping in parks and under bridges for a few weeks, she met a man who offered her a place to stay. At first they were boyfriend and girlfriend, but then he began demanding she have sex with his friends who paid him money. She spent the next 14 months engaged in prostitution. She did not leave out of fear of being returned to the group home from where she had run away (Urbina, 2009 October 26).

Another teen runaway was taken advantage of and victimized in Miami, Florida. Two adult males, whom she had met through a mutual friend, kidnapped her. She was 16 years old and had run away from home. The men drugged and beat her. They forced her into prostitution, making her have sex with 24 men a day. The men also threatened to kill her if she attempted to flee. She was finally able to escape, and the men are being charged with numerous felonies including human trafficking. They could be imprisoned for life (Zea, 2015 March).

Stories like these have led to arguments that juvenile prostitutes should not be treated and punished as offenders. A recent report published by the National Academy of Sciences argues that arresting and prosecuting these juveniles can actually do more harm by giving them criminal records that can make it even more difficult to get out of the sex trade industry.

A better response is to treat juveniles engaged in prostitution as victims and not prosecute them. This can ensure they receive the programming and help that they need to overcome their involvement in sex trafficking (Clayton, Krugman & Simon, 2013).

A major determiner of a runaway juvenile's likelihood of avoiding subsequent contacts with the juvenile justice system is reunification with his or her family. Although families with runaway youths tend to have issues with familial conflict, inadequate discipline, poor monitoring and supervision of children, and poor parent-child relationships (Dadds, Braddock, Cuers, Elliott & Kelly, 1993), research has found that the longer juvenile runaways spend on the streets, the more likely they are to engage in criminal activity (McCarthy & Hagan 1992). In situations when attempts at reunification are successful, on the other hand, youths can often avoid further involvement with the juvenile justice system. Therefore, efforts are usually put into place to increase the chances of successful reunification.

Thompson, Kost, and Pollio (2003) examined ethnic differences in the reunification process for runaway youths in four Midwest states. They found that Black and Hispanic youth were more likely to return home than White youths. There were no differences between White, Native American, and Asian youth in their likelihoods of returning home. For White and Hispanic youth, females were more likely than their male counterparts to return home. If Black, Native American, and Hispanic youths were living in an institutional setting (e.g., a group home) or on the streets prior to running away, they had the lowest probabilities of returning home. It appears, therefore, that barriers exists in runaway youths' abilities to successfully reunite with their families. This is especially problematic for minority boys who had not been living with their families prior to running away.

Ethnic differences in youths' likelihoods of returning home might be explained by differences in their risks factors. Additional research conducted by Slesnick, Vasquez, and Bittinger (2002) compared the needs of Hispanic and non-Hispanic White runaways. They found that Hispanic youths had stronger familial relationships and less familial conflict than White youths. For substance abuse, White juveniles used tobacco on more days than Hispanic youths. No differences were found between White and Hispanic youths living in two-parent families for marijuana use, but for youths in one-parent families, White youths smoked marijuana on more days than Hispanic youths. No differences were found for alcohol use. In regards to mental health, Hispanic runaways reported more depression than White runaways. The greater familial involvement in Hispanic youths' lives and the lower rates of substance use, might be some indication of why Hispanic youths were found to be more likely to return home than White runaways in Thompson et al.'s (2003) study.

Curfew Laws

Curfew laws are city ordinances that prohibited juveniles from being out in public and on the streets during a specified time period. These laws have been around for a long time, with the first curfew law being enacted in 1880 in Omaha, Nebraska (Hemmens & Bennett, 1999). In the 1990s they gained in popularity, with 60% of the 200 largest cities in the United States adopting or revising a curfew law (Ruefle & Reynolds, 1996). Since then, juvenile curfew laws have continued to be a popular mechanism to prevent juvenile crime. Eight percent of the 200 largest cities and 75% of 60 moderate-sized cities in the United States have curfew laws (Ruefle & Reynolds, 1996). It is believed that, if police enforce curfew laws, juveniles are removed from the streets and are cut off from the opportunity to commit crime. These laws also limit juveniles' time on the streets where they are at a greater risk of being victimized. Empirical examinations of the effectiveness of these laws to reduce juvenile crime, however, have not provided strong support for their effectiveness (Males and Macallair, 1999; McDowall, Loftin & Wiersema, 2000; Reynolds, Seydlitz & Jenkins, 2000).

McDowall, Loftin, and Wiersema (2000), examined the effects of juvenile curfew laws in 57 cities across the United States to determine if curfew laws affected juvenile arrests as measured by the UCR and number of homicides committed by juveniles according to the National Center for Health Statistics. The results provided weak support for the argument that curfew laws reduce juvenile crime. Only cities that had revised their laws experienced any reductions in crime. Those states that implemented curfew laws for the first time did not experience any reductions. The reductions that were experienced by cities with revised laws were for burglaries, larceny and simple assaults only. Homicides, rapes, robberies, aggravated assaults, motor vehicle thefts, vandalism, and weapon offenses were not affected. In addition, the researchers could not rule out the possibility that these reductions were simply due to chance and that the curfew laws were not the actual cause of the reductions.

Reynolds et al. (2000) examined the effectiveness of curfew laws to reduce juvenile offending and victimizations in New Orleans, Louisiana. New Orleans' curfew law went into effect in 1994 and is one of the most restrictive laws in the United States. On weekdays the curfew begins at 8:00pm and on weekends it begins at 11:00pm. When the curfew is under effect, juveniles are not allowed to be in any public space without a legal guardian or authorized adult. The law in New Orleans is also unique because the juvenile is not punished; she or he is either sent home or transferred to the curfew center. Parents of the juvenile, however, can be fined, ordered to attend parenting classes or counseling, or ordered to perform community service.

The researchers examined the effect of the law on juvenile property victimizations, juvenile violent victimizations, and juvenile arrests. They also examined the property and violent victimizations of people of all ages. They found that none of the outcomes, juvenile property and violent victimizations, property and violent victimizations of people of all ages, and juvenile arrests, were significantly reduced during the curfew hours. Changes that they did observe during curfew hours were small and only temporary, leading the researchers to conclude that the curfew law was not effective in reducing offending or victimizations.

Overall, it appears that curfew laws are not effective in reducing juvenile crime. However, these laws remain popular. It is also unclear as to what effect these laws have on juveniles of different races and ethnicities. Some have challenged curfew laws based on the premise that they violate juveniles' rights. This might be especially concerning if they are being used to target some groups more than others. It is important that future research examine this possibility, as these laws might actually be causing unnecessary harm in addition to being ineffective.

Status Offenders in the Juvenile Court System

The juvenile justice system was developed to focus on treatment as opposed to punishment. Early in the juvenile justice system's history, status offenses were added to the list of offenses that were under the jurisdiction of the juvenile court. Although these offenses applied to all juveniles, the court was more concerned with girls who engaged in these behaviors than boys. For boys, the court was more concerned about involvement in criminal activities (Schlossman, 1977).

As discussed in Chapter 9, juvenile justice practitioners may hold paternalistic attitudes toward girls that drive these practitioners to proscribe more punitive punishments to females in an effort to protect girls. Girls, therefore, are being incarcerated "for their own good" and to save them from their own immoral behavior (Abrams & Curran, 2000; Boritch, 1992). This might be especially prevalent with status offenders, as juvenile justice personnel might see an opportunity to save these girls from entering into a criminal lifestyle, whereas girls who are already engaged in delinquent behaviors might be viewed as lost causes. It can also be more problematic for status offenders, because judges typically have greater discretion in punishing juveniles for status offenses than they do for criminal offenses (Kim, 2010).

It appears that girls' engagements in status offenses are viewed as concerning and problematic, while boys' engagements in these same behaviors are viewed as acceptable or typical "boys will be boys" behavior. In fact, self-report surveys show that while boys and girls engage in status offenses at about the same rate, more girls are referred to the juvenile court for status offenses than boys (Chesney-Lind, 1997; Chesney-Lind & Sheldon, 2004; Kempf-Leonard & Sample, 2000). It is possible, therefore, that female status offenders are treated more harshly than male status offenders in an effort to save girls from further involvement in delinquency. Juvenile court workers might also be concerned with the risks of girls engaging in sexually promiscuous behaviors and in getting pregnant. Harsher treatment of girls, therefore, is used to protect girls from these ills (Schaffner, 2006).

It is also possible, however, that paternalistic attitudes toward girls could have the opposite effect on certain female status offenders. Juvenile court personnel might treat these girls more leniently than boys in an effort to protect them from the harsh realities and consequences of the system. This idea is termed selective chivalry (Dodge, 2002), and predicts that girls who appear more passive and submissive will be treated more leniently. Because these characteristics are typically more closely associated with White girls, they may receive leniency while minority girls, especially Black girls, are treated more harshly because they are less likely to exhibit these feminine behaviors (Horowitz & Pottieger, 1991). White girls, therefore, are viewed as amenable to treatment while Black girls are viewed as dangerous (Seitz, 2005).

An early study was conducted by Bishop and Frazier (1996) to determine whether race and gender affected the processing of status offenders. The study examined status offenders in Florida who were processed from 1985–1987. Two decision points were included; the first was the intake decision (i.e., whether to handle the case informally or petition it to the juvenile court), and the second was the final disposition (possible sanctions are community service, probation, or placement in non-secure facility). Their analysis indicated that Whites and females were more likely to be referred for formal processing at intake. Race and gender did not significantly impact the final disposition stage. Although this study was the first to examine the impact of race and gender on the processing of status offenders, it was limited to White and non-White measures for race and ethnicity. Other more recent studies have improved on this measure, allowing more precise examinations of how race and ethnicity impact the processing of status offenders.

Freiburger and Burke (2011) examined the treatment of status offenders in Arizona for Black, White, Hispanic, and Native American juveniles. Their analysis did not find a significant effect for gender, meaning male and female status offenders were treated similarly in the adjudication decision. For race and ethnicity, Hispanic status offenders were more likely to be adjudicated than White status offenders. When gender and race/ethnicity were examined together, however, they found that Native American boys were treated the harshest, followed by Black females, and Hispanic females.

Another study conducted by Peck, Lieber, and Brubaker (2014) in two Mid-Atlantic states similarly found disparities in the treatment of status offenders depending on the juvenile's race. Similar to Freiburger and Burke (2011), they did not find a significant effect for gender on the intake and adjudication decisions. During the intake decision, Black status offenders and status offenders of "other" ethnicities were treated similarly to White status offenders. In the adjudication decision, however, Black status offenders were 128% more likely to be adjudicated than White status offenders, and status offenders of "other" ethnicities were 46% less likely to be adjudicated than Whites. When race and gender interactions were examined, the results found that Black males were treated more leniently than any of the females and males of "other" ethnicities. For adjudication, similar to Freiburger and Burke's (2011) finding, Black females were the most likely to be adjudicated. Boys and girls of "other" ethnicities were significantly less likely to be adjudicated than White and Black status offenders.

Data on status offenders in Oklahoma found that girls were more likely than boys to be formally petitioned to the courts, but were less likely to be adjudicated. Gender was not significant in the decision to place the juvenile in custody. Black, Hispanic, and Native American status offenders were not treated significantly different than White status offenders in any of the three outcomes examined (Spivak, Wagner, Whitmer & Charish, 2014). Unfortunately, the authors did not examine race and ethnic dyads like Freiburger and Burke (2011) and Peck et al. (2014), so it is not known whether the effect of gender varied by the status offender's race and ethnicity.

Overall, research examining the effects of race and ethnicity on the juvenile court processing of status offenders is limited. The research that has been done highlights the importance of examining the effects of race and ethnicity in combination with gender, as the results of these studies show that race and ethnicity differently affect the processing of status offenders for boys and girls. Furthermore, while it appears that Black girls are typically treated more harshly for status offenses, consistent with selective chivalry, race, ethnicity and gender have different impacts on different decision theory.

The Detention of Status Offenders

As discussed earlier, many of the issues surrounding status offenders centered on girls and their behaviors. This led to girls being detained more often for status and minor offenses (Platt, 1977; Schlossman, 1977). Concern over the disproportionately high incarceration of girls for status offenses was one of the motivations for the Juvenile Justice and Delinquency Prevention Act of 1974. Implementation of this Act led to the deinstitutionalization of status offenders, meaning that juveniles could no longer be institutionalized (i.e., placed in secure detention) for status offenses. If states did not comply with this amendment, they risked losing federal funding (Belknap, 2007; Chesney-Lind, 2006).

The practice of detaining and incarcerating status offenders, however, was not completely eliminated by the JJDP Act. In 1980, an amendment was added to the Act allowing status offenders to be detained and incarcerated for violating procedural violations, even if these violations stemmed from status offenses. Therefore, a juvenile who is petitioned to the court for a status offense, such as running away, cannot be placed in a detention center for their offense. If the juvenile fails to follow a court order, however, they may be placed in secure detention for failing to follow that court order. An example of this would be a juvenile who is brought before the court for truancy. He or she cannot be detained for engaging in truancy, but the judge might order the youth to stop skipping school. After that order, if the juvenile is truant, the judge can order him or her to be detained for violating the order not to skip school.

It is estimated that in 2010, of the 137,000 status offense cases that were petitioned to the juvenile court, 10,400 involved detention and 6,100 resulted in an out-of-home placement (Puzzanchera & Hockenberry, 2013). In 2011, about 2,239 status offenders were being held in residential placement, with 1,876 of those being held in secure detention facilities. An additional 220 status offenders were being held while awaiting adjudication (Sickmund, Sladky, Kang & Puzzanchera, 2013). According to a report by the Coalition for Juvenile Justice, 31 states and Washington D.C. allow status offenders to be detained in secure detention facilities for violating a court order (VAC) or on a 24-hour hold. Table 10.3 presents the lists of these states.

Table 10.3. States that allow juveniles to be detained for violation of court orders or 24-hour hold

Alabama	Kentucky	South Carolina
Alaska	Louisiana	South Dakota
Arizona	Michigan	Tennessee
Arkansas	Mississippi	Texas
California	Missouri	Utah
Colorado	Nevada	Virginia
Georgia	North Carolina (limited to 24-hour hold on runaways)	Washington State
Idaho	Ohio	Washington D.C.
Illinois	Oklahoma (up to 24 hours)	Wisconsin
Indiana	Oregon	Wyoming
Kansas State (only for runaways)	Rhode Island	

Of the states that incarcerate status offenders, in 2012, Washington had the most cases of juveniles being detained for failing to follow a court order for a status offense with 2,705 cases. This was followed by Kentucky with 1,048, Arkansas with 747, and Colorado with 356 (Coalition for Juvenile Justice, 2014). Between 1995 and 2011, runaway cases were the most likely to involve detention, and truancy cases were the least likely to involve detention. In 2011, truancy (22%) was the most common offense for which status offenders were ordered into an out-of-home placement, followed by liquor law violations (21%) and running away (18%) (Hockenberry & Puzzanchera, 2014).

According to the Coalition for Juvenile Justice, of the 2,239 status offenders being held in 2011, 43.7% were White, 32.9% were Black, 10.2% were Hispanic, and 4.2% were American Indian. From these numbers, it appears that Black youths are overrepresented in this population comparative to their numbers in the general population (16.6% of youths age 12–17 were Black in 2011). Black youths were also overrepresented (38.6%) among the 220 juveniles being held while awaiting adjudication (Coalition for Juvenile Justice, 2014).

Alternatives to Detention

It might seem like the federal government should simply pass legislation requiring states to end the practice of using detention to punish violations of court orders (VCO). If the federal government were to do that, however, states would have to find an alternative way to handle these offenders. In recent years, three states, Florida, New York, and Connecticut, have taken the initiative and have put forth efforts to end the practice of detaining status offenders under VCO.

The state of Florida requires that status offenders (known as Children in Need of Services in the state) first try to resolve their problems with the help of Families in Need of Services (FINS). Once a status offender becomes a FINS case, the case is turned over to the Network. The Network is a private service provider containing 32 community-based agencies. Once referred to the Network, the youths and their families receive an assessment and are referred for services. In cases where there is no improvement in the juveniles' offending, the juveniles are then turned over to the juvenile court. It appears, however, that most juveniles in the program do improve and do not end up in the juvenile court. In 2005–2006, 98% of the youths in the Network were crime-free during the program; 90% completed services. Of those who completed their programs, 90% were crime-free six months after services were complete (Magulescu & Caro, 2008).

Orange County, New York, developed the Family Keys program to better serve the needs of status offenders (called Persons in Need of Supervision in New York) in 2003. With this program, the probation office refers families to the Family Keys program. The family then receives a visit from a case worker within 48 hours, instead of the long waiting period that occurred under the old system. After an assessment is completed by the case worker, a service plan is developed, and families are connected with services in the community.

This program also appears to be working. Of the youths referred to this program, 98% avoided out-of-home placements. Given its success, the program has since become a model for other jurisdiction in New York. Now, across the state, status offense cases referred to the court decreased by 41% from 2004 to 2006, and non-secure detention of status offenders decreased by 39% from 2005 to 2006 (Magulescu & Caro, 2008).

In 2007, Connecticut implemented the Families with Service Needs (FWSN) initiative to stop detaining juveniles who violated court orders for status offenses in secure detention facilities and to begin diverting them into alternative programming. An effort was also put into place to create more community-based treatment services available to these status offenders. The intention of these efforts was to reduce the amount of judicial involvement in status offender cases, reduce the number of status offense referrals, keep status offenders out of secure detention, and improve juvenile outcomes.

An evaluation of this initiative found that referrals for FWSN complaints decreased by 41% after its implementation. No status offenders were detained for order violations in the year following the FWSN initiative (compared to 14% detained the year before FWSN Initiative). The initiative was also successful in reducing the courts handling of FWSN referrals from 50% to 4%. Lastly, the Initiative effectively reduced recidivism from 32% to 26%; the number of youths adjudicated for another offense also decreased from 16% to 12% (Ryon, Devers, Early & Hand, 2012).

These findings indicate that states can successfully divert status offenders from detention and from the juvenile court system successfully. It also indicates that other methods of dealing with status offenders might be more effective in reducing subsequent referrals and arrests. Although each of these programs have unique qualities, they all involve treatment and work in partnership with community-based services. In addition, all three programs have costs less than traditional juvenile court services for their youths, effectively providing a cheaper and more effective method for dealing with status offenders (Magulescu & Caro, 2008).

Conclusion

Status offenders present unique challenges to the juvenile justice system. Although these offenses are typically not considered as serious as criminal offending, status offending can lead to subsequent involvement in the juvenile justice system, severed social bonds, other social ills such as unemployment, and even to the victimization of juveniles. It is important, therefore, that status offenses be addressed. However, in addressing these issues through the juvenile court, research has found that racial and ethnic differences exist in the processing of these cases. These differences especially disadvantage minority females. Additional issues also arise with minority overrepresentation when punitive sanctions are utilized by the court as well as by informal mechanisms of social control such as schools. These issues become even more glaring when detention is used as a way to end chronic status offending.

Ending the practice of detaining juveniles for violating court orders will likely not be as simple as mandating that the practice cease, as the court would still be faced with the issue of dealing with chronic status offenders. A few states, however, have implemented alternative programming that focuses on treatment instead of punitive punishments. These states have found success with these programs. After continued and rigorous evaluations of these programs, they should serve as models for other states to better handle status offenders.

Discussion Questions

1. Should states be allowed to detain status offenders for violating court orders for status offenses or should this be considered a violation of the 1980 amendment to the Juvenile Justice and Delinquency Prevention Act?
2. Should the juvenile court handle status offenses or should they be treated informally within families? What are some advantages and disadvantages to having the court involved?
3. Do you agree that status offenses can lead to more serious criminal behavior? Why or why not?
4. What can the juvenile court system do to reduce gender and racial disparities in court processing decisions?
5. If the use of secure detention for status offenders who violate court orders is eliminated, what should the juvenile justice system do about juveniles who are chronic status offenders? Given the success of programs in Florida, New York, and Connecticut, why do you think more states have not adopted similar strategies?

References

Abrams, L.S. & Curran, L. (2000). Wayward girls and virtuous women: Social workers and female juvenile delinquency in the progressive era. *Affilia, 15*(1), 49–64.

American Civil Liberties Union. (n.d.). *School-to-prison pipeline.* Retrieved on June 29, 2015 from: https://www.aclu.org/issues/racial-justice/race-and-inequality-education/school-prison-pipeline.

Aud, S., KewalRamani, A. & Frohlick, L. (2011). *America's youth: Transitions to adulthood* (NCES 2012-026). U.S. Department of Education, National Center for Education Statistics. Washington D.C.: U.S. Government Printing Office.

Baron, S.W. & Hartnagel, T.F. (1998). Street youth and criminal violence. *Journal of Research in Crime and Delinquency, 35,* 166–192.

Belknap, J. (2007). *The invisible woman: Gender, crime and justice*. Belmont, CA: West/Wadsworth.

Bishop, D.M. & Frazier, C.E. (1992). Gender bias in juvenile justice processing: Implications of the JJDP Act. *The Journal of Criminal Law & Criminology, 82*(4), 1162–1186.

Bishop, D.M. & Frazier, C.E. (1996). Race effects in juvenile justice decision-making: Findings of a statewide analysis. *The Journal of Criminal Law & Criminology, 86*(2), 392–414.

Boritch, H. (1992). Gender and criminal court outcomes: An historical analysis. *Criminology, 30*(3), 293–325.

Caswell, C. (2012 May 23). Mother sentence over truancy. Charleston Daily Mail. Retrieved from http://www.charlestondailymail.com/News/2012 05230255.

Chesney-Lind, M. (1997). The female offender: Girls, women, and crime. Thousand Oaks, CA: Sage.

Chesney-Lind, M. (2006). Patriarchy, crime and justice: Feminist criminology in an era of backlash. Feminist Criminology, 1, 6–26.

Chesney-Lind, M. & Shelden, R.G. (2004). *Girls, delinquency, and juvenile justice 2nd Ed.* Pacific Grove, CA: Brooks/Cole.

Civil Rights Data Collection. (n.d.). State and national estimations. Retrieved on April 14, 2015 from: http://ocrdata.ed.gov/StateNationalEstimations.

Clayton, E.W., Krugman, R.D., Simon, P. (2013). Confronting commercial sexual exploitation and sex trafficking of minors in the United States. Washington, D.C.: National Academics Press.

Coalition for Juvenile Justice. (2014). Disproportionate minor contact and status offenses. Emerging Issues Policy Series, 2, Available at: http://www.juvjustice.org/sites/default/files/resource-files/DMC%20Emerging%20Issues%20Policy%20Brief%20Final_0.pdf.

Cuevas, M. (2014 March 4). 10-year-old suspended for making fingers into shape of gun. CNN. Retrieved on March 10, 2015 from: http://www.cnn.com/2014/03/04/us/ohio-boy-suspended-finger-gun/.

Dadds, M.R., Braddock, D., Cuers, S., Elliot, A., Kelly, A. (1993). Personal and family distress in homeless adolescents. Community Mental Health Journal, 29, 413–422.

Dodge, M.L. (2002). Whores and thieves of the worst kind: A study of women, crime and prisons (1835–2000). Dekalb, IA: Northern Illinois University Press.

Flannery, K.B., Frank, J.L. & Kato, M.M. (2012). School disciplinary responses to truancy current practice and future directions. Journal of School Violence, 11, 118–137.

Freiburger, T.L. & Burke, A.S. (2011). Status offenders in the juvenile court: The effects of gender, race, and ethnicity on the adjudication decision. Youth Violence and Juvenile Justice, 9(4), 352–365.

Golgowski, N. (2013 June 5). Kids suspended for bringing Nerf guns to school with teacher's permission. Daily News. Retrieved online on June 29, 2015 from: http://www.nydailynews.com/news/national/students-suspended-nerf-gun-article-1.1363552.

Hagan, J., and B. McCarthy (1997). Mean streets: Youth crime and homelessness. New York: Cambridge University Press.

Heck, R.H. & Mahoe, R. (2006). Student transition to high school and persistence: Highlighting the influences of social divisions and school contingencies. American Journal of Education, 112(3), 418–446.

Heilbrunn, J (2007) Pieces of the truancy jigsaw: A literature review. Denver: National Center for School Engagement.

Hemmens, C. & Bennet, K. (1999). Juvenile curfews and the courts: Judicial response to a not-so-new crime control strategy. Crime & Delinquency, 45, 99–121.

Henry, K.L. & Thornberry, T.P. (2010). Truancy and escalation of substance use during adolescence. Journal of Studies on Alcohol and Drugs, 71(1), 115–124.

Hockenberry,S. & Puzzanchera, M. (2014). Juvenile court statistics 2011. Pittsburgh, PA: National Center for Juvenile Justice.

Horowitz, R. & Pottieger, A.E. (1991). Gender bias in juvenile justice handling of serious crime-involved youth. Journal of Research in Crime and Delinquency, 28, 75–100. doi: 10.1177/0022427891028001005.

Kaufman, J.G. & Widom, C.S. (1999). Childhood Victimization, Running Away, and Delinquency. *Journal of Research in Crime Delinquency*, 3e, 347–370.

Kelley, T.M. (1983). Status offenders can be different: A comparative study of delinquent careers. Crime & Delinquency, 29(3), 365–380.

Kempf-Leonard, K. & Sample, L. (2000). Disparity based on sex: Is gender-specific treatment warranted? Justice Quarterly, 17(1), 89–128.

Kim, J.J. (2010). Left behind: The paternalistic treatment of status offenders within the juvenile justice system. Washington University Law Review, 87(4), 843–867.

Males, M. & Macallair, D. (1999). An analysis of curfew enforcement and juvenile crime in California. Western Criminological Review, 1(2), Available at: http://www.westerncriminology.org/documents/WCR/v01n2/Males/Males.html.

Maxson, C.L. & Klein, M.W. (1997). Responding to troubled youth. New York: Oxford University Press.

McCarthy, B. & Hagen, J. (1992). Mean Streets: The Theoretical Significance of Situational Delinquency among Homeless Youths. *American Journal of Sociology*, 98(3):597–627.

McDowall, D., Loftin, C., Wiersema, B. (2000). The impact of youth curfew laws on juvenile crime rates. Crime & Delinquency, 46, 76–91.

Mogulescu, S & Caro, G. (2008). Making court the last resort: A new focus for supporting families in crisis. New York: Vera Institute.

Monahan, K.C., VanDerhei, S., Bechtold, J. & Cauffman, E. (2014). From the school yard to the squad car: School discipline, truancy, and arrest. Journal of Youth Adolescence, 43, 1110–1122.

Newsome, W.S., Anderson-Butcher, D., Fink, J., Hall, L. & Huffer, J. (2008). The impact of school social work services on student absenteeism and risk factors related to school truancy. School Social Work Journal, 32(2), 21–38.

Office of Juvenile Justice and Delinquency Prevention. (n.d.). Delinquency cases involving Hispanic youth. Retrieved on March 15, 2015 from: http://www.ojjdp.gov/ojstatbb/special_topics/qa10605.asp?qaDate=2012.

Parents Could Face Charges for Truant Children. (2009, September 10). WBNS-10TV. Retrieved from http://www.10tv.com/content/stories/2009/09/10/story_truancy.html.

Peck, J.H., Leiber, M.J. & Brubaker, S.J. (2014). Gender, race, and juvenile court outcomes: An examination of status offenders. Youth Violence and Juvenile Justice, 12(3), 250–267.

Platt, A.M. (1977). The child-savers: The invention of delinquency. Chicago: University Chicago Press.

Powell, T. (2014 July 24). My son has been suspended five times. He's 3. The Washington Post. Retrieved on June 29, 2015 from: http://www.washingtonpost.com/posteverything/wp/2014/07/24/my-son-has-been-suspended-five-times-hes-3/.

Puzzanchera, Charles, and Sarah Hockenberry. 2013. Juvenile Court Statistics 2010. Pittsburgh, PA: National Center for Juvenile Justice. Available at http://www.ojjdp.gov/pubs/243041.pdf.

Reynolds, K.M., Seydlitz, R. & Jenkins, P. (2000). Do juvenile curfews work? A time series analysis of the New Orleans Law. Justice Quarterly, 17(1), 205–230.

Ruefle, W.J. & Reynolds, K.M. (1996). Keep them at home: Juveniles curfew ordinances in 200 American Cities. American Journal of Police, 15, 63–84.

Ryon, S.B., Devers, L., Early, K.W. & Hand, G.A. (2012). Changing how the system responds to status offenders: Connecticut's Families with Service Needs Initiative. Juvenile and Family Court Journal, 63(4), 37–46.

Schaffner, L. (2006). Girls in trouble with the law. New Jersey: Rutgers University Press.

Schaffer, D. & Caton, C.L.M. (1984). Runaway and homeless youth in New York City: A report to the Ittleson Foundation. New York: Division of Child Psychiatry.

Schlossman, S.L. (1977). Love and the American delinquent: The theory and practice of "progressive" juvenile justice 1825–1920. Chicago: University of Chicago Press.

Seitz, T. (2005). The wounds of savagery: Negro primitivism, gender parity, and the execution of Rosanna Lightner Phillips.Women and Criminal Justice, 16, 29–64.

Sheehy, K. (2012 August 13). Skipping high school can lead to fines, jail for parents. U.S. News & World Report. Retrieved from: http://www.usnews.com/ education/blogs/high-school-notes/2012/08/13/skipping-high-school-can-lead-to-fines-jail-for-parents.

Shelden, R.G., Horvath, J.A. & Tracy, S. (1989). Do status offenders get worse? Some clarifications on the question of escalation. Crime & Delinquency, 35(2), 202–216.

Sickmund, M., Sladky, T.S., Kang, W., & Puzzanchera, C. (2013). Easy access to the census of juveniles in residential placement. Available: http://www. ojjdp.gov/jstatbb/cazcjrp.

Slesnick, N., Vasquez, C. & Bittinger, J. (2002). Family functioning, substance use and related problem behaviors: Hispanic vs. Anglo runaway youths. Journal of Ethnicity in Substance Abuse, 1(4), 83–101.

Skiba, R.J., Michael, R.S., Nardo, A.C., Peterson, R. (2002). The color of discipline: Sources of racial and gender disproportionality in school punishment. The Urban Review, 34(4), 317–342.

Skola, E.P. & Williamson, K. (2012). The truancy intervention project: Our tips for success. Family Court Review, 50(3), 405–412.

Soivak, A.L., Wagner, B.M., Whitmer, J.M. & Charish, C.L. (2014). Gender and status offending: Judicial paternalism in juvenile justice processing. Feminist Criminology, 9(3), 224–248.

Spivak, A., Wagner, B., Whitmer, J., & Charish, C. (2014). Gender and status offending: Judicial paternalism in juvenile justice processing. *Feminist Criminology*, 9(3), 224–248.

Thompson, S.J., Kost, K.A. & Pollio, D.E. (2003). Examining risk factors associated with family reunification for runaway youth: Does ethnicity matter? Family Relations, 52, 296–304.

Urbina, I. (2009 October 26). For runaways, sex buys survival. The New York Times. Retrieved from: http://www.nytimes.com/2009/10/27/us/27runaways.html?pagewanted=all&_r=0.

Whitbeck, L.B., Hoyt, D.R. & Ackley, K.A. (1997). Abusive family backgroups and later victimization among runaway and homeless adolescents. Journal of research on Adolescence, 7, 375–392.

Wu., S, Pink, W., Crain & Moles, O. (1982). Student suspension: A critical reappraisal. The Urban Review, 14(4), 245–303.

Zea, N. (2015 March 3). Brothers charged with trafficking underage girl. CBS Miami. Retrieved on June 2, 2015 from: http://miami.cbslocal.com/2015/03/03/brothers-charged-with-trafficking-underage-girl/.

Chapter 11

Where Do We Go from Here?

Introduction

The problems facing historically marginalized racial/ethnic groups in America are troublesome. With current societal events (e.g., the Michael Brown shooting, the killings of Eric Garner, Trayvon Martin, and Freddie Gray, and the mass murder of nine African-Americans in a South Carolina church) bringing racially charged issues to the forefront, there is now a new (or renewed) focus on racial issues in the United States. People from all races, nationalities, and cultures are questioning the behavior and decision-making of individuals who have contact with the criminal justice system. They are also now examining the drives and motivations of those who actually work in this system. Additional consideration is being given to the informal mechanisms through which discrimination can operate to indirectly affect behaviors and decision-making.

The purpose of this book is to examine race issues in the juvenile justice system. While there are multiple books on juvenile delinquency, we provide an empirical examination of how race and ethnicity impacts the decision-makers in the juvenile justice system. In other words, the focus shifts from explaining the behavior of juveniles to explaining the behavior of the intake workers, prosecutors, judges, and other practitioners within the juvenile court process. We also grounded those empirical results in theories of juvenile justice decision-making. Instead of simply reporting the findings of race and ethnicity, we used theory to help make sense of what is observed in the literature. We also discussed special populations in the juvenile justice system, specifically juveniles, females, status offenders, and those who are transferred to the adult court. We further discussed the history of these groups and how race intertwines with these populations in examining decision-making of those in the system.

A final contribution of this book is that it is well grounded in a historical context. This is an issue that Hawkins (1987) advanced. He mentioned how the results from race scholarship should be framed in this context. We do this in this book. We provide a chapter tracing the factors leading up to the creation of the juvenile court, the actual implementation of the court, and the aftermath of its creation. We further integrated a strong discussion of race throughout the chapter at every turn, so readers can understand the role that race has played throughout the history of the juvenile system.

Racial Bias in the System?

In his seminal work *The Souls of Black Folk*, W. E. B. Du Bois (1903) indicated that "[t]he problem of the Twentieth Century is the problem of the color-line, the relation of the darker to the lighter races of men in Asia and Africa, in America and the islands of the sea. It was a phase of this problem that caused the Civil War; and however much they who marched South and North in 1861 may have fixed on technical points ... as we know, that the question of Negro slavery was the real cause of conflict" (p. 8). In his book *Race Matters*, Cornel West (1994) stated that, " ... the aim of a constitutional democracy is to safeguard the rights of the minority and avoid the tyranny of the majority" (p. 102). Despite there being an almost one century difference between each of these profound scholarships, they are discussing the same issues. The issues of race may be so entrenched in the fabric of America's justice system, notably the juvenile justice system that ignoring this existence is no longer possible.

The DMC data indicates that Blacks are over-represented at many stages of the juvenile justice system. Individual state data in some jurisdictions demonstrates that Hispanics are also greatly over-represented in the system. The issue *may* appear, then, to determine whether that disparity is due to discrimination. Walker, Spohn, & Delone (2012) caution against making this surface-level analysis. In essence, this provides the argument that the disparity is due to either no bias (i.e., differential offending between race/ethnicities) or a discriminatory system that specifically targets racial minorities. This position was elaborated upon by Tracy (2005):

> ... I would also suggest that, in an effort to subscribe to the tenets of political correctness, criminologists have avoided confronting the overwhelming evidence surrounding race and involvement in crime, particularly violent crimes against the person, drug-related offenses and weapons offenses. Researchers have focused instead on the alleged system biases and discrimination in the processing of offenders like those that are subsumed in the DMC initiative. The consequence, unfortu-

nately, is that this diverts scholarly attention away from the crucial questions surround[ing] race/ethnicity and crime, and fosters instead the study of highly peripheral issues that bring us further and further away from the "right stuff." (p. 340)

This conclusion and others like it are not taking full account of all the factors at play in the juvenile system and how race and ethnicity factor into decision-making. The formal legal theory suggests that any disparity is due to differential offending. However, after controlling for legal factors, the overwhelming evidence continues to find a race effect across the different outcomes. Therefore, researchers need to examine both the disparity-discrimination continuum and the multiple theoretical explanations for juvenile justice decision-making. Again, dismissing the examination of the juvenile justice decision-makers when these are the people whose job it is to ensure "justice" and "fairness" appears borderline research malpractice. It provides an assumption (which is not grounded in literature) that practitioners carry no bias or stereotypes which influence their decisions at particular outcomes.

Even prior to OJJDP identifying DMC as a mandate and eventual core requirement for states to get federal funding for their juvenile programs, researchers have examined the indirect racial and ethnic effects in court outcomes. The evidence from this body of literature is also fairly convincing. Racial and ethnic minorities (namely Black and Hispanic youth) are more likely to experience more punitive sentences early in the process, such as with the pre-adjudication detention. Regardless of what occurs after that point regarding race, the detention decision then has a direct negative effect on subsequent outcomes (i.e., adjudication and disposition). This line of analyses is consistent with Walker et al.'s (2012) institutionalized discrimination. As mentioned in Chapter 3, this form of discrimination stems from disparities hidden in racially neutral factors. The detention of youth is a racially neutral factor that has an influence on the guilt determination and sentencing of youth, but Blacks and Hispanics are more likely to get detained. Therefore, Blacks and Hispanics are more likely to be convicted and placed outside of the home if convicted. An insignificant race effect, alone, on any juvenile justice outcome is not enough to demonstrate that it has no impact.

Furthermore and perhaps even more concerning, the formal legal perspective ignores all the social mechanisms in which race and ethnicity operates. Although we present issues in race and ethnicity in chapters separately, many of these processes work in unison. Minority juveniles are disproportionately born into poverty, into single-female-headed households, and in neighborhoods that are socially disadvantaged. When growing up in these neighborhoods, juveniles are more likely to be approached by the police, and are more likely to experience a police interaction that is negative. As the frequency of these encounters increase, these juveniles' perceptions of the police become more negative. Because they have negative perceptions of the police, they are then more likely to act disrespectful during a police encounter. Acting disrespectful then increases their likelihood of being arrested. Once arrested, they are more likely to receive severe dispositions in the juvenile court. These dispositions can be directly impacted by race but are also impacted by the lack of family supports available to minority juveniles who are born into single parent households that are struggling financially. Being from a disadvantaged community again disadvantages minorities during this process because the high levels of crime and the lack of treatment resources in those areas make these juveniles appear to be at a greater risks of recidivating. Harsher punishments are also often found to increase juveniles' likelihoods of being involved in subsequent criminal behavior, resulting in further involvement in the criminal justice system.

Clearly, the impact that race and ethnicity have on the processing of juveniles is highly complex—even more complex than what is discussed here. Overlooking this complexity and simply focusing on one decision point, ignores these issues and will likely result in the further exacerbation of disproportionate minority contact in the system.

Role of Theory

Theory plays an important role in understanding how race and ethnicity are linked to juvenile justice decision-making. As mentioned in Chapter 3, delinquency theories (i.e., why youth engage in crime) are well developed. We understand the context in which delinquency is more likely to occur, in terms of neighborhood, delinquent friends, environment, school, and other factors. However, we understand very little about the decision-makers in the system, from police officers to judges. A heavy focus of research in this area is thus needed.

The multiple theories we discussed throughout the book are the main ones used to explain the link between race/ethnicity and juvenile justice outcomes. While these theories are useful, they have not been developed enough to fully place the relationship between race/ethnicities and decision-making into proper context. To date, the empirical research shows a clear relationship between juveniles' race and court outcomes. Theory can provide the lens through which to view and understand this relationship, to realize the possible connection between race/ethnicity and perceived dangerousness, and to study whether certain youth are more or less likely to be labeled with internal/external attributions, which then affect sentence severity.

One issue with theories of juvenile justice decision-making is that there are only a few theories, and they all attempt to explain several different outcomes among different actors in the juvenile system. Bernard and Engel (2001) mention how criminal justice (in our case juvenile justice) theories should be based first on their outcomes (e.g., detention or arrest or disposition, etc.). They should then be based on their independent variables (possible causes). This way, the theory will be specific and highly focused. They further argue that criminal justice theories are too broad and attempt to explain too much, resulting in theories that do not appear empirically supported.

As mentioned in Chapter 3, we agree that the theories need additional development. Although this is mentioned in the chapter, it warrants additional discussion here. While the body of delinquency theories captures data on the group in which researchers are trying to draw conclusions (i.e., the juvenile), researchers have not routinely captured demographic characteristics of police officers, probation officers, prosecutors, intake workers, and judges. For instance, research has shown that judges are influenced by their own personal characteristics (e.g., age and political affiliation) when making decisions (Rowland & Carp, 1996; Kulik, Perry & Pepper, 2003). Decision-making theories will remain under-developed until they include characteristics of the practitioners. If these changes are included in research, it should shed a significant amount of light on theory development for explaining how race is involved in juvenile process outcomes.

Historical Context

One goal we hope to accomplish in this text is to frame the juvenile court's history in light of race and ethnicity. History is often forgotten or simply ignored when reporting the results of race-based research. Hawkins (1987) mentioned that race research must be placed in the context of history in order to truly understand its effect. We agree with his point. From the beginning of the juvenile court, minorities were over-represented in the juvenile justice system. Does this suggest that being Black or Hispanic is synonymous with delinquency or criminality? If one looks at the history, it may place the findings in greater context.

For instance, the antecedents of the juvenile court were not designed for Black children. As mentioned in other chapters, slavery was alive and well during early times, so "slave justice" was used to correct the misbehaviors of most Black children. What was imposed on Black children during that time were lynchings, beatings, lashings, and shootings. Also, the U.S. Supreme Court was reminding the country of Blacks' proper "place" in their rulings, further reinforcing the view that Blacks belong to a class that was often forgotten, abused, and killed. While all of this was going on, there was discussion of beginning a juvenile court or some type of separate system for youth.

It appears, therefore, that the juvenile system was not meant to serve the needs of minority youth. When the system began including Black youth, the facilities were of significantly lower quality than the facilities for White youth. Therefore, the system began by treating minority youth differently from White youth. One cannot ignore this history and the manner in which this view would have carried through the years and continue to affect the views and subsequent treatment of minority juveniles in present times.

Final Thoughts and Directions
for Future Research

Overall, we believe that there is enough evidence to suggest that some form of discrimination in the juvenile justice system exists. There is, however, debate on whether the effects are direct or indirect. We do not agree with researchers who dismiss the value of conducting race and ethnicity research with a focus on the juvenile justice system. The workers in the system are human; therefore, they are open to biases, prejudices, favoritism, etc. It is important to examine their actions in much the same way that researchers examine the actions of offenders.

The issue then becomes focused on what must be done to combat the issue of discrimination (whether direct or indirect) that exists in the juvenile justice system. Because the race/ethnicity effect may operate indirectly through earlier court decisions to detain a juvenile prior to adjudication, the Annie E. Casey Foundation launched a project called the Juvenile Detention Alternative Initiative (JDAI). Starting almost twenty years ago, the goal was for juvenile court systems across the nation to reduce the reliance on pre-adjudication-detention, given its negative effect on subsequent court outcomes. It is based on the eight core strategies identified below (see http://www.aecf.org/work/juvenile-justice/jdai/). Through reducing pre-adjudication detention, *indirect* discrimination can be reduced a great deal.

- Promoting collaboration between juvenile court officials, probation agencies, prosecutors, defense attorneys, schools, community organizations and advocates
- Using rigorous data collection and analysis to guide decision making
- Utilizing objective admissions criteria and risk-assessment instruments to replace subjective decision-making processes to determine whether youth should be placed into secure detention facilities
- Implementing new or expanded alternatives to detention programs—such as day and evening reporting centers, home confinement and shelter care—that can be used in lieu of locked detention
- Instituting case processing reforms to expedite the flow of cases through the system
- Reducing the number of youth detained for probation rule violations or failing to appear in court, and the number held in detention awaiting transfer to a residential facility
- Combatting racial and ethnic disparities by examining data to identify policies and practices that may disadvantage youth of color at various stages of the process, and pursuing strategies to ensure a more level playing field for youth regardless of race or ethnicity
- Monitoring and improving conditions of confinement in detention facilities

—The Annie E. Casey Foundation

Even if the detention issue was not a concern, the biases occurring at the beginning stages of the process must be addressed. Youth of color are more likely to experience negative outcomes at the arrest stage and intake decisions, which are prior to when detention decisions are made. This concern requires stakeholders from multiple areas to have a strong investment in change. Legislatures (both state and federal) need to examine the laws and policies that place police agencies in inner city, urban, and disproportionately minority neighborhoods all too often. More frequent contacts alone will increase the likelihood of juveniles in those areas being arrested. Again, Walker et al. (2012) discussed how seemingly racial "neutral" policies, in essence, result in discriminatory practices and outcomes. As discussed in Chapter 5, practices such as these are why many youth (especially those of color) do not have overly favorable views of police.

An additional stakeholder is police agencies. Whether bias and stereotyping are acts of individual or institutional discrimination, denying their existence simply exacerbates the issue. As researchers, we must recognize potential biases we may have so we can minimize their effect on studies and ultimately the results. Given that police are the main referral source and gateway to the juvenile justice system, they must also recognize their personal and professional biases. They must acknowledge the influence of experiences, stereotypes, policies, and practices on how perceptions of racially and ethnically marginalized groups are portrayed and treated. Without admitting the bias, nothing will change and the problem will worsen, resulting in more police contact, more arrests, and more negative experiences in the juvenile system.

A final stakeholder is the community, including minority youth. We do not deny that the over-representation of minority youth in the juvenile system is *partially* due to these groups engaging in a disproportionate amount of offenses that are more likely to come to the attention of police. The communities where these youth live must invest in opportunities that will decrease the risk factors for delinquent behavior. Gabbidon and Taylor Greene (2013) stated it well: "... racial minorities must continue to look beyond governmental institutions to provide the impetus for change. By now it should be clear that the government offers no panacea and that such expectations are unrealistic" (p. 314). In other words, if minorities are waiting for parity, it is probably not going to occur. Therefore, communities must find ways to protect, guide, and mentor their youth, giving them a lower chance of having contact with police agencies.

In light of all the issues discussed in this book, we hope scholars will find opportunities to continue building upon this body of work. First, it is important that more research be conducted that examines juveniles of different ethnicities. Many studies have focused on Black and White juveniles. Hispanic juveniles and juveniles of other ethnicities are either not included in these studies or are lumped together in the minority category. It is important that future research be conducted that is able to distinguish between juveniles in these groups and to examine their experiences separately. This is especially important for Hispanic juveniles, as their presence in cities and in the criminal justice system is increasing. There is further reason to expect the experiences of Black and Hispanic juveniles to be different. Conflict theory scholars have argued that skin tone is a strong indicator of distance from the dominant culture, with those of darker skin tones further from the dominant group (Portes & Rumbaut, 2001). Therefore, Black individuals would be expected to be more threatening to the White dominant culture than Hispanics. In addition, Blacks have a history of extreme subordination through slavery that Hispanics do not. This history can affect their current level of power in our society as well as the symbolic threat that they pose to the dominant class. Because of this, it is expected that Black juveniles will be the most subjected to harsh treatment, Hispanic juveniles will fall in the middle, receiving better treatment than Black juveniles but not as favorable treatment as White juveniles.

Second, researchers must continue to develop theories that can help frame and explain the findings pertaining to race and the juvenile justice process. Also, scholars and practitioners must not ignore the role of history in explaining the current discriminatory practices that are clearly observed in the juvenile justice system. In addition, research should further be expanded to include more recent data. Many of the data sources utilized in research examining the processing of juveniles is dated, especially in the observations of police and juvenile interactions. Instead of relying on secondary data, we encourage researchers to collect more recent data on these issues. Although these inquiries will likely be focused on specific juvenile justice system jurisdictions which will limit generalizability, they will provide a much more accurate picture of how race and ethnicity is affecting decisions in the juvenile system today. Finally, researchers should continue exploring multiple decision points in the juvenile justice system, because true effects cannot be assessed at one decision point. Related to this, scholars should begin building the knowledge base on the influence of race on sentencing outcomes. To date, most research examines out-of-home placements, but those could include group homes, foster care, boot camp, secure correctional confinement, living with another relative outside of the home, etc. (see Feld, 1995 for notable exception). We need to understand, specifically, what happens to these youth once they are adjudicated. The adult literature is fairly robust in this area. It is time for juvenile justice scholars to appropriately follow suit.

References

Bernard, T.J. & Engel, R.S. (2001). Conceputualizing criminal justice theory. *Justice Quarterly, 18*(1), 1–30.

Du Bois, W.E.B. (1903). *The souls of Black folk.* Chicago: A.C. McClurg & Co.

Feld, B.C. (1995). The social context of juvenile justice administration: Racial disparities in an urban juvenile court. In K.K. Leonard, C.E. Pope, & W. Feyerherm (Eds.)., Minorities in juvenile justice (pp. 66–97). Thousand Oaks, CA: Sage.

Gabbidon, S.L. & Taylor Greene, H. (2013). *Race and crime* (3rd ed.). Thousand Oaks, CA: SAGE.

Hawkins, D.F. (1987). Beyond anomalies: Rethinking the conflict perspective on race and criminal punishment. *Social Forces, 65*(3), 719–745.

Kulik, C.T., Perry, E.L. & Pepper, M.B. (2003). Here comes the judge: The influence of judge personal characteristics on federal sexual harassment case outcomes. *Law and Human Behavior, 27*(1), 69–86.

Portes, A. & Rumbaut, R.G. (2001). Legacies: The story of the immigrant second generation. New York: Russell Sage Foundation.

Rowland, C.K. & Carp, R.A. (1996). Politics and judgment in federal district courts. Lawrence, KS: University Press of Kansas.

Tracy, P.E. (2005). Race, ethnicity, and juvenile justice: Is there bias in postarrest decision making. In D.F. Hawkins & K. Kempf-Leonard (Eds.), *Our children, their children: Confronting racial and ethnic differences in American juvenile justice* (pp. 300–347). Chicago: The University of Chicago Press.

Walker, S., Spohn, C. & DeLone, M. (2012). *The color of justice: Race, ethnicity, and crime in America.* Belmont, CA: Wadsworth.

West, C. (1994). *Race matters.* New York: Vintage Books.

Index